The Secret Garden

The Secret Garden

An Anthology in the Kabbalah

Edited by
David Meltzer

STATION HILL OPENINGS
BARRYTOWN, LTD.

Published under the Station Hill Arts imprint of Barrytown, Ltd.,
Barrytown, New York, 12507, as a project of The Institute for Pub-
lishing Arts, Inc., a not-for-profit, federally tax exempt, educational
organization.

Web: www.stationhill.org
E-mail: Publishers@stationhill.org

Grateful acknowledgement is due to the National Endowment for
the Arts, a Federal Agency in Washington, DC, and to the New York
State Council on the Arts for partial financial support of the publish-
ing program of The Institute for Publishing Arts.

Cover design by Susan Quasha

Library of Congress Cataloging-in-Publication Data

The secret garden : an anthology in the kabbalah / edited by David
    Meltzer.
       p. cm.
    Previously published: New York : Seabury Press, c1976.
    Includes bibliographical references.
    ISBN 1-886449-53-8 (alk. paper)
    1. Cabala—Translations into English. I. Meltzer, David.
BM525.A2S4   1998
296. 1'6—dc21   98-7237
                                     CIP

*This beginning is for J. A. H.,
comrade in the treetops.*

The secret Garden
In worlds of light hidden
—Two hundred and fifty
Encompassing worlds—
Where Shekinah's splendor
From splendor proceeding
Its splendor sends forth
To the ends of creation,
In the fullness of glory
Is revealed in its beauty
To the eyes made seeing—
The garden of Eden.

The Ancient, the Father,
The Holy One speaks
His Name again pronouncing,
"Yod He Vau He" again
Gloriously crying.
Then speak the lightful Hosts
Making brave music:
His thirteen paths of mercy
They gladly proclaim.

Who sees the mighty ones
High in the Heavens
Mighty in beauty?
Who sees the Chariots
Holy and glorious?
Who sees the Hosts in
The bright courts of glory
Exalting and praising
In awe and in fear
In joy and in wonder
The Holy One's Name?

                    —From The Zohar (III, 4a–4b),
                    Translated by Maurice Simon,
                    Harry Sperling and Paul Levertoff

CONTENTS

PUBLISHER'S FOREWORD

It was a different world when David Meltzer first published *The Secret Garden*. In 1976 we did not have easy access to English language versions of Kabbalistic texts from the Jewish tradition (with few exceptions such as the partial translation of *The Zohar* by Sperling and Levertoff, the latter, incidentally, the father of the poet, the late Denise Levertov). Rumor of a wealth of splendid esoteric and imaginative material from all periods of Jewish Kabbalistic writing circulated among us, mainly through the work of Gersholm Scholem and the various Western "occult" traditions, ranging from famous references to the Kabbalah in Pico Della Mirandola down to the rituals of the Hermetic Order of the Golden Dawn, familiar to readers of William Butler Yeats and Charles Williams. How fortunate we were to finally gain access to Kabbalah by way of David Meltzer's refined ear for language, so that it entered directly into the stream of emergent poetry.

There was, in fact, something of a sub-community among the American poets of the 50s, 60s, and 70s—including (besides David Meltzer) Robert Duncan, Jack Hirschman, Diane di Prima, Jerome Rothenberg, Nathaniel Tarn, and others (ourselves too, in fact)—whose life in poetry brought essential involvement with the imaginal worlds of Kabbalistic writings. David Meltzer sought both to feed our hunger for this material and provide contexts for the articulation of its relevance to contemporary poetry. This contribution continues both through the impact he has made on American poets and readers of poetry and through the texts themselves which, in the refined and literary focus they share, still serve anyone interested in Kabbalah: hence the importance of keeping this seminal book in print.

We owe a great deal to David Meltzer for riches received not only through his anthology, *The Secret Garden,* but as well through his magazine *Tree* (including Tree Books, introducing us, for instance, to the works of Edmond Jabès, some of which we later published at Station Hill Press) and indeed his own writing. Addressing *The Secret Garden* in the context of David Meltzer's work, poet/anthologist Jerome Rothenberg (editor of *A Big Jewish Book* [1978], which owes so much to Meltzer's precedent) has said:

> David Meltzer's gift—one among his many—has been to link old mysteries & poetries with the world of daily living & with the way we've come to do our work as poets in the here & now. A proponent over the last thirty years of an enlightened "bop kabbalah,"

Meltzer in *The Secret Garden* offers us a treasury of those basic works of Jewish mysticism that have sparked his own writing & that of many of his fellow poets. Beautifully gathered and translated, here is a classic example of the anthologizer's art.

And when we approached David Meltzer about reprinting his classic collection, we asked him to speak to the "inspiration" for this work that is, in fact, the fruit of many years of work and personal engagement:

This book was compiled at the outset of an involvement with Kabbalah as a critical, theoretical, hermeneutic, social and personal practice; yet one outside of any apparent orthodoxy other than poetry which knows better, or should. At the root, for me, was the power and powerlessness of spoken and written language; a richly facile mysticism of language with infinite attention paid to its very molecules: the alphabet. A philosophical & mystical (mystery-embracing) engagement which I still think leads towards social transformation, collectively and individually, whose telos is revolution, actual and meta-actual.

My two mentors were Abraham ben Samuel Abulafia—a 13th century communist language mystic whose works made available the means of production for anyone willing to enact, embody, and internalize rituals it clearly described in how-to manuals of methods to achieve the blank-page state of prophetic reception and therefore self and societal transformation—and Isaac Luria—the Ari, the lion, whose 16th century grand theory of exile and redemption remain one of Kabbalah's high mythopoetic programs of purpose and social consciousness. Connecting these two inspired intelligences were two books—one, the microcosmic *Sephir Yetzirah*, a counter cosmogony which states that YHVH wrote being into being rather than speaking it, sounding it, and the other, a macrocosmic midrashim whose five-volume English translation only partially represents its abundance, was *The Zohar* (which my exemplar Robert Duncan called "the greatest mystical novel ever written")—an anthology of treatises composed in the 13th century primarily by Moses De Leon, an inspired trickster of endless profundity. Before Gersholm Scholem's orthographic analysis of the pseudo-Aramaic "ancient manuscripts," *The Zohar* was rumored to have been written by Abulafia.

Today, scholarship on the Kabbalah in English has flourished through the work of Moshe Idel and many others, but the general availability of readable translations of the texts themselves remains, at best, uneven. In a tradition in which language itself embodies the possibility of access to the mystery of being*, it is vitally important that we have texts rendered with that possibility in mind. David Meltzer gave us the first collection of such texts and, as far as we know, the only collection based on that principle. Whatever chance we have of knowing Kabbalah in English would seem to rest as much in the hands of poets as scholars, and *The Secret Garden* will not let us forget this.

George Quasha and Charles Stein

---

* That the Mystery is knowable through language/text has suggested to certain poets that Kabbalah itself is already poetic doctrine; certainly Duncan and Meltzer shared this Blakean view regarding sacred/visionary texts generally, indicating a primary and extra-traditionary path in poetry with its own *gnosis*. Of course this very complex matter cannot be represented in simple notions, but it is important to register that it is hardly about a reduction of Kabbalah to literature or even modernist/post-modernist experimental poetry. One might look instead for an enhanced inquiry into the possibility of poetry itself, a metapoetic possibility that is *liminal* to literary and religious traditions as such. Edmond Jabès sought such a possibility in the nature of the Book. One might point as well, neologistically, toward a pre-definitional sense of "gnosemic language," where the very particles of text or utterance are charged with a gnosis special to that text or utterance, or, more generally, "lognosis," where radically poetic language and "gnoetic" insight are permitted to embody each other.

INTRODUCTION

The Kabbalah, as much as poetry, is the study of and submission to the mysteries of the word. The language used by Kabbalists is so intricately dimensional that it is almost impossible to fully convey the simultaneous layers of meaning revealed in the simplest of words. It is said that one word is the seed of a particular universe, a system of interactions and realities as complex as the birth and death of a sun.

Much of what is of utmost significance in the Kabbalistic tradition never approaches the page. Its deepest secrets can only be set free beyond the page. The oral transmission of Kabbalistic mysteries remains a series of moments between a master and his disciples, moments that transcend the limits of written language.

Many of the selections included in this book were not written to serve the continuity of a literary tradition; instead, they take the form of notes for the actual teaching which takes shape only in the context of a sharing-of-breath experience between teacher and student. With few exceptions these texts remain as the aftermath of the actual teaching—they are shadows, ghosts.

The Kabbalist is not unlike the poet or shaman in the risks taken in creation. Whether spoken or written, the emergence of a word becomes a momentous event. The Kabbalist's devotion leads him into a deeper comprehension of each word he confronts. He knows that when words are combined into a sequence their overall impact often transforms the immediate reality. Through creation inspired by the words within the Torah and through endless meditation upon the meaning of each letter, each word, each sentence, chapter, book, even each vowel-point, the Kabbalist hopes to penetrate through the folds and veils to enter other realms, to ascend new rungs of consciousness and to ultimately reach emersion and dispersal into the highest source of his yearning's goal. Creation—for the Kabbalist or poet or shaman—is the ability to receive the word, as well as being responsive to his capacity as word-creator. To embody the book, to be filled with vision, truth, compassion; to live in such a way that no spot within or without is unblessed by word. As a contemporary Kabbalist once wrote to me, echoing the traditional longing, "to be walking, breathing Torah." To be as we are: organisms guided by light to light.

Yet the paradox of the Kabbalah is that of all mystical traditions: the intensive study of the book, the books, the books within books, words within words, meanings within meanings, serves as a process which leads beyond the book, the words, to a point of complete word-less-ness. You ascend to a plateau of profound blankness, the blankness of a piece of paper before words are engraved into it.

* * * *

This collection of Kabbalistic texts in translation, concluding with a group of texts from the Sabbatian movement of the seventeenth century, should be regarded only as a source book, an attempt to approach the written element of the Kabbalah. It is in no way comprehensive or definitive. Many will find this book to be another distraction or misrepresentation of the Kabbalah, whose works can only be fully known in their original language. For this I apologize in advance and take full responsibility for all errors. Nevertheless I hope the presence of this book fills a small part in the void of contemporary scholarship dealing with the translating of writings by the Kabbalists.

My interest in and devotion to Kabbalah as both process and metaphor have preoccupied me for over a decade, and have been absorbed not only into my work as a poet but in the way I receive or intuit reality. It is therefore with great humility and reverence for tradition that I offer this book.

* * *

I must thank those people who have kept me alert and true during the assemblage of this volume:

Jack Hirschman, Rabbi Zalman M. Schachter, J. R. Willems, Jerome Rothenberg, Joachim Neugroschel, Harris Lenowitz, Asa and Pip Benveniste, Samuel Avital, Carlo Suares, Anthony Rudolf, Daniel Bloxom, The Work of the Chariot, Yehuda Shamir, Peter Marin, Stephen Pickering, Howard Schwartz, Steven L. Maimes, Edmond Jabes, Siegfried Hessing, the works of Gershom G. Scholem first and foremost, and Robert Duncan for introducing me to Scholem's works many years ago. May you all be pleased with what the garden offers.

Richmond, California
Fall, 1975

The Secret Garden

Part One

$\mathcal{R}$abbi [*Judah the Prince*] *had a worthy disciple who once recited before him a passage from the Merkabah mystery. Rabbi did not agree with it, and he was smitten with boils. This mystical doctrine can be compared to two paths, one of which leads into fire (or "light"), the other into ice (or "snow"). Whoever strays into the former perishes in fire, and whoever strays into the latter perishes in ice. What should the student do? He should walk in the middle.*

BARAITA ON THE WORK OF CREATION

(Baraita de Ma'aseh Bereshit)

(C. EIGHTH CENTURY)

EDITOR'S NOTE. The two earliest forms of Jewish mysticism were *ma'aseh merkabah,* writings which explored the mysteries of the Throne on its Chariot as revealed in the first chapter of Ezekiel, and *ma'aseh bereshith,* speculations on the first chapter of Genesis with special emphasis placed on cosmology and cosmogony.

These two esoteric disciplines were connected in the sense that, according to mystical cosmogony, the heavens and spheres of the Divine Throne were situated "above" the earth and firmament. Practitioners of ecstatic Merkabah mysticism experienced an ascent of the soul, in which they passed through various heavenly spheres until they finally beheld the vision of the Throne of Glory. Gershom Scholem equates the mysteries of the Throne and the Divine Glory revealed there to be parallel in Jewish esoteric tradition to the revelation of the Divine in Gnosticism.

The study and teaching of both forms were highly restricted and not to be taught in public.

"Thou art not allowed to investigate that which is below, that which is before (in the ultimate future), and that which is behind (at the beginning of things), but only that which is from Creation on." (*Genesis Rabba,* 1).

O ur Rabbis taught: Four men entered the Garden [PaRDeS], namely, Ben Azzai and Ben Zoma, Acher and R. Akiba. R. Akiba said to them: When ye arrive at the stones of pure marble, say not:

3

Water, water. For it is said: He that speaketh falsehood shall not
be established before mine eyes *(Psalms 101:7). Ben Azzai cast a
look and died. Of him Scripture says:* Precious in the eyes of the
Lord is the death of His saints *(Psalms 116:15). Ben Zoma looked
and became demented. Of him Scripture says:* Hast thou found
honey? Eat as much as is sufficient for thee, lest thou be filled
therewith and vomit it *(Prov. 25:16). Acher mutilated the shoots. R.
Akiba went up unhurt, and went down unhurt.*

—*Chagigah, 14b.*

IN THE BEGINNING GOD CREATED THE HEAVEN AND THE EARTH;
you shouldn't read BERESIT as *in the beginning* but BERA SIT, *He
created six.* And in effect you will find that it is written, *He created
six.* If the Writing says BERA SIT, that means he created six letters;
and through them were the heavens and the earth formed, as it is
said: FOR THROUGH YH YHWH He formed the worlds. YH are two
letters, YHWH are four, thus there are six. So you must understand
that it is through six letters that God created the heavens and the
earth. If you say, is it only the heavens and the earth that were
created through these six letters, through the writing THROUGH YH
YHWH HE FORMED THE WORLDS, understand as well that two
worlds were created by these six letters: the world here and now,
and the world that will be.

It is said: IN THE BEGINNING. What exactly was there in the
beginning? God created the heavens and the earth through a single
letter, and sealed it with fire. What is that unique letter by which
the heavens and the earth were created? It is the letter *He* as it is
said: BEHOLD THE ORIGINS OF THE HEAVENS AND THE EARTH
WHEN THEY WERE CREATED. You shouldn't read: WHEN THEY
WERE CREATED, but THROUGH THE LETTER *HE* DID HE CREATE
THEM. It is through this letter God created the heavens and the
earth, the world here and now and the world that will be.* He
sealed them with the fire of Gehenna, which is half flame and half
hail. Sinners are chastised with burning hail, which scorches them
like flame, and with flame that devours them like hail. (Another
version is that they are condemned to hail, then pass from the hail

*Another version says the here and now was created by *He* and the world to come
by *Yod.*

into the burning flame and from the burning flame into the hail.)

The destroying angels come down to them and withhold their souls in their bodies, as it is said: FOR THEIR MAGGOT SHALL NOT PERISH. The destroying angels come down one day, and one day the angel of death comes down for them and drives them from the hail to the flame and from the flame to the hail, like a shepherd who moves his flock from one mountain to another, as it is said: AS THE SMALL BEAST THAT DEATH PLACED IN SHEOL.

The destroying angels come down and chastise them in Gehenna for 12 months. At the end of the 12 months they have to descend to the gates of the SHADOW OF DEATH.

At the gates of the SHADOW OF DEATH they are chastised for 12 months. At the end of the 12 months they have to descend to the GATES OF DEATH.

At the GATES OF DEATH they are chastised for 12 months. At the end of the 12 months they have to descend to the filth of mire.

In the filth of mire they are chastised for 12 months. At the end of the 12 months they have to descend to the whirlpool of destruction.

In the whirlpool of destruction they are chastised for 12 months. At the end of the 12 months they have to descend to the place of perdition.

In the place of perdition they are chastised for 12 months. At the end of the 12 months they have to descend to lower Sheol.

In lower Sheol they are chastised for 12 months, at which point all the righteous behold them and say to those whose compassion extends over all their works: Begin the trial! The Holy Spirit then answers: No, my soul is not yet calm, for they have destroyed my house and murdered my son, as it is said: THE FURY OF THE ANGER WILL NOT FORESHORTEN THE TIME OF THE ACTION BY WHICH THE INTENTION OF HIS HEART IS REALIZED.

At the end of the 12 months, they have to descend into the territory under the river which has its origins under the throne of Glory, as it is said: BEHOLD THE TEMPEST OF YHWH WHICH SPLINTERS, THE HURRICANE WHICH BREAKS LOOSE, UPON THE HEAD OF THE UNGODLY, BREAKING INTO THEM. That which descends into the territory does not reascend, as it is said: THE GODS WHO HAD NO PART IN MAKING THE HEAVENS AND THE EARTH PERISH UPON LEAVING THE ARQA.

This is the fifth abyss.

Above the territory there is an abyss,
above the abyss there is Tohu,
above Tohu there is Bohu,
above Bohu there is a sea,
above the sea there are streams,
above the streams there is a world
and upon this world there are mountains,
hills and their inhabitants, as it is said:
THE MOUNTAINS WILL TREMBLE BEFORE ME
AND THE HILLS WILL BE FOUNDED.
This is the sixth abyss.
Above this world there is another abyss,
above the abyss there is Tohu,
above Tohu, Bohu,
above Bohu, a sea,
above the sea, streams

and amidst these streams there is land, there is man, domestic animals, beasts of the field, sky birds, fish of the sea, Laws, good actions and heavenly dread, as it is said: LEND YOUR EAR, O YOU INHABITANTS OF EARTH. This is the seventh abyss.

Above this land there is a curtain which is closed at evening and which opens at dawn each day renewing the creation.

Above the curtain there are heavens, as it is said: HE EXTENDS THE HEAVENS AS A VEIL. Why are these called heavens? It is because the Holy One, blessed be He, had mingled the fire with the water, spreading out the one with the other in creating the heavens, as it is said: IT IS MY HAND WHICH HAS FOUNDED THE EARTH AND MY RIGHT HAND WHICH HAS STRETCHED OUT THE HEAVENS. You shouldn't read it as "heavens" but as "fire and waters."

Above these heavens there is a sea; where there is wheat, wort and oil. When the Holy One, blessed be He, wishes to bless the earth, he does so from time to time in the form of dew and rainfall.

Above the sea there are streams and below the streams a firmament. Between the streams and the firmament the sun-disk, the moon, the planets and the fixed stars are suspended. It is from there that the entire world receives its light. They rule over all the abysms and their light descends to the lower earth, as it is said: AND GOD PLACED THEM . . .

Above the sea are the streams. Between the streams and the sea there is the place of hailstones, and lightning flashes making a roofing for all, and subtle walls of fire surrounding them, as it is said: THE HEAVENS AND THE HEAVENS OF HEAVENS.

At the gates of the heavens, in the direction of the northwind, angels are appointed. Their names are:
1. ALEPH-LAMED-ALEPH-LAMED
2. ALEPH-LAMED-BETH-YOD-MEM
3. BETH-LAMED-YOD-ALEPH-LAMED
4. BETH-LAMED-YOD
5. BETH-SAMEKH-LAMED-YOD-ALEPH-LAMED

They guard the exits of the northwind.

At the gates of the southwind angels are also appointed. Their names are:
1. DALETH-VAV-RESH-NUN-YOD-ALEPH-LAMED
2. DALETH-RESH-KOPH-YOD-ALEPH-LAMED
3. HAY-MEM-VAV-NUN
4. DALETH-VAV-NUN-YOD-ALEPH-LAMED
5. GHIMEL-HAY-NUN-YOD-ALEPH-LAMED

They guard the exits of the southwind.

At the gates of the eastwind angels are also appointed. Their names are:
1. DALETH-VAV-RESH-NUN-YOD-ALEPH-LAMED
2. GHIMEL-BETH-RESH-YOD-ALEPH-LAMED
3. GHIMEL-DALETH-RESH-YOD-ALEPH-LAMED
4. AYIN-DALETH-RESH-YOD-ALEPH-LAMED
5. MEM-VAV-DALETH-YOD-ALEPH-LAMED
6. RESH-HAY-MEM-YOD-ALEPH-LAMED
7. HAY-NUN-YOD-ALEPH-LAMED

They guard the exits of the eastwind.

At the gates of the westwind angels also are appointed. Their names are:
1. YOD-ALEPH-LAMED-SAMEKH-NUN
2. SAMEKH-VAV-KAPH-YOD-ALEPH-LAMED
3. TSADEE-NUN-SAMEKH-YOD-ALEPH-LAMED
4. BETH-HAY-YOD-ALEPH-LAMED
5. BETH-KAPH-TAV-MEM-YOD-ALEPH-LAMED
6. TAV-RESH-PHEY-NUN-YOD-ALEPH-LAMED

They guard the exits of the westwind.

Above the firmament there are heavens where the sun, the moon and the stars are fixed. The extremities of the firmament resemble a vault. The sun, the moon, the planets, the stars and the firmament arch govern all the abysms. Their light descends to the lower earth, as it is said: GOD PLACED THEM IN THE FIRMAMENT OF THE HEAVENS.

At the gate of the firmament, in the direction of the northwind, angels are appointed. Their names are:

1. TAV-YOD-ALEPH-LAMED
2. AYIN-NUN-YOD-ALEPH-LAMED
3. NUN-NUN-ALEPH-LAMED
4. HAY-LAMED-KAPH-YOD-MEM
5. HAY-NUN-YOD-ALEPH-LAMED

They guard the exits of the northwind.

At the gates of the southwind angels are also appointed. Their names are:

1. CHETH-LAMED-ALEPH-HAY
2. BETH-HAY-LAMED-YOD-ALEPH-LAMED
3. BETH-LAMED-HAY-YOD-ALEPH-LAMED
4. LAMED-VAV-ALEPH-LAMED
5. YOD-LAMED-YOD-ALEPH-LAMED
6. NUN-KAPH-RESH-YOD-ALEPH-LAMED

They guard the exits of the southwind.

At the gates of the eastwind angels also are appointed. Their names are:

1. MEM-SAMEKH-YOD-MEM
2. CHETH-RESH-MEM-YOD-ALEPH-LAMED

It is sealed with the seal: I AM THAT I AM. Why is it so sealed? Because had He not sealed it with such a seal each creature would not have been able to fathom His letters on account of the violence of the fire. And whomsoever would be kept from fathoming His letters would be immediately invaded by the fire. That is the reason why He smothered it with His letters and sealed it with His seal.

So it is said, "in the beginning." What is it that is "in the beginning"? Firstly, He created the heavens and the earth, He established the abodes and the abysms spelling out of them, He formed seven abodes on high to which correspond seven abysms below:

> He stretched the heavens above and, as if in retort,
> founded the earth below,

He let out the storm clouds above, and, as if in retort,
    founded the dry land below,

He fixed an abode above, and as if in retort,
    founded the territory below,

He stretched another abode out above and, as if in retort,
    He founded the world below,

He stretched the mist above and, as if in retort,
    founded the world below,

He let out his throne above and, as if in retort,
    He stretched a part of HIS GLORY below.
    These the works of the first day.

The second day He parted the waters. He placed a part of them below and kept a part of them above, as it is said: GOD MADE THE FIRMAMENT AND SEPARATED THE WATERS.

The third day He collected the waters in a single place, made the dry land appear and called it "earth." And He made the trees thrust up, and the herb and all sorts of seeds, and fruit trees and plants of every species with their leafage and blossom, as it is said: THAT THE EARTH GAVE FORTH ITS GREEN: THAT THE HERB BORE SEED AFTER ITS KIND.

The fourth day He created the luminaries to divide the day from the night. He made the sun rule the day and the moon and the planets the night, as it is said: GOD CREATED THE TWO LUMINARIES.

The fifth day He created the fish and all the water reptiles and the bird that flies above the earth, as it is said: THE WATERS SWARM WITH A TEEMING OF LIVING BEINGS AND THE BIRD FLIES OVER THE EARTH.

The sixth day He created the domestic animals and the savage beasts and insects, as it is said: THE EARTH PRODUCED A LIVING SOUL AFTER ITS KIND.

After all these beings, He created man to govern them.

He established his armies, gave them orders with respect to His service, and placed an angel at their head. Next the tempest and the thunderstorm formed a circle around them. Next those who said "Holy" and those who said "Blessed" formed a circle, as it is said: THE EARTH IS ABUNDANT WITH HIS PRAISE.

This is the lower abyss.

Above the abyss there is Tohu,
above Tohu, Bohu,
above Bohu, there is a sea,
above the sea, streams,
above the streams, a desert
and in the desert there are rivers,
and the quarries of the abyss,
as it is said:
I WILL CHANGE THE RIVERS INTO DESERT.

This is the third abyss.

Above the desert there is an abyss,
above the abyss, Tohu,
above Tohu, Bohu,
above Bohu, a sea,
above the sea, streams,

and amidst the streams, dry land, and upon the dry land there are other water bodies, and rivers and snowdrifts, as it is said: THE SEA BELONGS TO HIM, IT IS HE WHO HAS MADE IT, AND ALSO THE DRY LAND HE HAS FORMED.

This is the fourth abyss.

Above the dry land there is an abyss,
above the abyss, Tohu,
above Tohu, Bohu,
above Bohu, a sea,
above the sea, streams,
and on the streams there is the territory
and on the territory
        the lower Sheol,
        the place of perdition,
        the whirlpool of destruction,
        the filth of mire,
        the gates of the dead,

> the gates of the shadow
> of death
> and Gehenna.

Angels of destruction are appointed for the sinners who are found there.
The highermost station is the lower Sheol,
its depth is 300 years long;
the second station is the place of perdition,
its depth is 300 years long;
the third station is the whirlpool of destruction,
its depth is 300 years long;
the fourth station is the filth of mire,
its depth is 300 years long;
the fifth station is the gates of the dead,
its depth is 300 years long;
the sixth station is the gates of the shadow of death,
its depth is 300 years long;
the seventh station is Gehenna,
its depth is 300 years long.

The fire of lower Sheol is 61 times stronger than the fire of the place
of perdition;
the fire of the place of perdition is 61 times stronger than the fire
of the whirlpool of destruction;
the fire of the whirlpool of destruction is 61 times stronger than the
fire of the filth of mire;
the fire of the filth of mire is 61 times stronger than the fire of the
gates of the shadow of death.

ARIEL is at the head of those angels who have all the hymns of songs and praise upon their lips. He forces his way through them and opens the paths for them. The angels say to one another: What should we do? A radiant angel shows them. They construct ladders by which they ascend and descend; that is, by ascending they speak words of praise, and by descending they bring peace to the world.

The length of the world is 508 years long, and its breadth is 518 years. It is round and the great sea entirely encircles it. The whole forms a sort of vault and is everywhere held erect. The whole world fits into the fins of Leviathan. Leviathan lies in subterranean waters, in the waters of the pure fish, in the middle of the sea.

The subterranean waters are, in harmony with the waters of creation, like a small fountainhead at the edge of the sea; the ocean is, in harmony with streams that weep, like a small fountainhead at the edge of the sea.

Why are they called the *streams that weep?* Because when the Holy One, blessed be He, divided the waters, He took one part and placed it above and the other part he sent below. The streams placed below are emotional: they lament, weep, grieve, and in weeping they cry out: We are not worthy of being close to our creator. And what do they do? They had the audacity to fight their way across the abysms in order to try to attain the world above, until the Holy One, blessed be He, roared at them and drove them back, as it is said: BEFORE THE VOICE OF THE GREAT STREAMS, THE MAJESTIC WAVES OF THE SEA, and afterward: YHWH IS MAJESTIC IN THE HEIGHTS. Don't read it as "waves" but as "before the voice of song" that the streams will sing; afterward the upper streams will ask of the word and will say in their turn: YHWH IS MAJESTIC IN THE HEIGHTS. And that is the reason for the designations of "the streams that weep."

The streams that weep are suspended above the lower earth; the lower earth stretches above the streams; the streams are connected to the columns of HASMAL; the columns of HASMAL are connected to mountains of hail; the mountains of hail are connected to treasuries of snow; the treasuries of snow are connected to the streams; the streams are connected to the fire and the fire above to the abyss.

The abyss is connected to Tohu. Tohu to Bohu. Bohu to the wind,
The wind is suspended from the storm and attached to the vault of earth,
The earth is suspended from the storm and attached to the vault of the desert,
The desert is suspended from the storm and attached to the vault of dry land,
The dry land is suspended from the storm and attached to the vault of the territory,
The ARQA is suspended from the storm and attached to the vault of the world,
The world is suspended from the storm and attached to the vault of the earth,

The earth is suspended from the storm and attached to the vault
  of the heavens,
The heavens are suspended from the storm and attached to the
  vault of the firmament,
The firmament is suspended from the storm and attached to the
  vault of the thunderclouds,
The thunderclouds are suspended from the storm and attached to
  the vault of the foundation,
The foundation is suspended from the storm and attached to the
  vault of the abode,
The abode is suspended from the storm and attached to the vault
  of the mists,
The mists are suspended from the storm and attached to the power-
  ful arm of the Holy One, blessed be He,
as it is said: THE COLUMNS OF THE HEAVENS WILL BE SHAKEN
WHEN HE THREATENS. It is said for that purpose that it is also
said: YOUR WORKS ARE NUMEROUS O YHWH; YOU HAVE
CREATED THEM ALL WITH WISDOM.

> Then the fire and the water form
> a circle around the lower earth,
> then the tempest and storm form
> a circle around the fire and water,
> then those who make a great noise
> form a circle round the tempest and storm,
> then the cherubim who fly about
> form a circle round the noisemakers,
> then those with the quality of living creatures
> form a circle round the flying cherubim,
> then those who rush up and retort form
> a circle round those with living qualities,
> then those who say "holy" and "blessed"
> form a circle round those who rush up and retort.

The lower earth contains the holy living creatures, the OFANIM
and the throne of Glory. The throne of Glory is the staircase from
the feet of the Almighty to all earth, as it is said: THE HEAVENS
ARE MY THRONE AND THE EARTH THE STEPS TO MY FEET;
and as it is furthermore said: AND I LOOK UPON AND BEHOLD
THE LIVING CREATURES AND AN OFAN ON THE EARTH. And just
as His Shekinah is found on high so is she found below, as it is

said: AND THE NAME OF THE CITY HEREAFTER WILL BE HIS SHEKINAH.

18,000 worlds form a circle around her, as it is said: EIGHTEEN THOUSAND WORLDS AROUND;
four-thousand five-hundred from the north, four-thousand five-hundred from the south, four-thousand five-hundred from the west, four-thousand five-hundred from the east,
all comprising the eighteen thousand worlds.
The world of the northwind is full of praise and glory, power and valor, eulogy and song.
The world of the southwind is full of praise and glory, power and valor, eulogy and song; it is as well abundant with majesty and beauty, joy and fame, pride and exaltation.
 The world of the eastwind is full of holiness and purity, power and justice, victory and valor.
 The world of the westwind is full of beauty and ornament containing the royal crown and the voice of the subtle silence.
 Those 18,000 worlds are then surrounded by fire and the water; after the fire and water there are:
 1. TAV-HAY-RESH-YOD-ALEPH-LAMED
 2. NUN-VAV-RESH-YOD-ALEPH-LAMED
 3. VAV-GHIMEL-BETH-RESH-YOD-ALEPH-LAMED

> The fire and the water form a circle
> round the 18,000 worlds; then
> the tempest and storm form a circle
> the rumbling and trembling form a circle
> round the tempest and the storm; then
> terror and dread form a circle
> round the rumbling and trembling; then
> thunder and lightnings form a circle
> round the terror and the dread; then
> the wings of the wind form a circle
> round the thunder and lightning; then
> the rivers of flame form a circle
> round the wings of the wind; then
> the rivers of the sea form a circle
> round the rivers of flame; then
> the rivers of rain form a circle
> round the rivers of the sea.

Beyond the rivers of rain there is nothing but night without end, without number, without quality or quantity, incalculable, as it is said: HE MAKES THE NIGHTS HIS WITHDRAWAL, THE TENT AROUND HIMSELF.

Those who encircle the nights are:

1. NUN-VAV-RESH-YOD-ALEPH-LAMED
2. TOV-HAY-RESH-YOD-ALEPH-LAMED
3. GHIMEL-BETH-RESH-YOD-ALEPH-LAMED
4. NUN-VAV-HAY-RESH-YOD-ALEPH-LAMED
5. NUN-GHIMEL-BETH-YOD-ALEPH-LAMED

They guard the exits of the eastwind.

At the gates of the westwind angels are appointed. Their names are:

1. KAPH-VAV-RESH-YOD-ALEPH-LAMED
2. PHEY-DALETH-YOD-ALEPH-LAMED
3. SAMEKH-CHETH-NUN-YOD-ALEPH-LAMED
4. AYIN-NUN-YOD-ALEPH-LAMED

They guard the exits of the westwind.

Above the firmament are the clouds. There are found the treasuries of snow, of hail, of dew, of manna, of the balms of the resurrection of the dead; as it is said: AND THE CLOUDS IN HIS MAJESTY.

At the gates of the clouds, in the direction of the northwind, angels are appointed. Their names are:

1. PHEY-NUN-YOD-YOD-ALEPH-LAMED
2. PHEY-NUN-ALEPH-LAMED
3. RESH-PHEY-ALEPH-LAMED
4. RESH-MEM-YOD-ALEPH-LAMED
5. DALETH-RESH-MEM-YOD-ALEPH-LAMED

They guard the exits of the northwind.

At the gates of the southwind angels are appointed. Their names are:

1. TSADEE-DALETH-KAPH-YOD-ALEPH-LAMED
2. KAPH-DALETH-YOD-SHIN-ALEPH
3. TOV-YOD-RESH-TETH-ALEPH-LAMED
4. TOV-RESH-NUN-YOD-ALEPH-LAMED
5. SHIN-MEM-AYIN-YOD-ALEPH-LAMED

They guard the gates of the southwind.

At the gates of the eastwind angels are appointed. Their names are:

1. PHEY-RESH-VAV-ALEPH-LAMED
2. SAMEKH-RESH-YOD-ALEPH-LAMED

3. KAPH-NUN-YOD-ALEPH-LAMED
4. SHIN-SAMEKH-TOV-NUN-YOD-ALEPH-LAMED
5. SHIN-MEM-AYIN-YOD-ALEPH-LAMED
6. SHIN-MEM-AYIN-ALEPH-LAMED

They guard the exits of the eastwind.

At the gates of the westwind angels are appointed. Their names are:

1. TETH-VAV-RESH-NUN-YOD-ALEPH-LAMED
2. KAPH-RESH-NUN-YOD-ALEPH-LAMED
3. RESH-CHETH-YOD-ALEPH-LAMED
4. MEM-LAMED-TETH-YOD-ALEPH-LAMED
5. PHEY-LAMED-TETH-YOD-ALEPH-LAMED

They guard the exits of the westwind.

Above the clouds is found the foundation where He has constructed a sanctuary, an altar of incense and an altar of sacrifices. MICHIAL, the great prince, burns incense on the altar and presents an offering on the altar of sacrifice, as it is said: A PLACE WHERE YOU HAVE MADE YOUR ABODE, YHWH, A SANCTUARY, ALMIGHTY ONE, THAT YOUR HANDS HAVE PREPARED.

At the gates of foundation, in the direction of the northwind, angels are appointed. Their names are:

1. RESH-CHETH-VAV-MEM-YOD-ALEPH-LAMED
2. CHETH-NUN-VAV-NUN-YOD-ALEPH-LAMED
3. BETH-HAY-YOD-ALEPH-LAMED
4. SHIN-RESH-PHEY-YOD-ALEPH-LAMED
5. MEM-SAMEKH-YOD-ALEPH-LAMED
6. SHIN-RESH-ALEPH-LAMED

They guard the exits of the northwind.

At the gates of the southwind, angels are appointed. Their names are:

1. TETH-HAY-VAV-RESH-YOD-ALEPH-LAMED
2. MEM-CHETH-NUN-YOD-ALEPH-LAMED
3. GHIMEL-DALETH-YOD-ALEPH-LAMED
4. HAY-VAV-SHIN-YOD-ALEPH-LAMED
5. VAV-AYIN-NUN-MEM-ALEPH-LAMED
6. VAV-KAPH-SHIN-YOD-ALEPH-LAMED

They guard the exits of the southwind.

At the gates of the eastwind angels are appointed. Their names are:

1. TETH-RESH-PHEY-ALEPH-LAMED
2. BETH-HAY-LAMED-YOD-ALEPH-LAMED

3. BETH-GHIMEL-GHIMEL-ALEPH-LAMED
4. RESH-MEM-MEM-ALEPH-LAMED
5. KAPH-LAMED-BETH-SAMEKH
6. ALEPH-SAMEKH-RESH-VAV-NUN

They guard the exits of the eastwind.

At the gates of the westwind angels are appointed. Their names are:

1. ALEPH-LAMED-MEM-HAY-KAPH-NUN-ALEPH-LAMED
2. ALEPH-SAMEKH-CHETH-KAPH-NUN-ALEPH-LAMED
3. LAMED-VAV-BETH-KAPH-YOD-MEM
4. SAMEKH-VAV-MEM-CHETH-MEM
5. YOD-HAY-LAMED-ALEPH

They guard the exits of the westwind.

Above the base there is an abode containing angels, legions and the entire army of the upper world, as it is said: TO THE ABODE OF THE GODS OF FORMER TIMES.

At the gates of the abode, in the direction of the northwind, angels are appointed. Their names are:

1. ALEPH-CHETH-YOD-ALEPH-LAMED
2. ALEPH-NUN-YOD-ALEPH-LAMED
3. CHETH-TSADDE-KAPH-YOD-ALEPH-LAMED
4. MEM-RESH-GHIMEL-BETH-YOD-ALEPH-LAMED
5. SHIN-TAV-PHEY-YOD-ALEPH-LAMED
6. VAV-MEM-TAV-NUN-YOD-ALEPH-LAMED

They guard the exits of the northwind.

At the gates of the southwind angels are appointed. Their names are:

1. NUN-CHETH-BETH-DALETH-YOD-ALEPH-LAMED
2. NUN-PHEY-LAMED-YOD-ALEPH-LAMED
3. KAPH-DALETH-SHIN-YOD-ALEPH-LAMED
4. HAY-VAV-DALETH-RESH-YOD-ALEPH-LAMED
5. NUN-CHETH-MEM-YOD-ALEPH-LAMED
6. MEM-LAMED-CHETH-YOD-ALEPH-LAMED

They guard the exits of the southwind.

At the gates of the eastwind angels are appointed. Their names are:

1. SHIN-MEM-SHIN-YOD-ALEPH-LAMED
2. BETH-RESH-KAPH-YOD-ALEPH-LAMED
3. YOD-RESH-AYIN-SHIN-YOD-ALEPH-LAMED
4. CHETH-DALETH-RESH-YOD-ALEPH-LAMED
5. SHIN-RESH-PHEY-YOD-ALEPH-LAMED

    6. YOD-HAY-NUN-KAPH

    7. RESH-BETH-ALEPH

They guard the exits of the eastwind.

    At the gates of the westwind angels are appointed. Their names are:

    1. ALEPH-NUN-CHETH-ALEPH-LAMED

    2. PHEY-LAMED-LAMED-ALEPH-LAMED

    3. PHEY-LAMED-LAMED-ALEPH-LAMED

    4. TSADDE-VAV-RESH-TAV-KAPH

    5. SHIN-MEM

    6. KAPH-DALETH-VAV-SHIN

    7. TAV-YOD-PHEY-CHETH

    8. PHEY-YOD-LAMED-LAMED-ALEPH-LAMED

    9. CHETH-ALEPH-LAMED

    10. SHIN-MEM-HAY-SHIN-MEM

They guard the exits of the westwind.

    Above this abode there is another, of which it is said: BEHOLD THE HEAVENS, SEE YOUR HOLY AND MAGNIFICENT ABODE. Above this abode are the clouds, as it is said: SING TO THE LORD, CELEBRATE HIS NAME, OPEN A PATH FOR THE HORSEMAN OF THE CLOUDS. In the clouds are found justice, charity, judgment, the treasuries of life, benediction and peace, and the souls of the Just, the dew with which the Holy One, blessed be He, revives the bodies of the dead for the LIGHT.

    The span of the arc rests upon the clouds. Lofty with thousands of myriads of measures, it corresponds to the watchmen and to the angels. Above it are found the wheels of *ofanim* resting on the arc. Lofty with thousands of myriads of measures, the wheels correspond to the seraphim, to the ofanim and to the legions. Above that are found the feet of the living creatures, resting on the wheels of the ofanim. Lofty with thousands of myriads of measures, they correspond to the great princes.

    The summit of the arc rests on the head of the living creatures, from which radiates the rays of majesty. The firmament is like a formidable mirror extending above the rays of majesty. Lofty with thousands of myriads of measures, it corresponds to the princes of purification. Above the firmament is found a foundation and a luminous likeness situated upon the formidable mirror. Lofty with thousands of myriads of measures it corresponds to the verse: THE CHARIOTS OF GOD ADD UP TO THOUSANDS OF MYRIADS.

Above this is found an abode which is like fire. Placed upon the luminous likeness it is lofty with thousands of myriads of measures. It corresponds to the majestic rays and to the rains of glory. Above this abode there is a throne of sapphire resting on the likeness of the fire. Lofty with thousands of myriads of measures it corresponds to "strength" and to "power."

Above the throne of sapphire is the throne of Glory itself. Situated on sapphire stone it is lofty with thousands of myriads of measures. It is like the Lord of the entire world whose Glory is established on the throne, as it is said: I SEE YHWH SITTING ON THE LOFTY AND ELEVATED THRONE. Moreover it is said: A WORK OF TRANSPARENT SAPPHIRE WAS AT HIS FEET. The entire world like a talisman hangs from His powerful arm, as it is said: AND AT HIS FEET: THE WORLD.

The throne of Glory is encircled by the tents of splendor, with sapphire and emerald which conceal it from view, as it is said: THE EYE SHALL IN NO WAY SEE ME. FOR I WILL INVOKE THE NAME OF YHWH TO MAGNIFY OUR LORD GOD.

This prayer should be recited with fervent intention: You are blessed YHWH, our God, God of our fathers, God of Abraham, God of Isaac and God of Jacob, the great strong and awesome God, God Above All, who has created the heaven and the earth through His compassion! You are the King of kings, the Holy One, blessed be He!

Blessed be Your Name! Honored be Your Name! Venerated be Your Name! United be Your Name! That Your Name triumph! Praised be Your Name! Adored be Your Name! That Your memory continue through all eternity! You are seated on the throne of Glory and the living creatures ascend before You.

You are made of fire! Your throne is iron! The holy living creatures are aflame! Your servants are of consuming flame! You are the Prince above all other princes! Your chariots are above the ofanim! Send David to me, the son of Zalmath, your servant, to lead me to the wise at heart who are ordained for the servants of YH. That he expand my heart and my lips like a fountain that overflows the brim, LIKE A FOUNTAINHEAD WHOSE WATERS NEVER DRY UP!

> You are blessed, YHWH!
> Your great Name is above all other names!

Rise up, YHWH, in your power!
We want to sing and celebrate your valor!
Celebrate your great and formidable Name!
It is holy. I want to sing YHWH all the days of my life,
celebrate YHWH as long as I live!

—Translated by Jack Hirschman
from a French translation of
the original Hebrew

R. Akiba said: "In that hour when I ascended on high, I made marks at the entrances of heaven more than at the entrances of my own house, and when I came to the curtain, the angels of destruction went forth to destroy me. God said to them: 'Leave this elder alone, for he is worthy to contemplate my glory.' "

R. Akiba said: "In that hour when I ascended to the Merkabah, a heavenly voice went forth from under the throne of glory, speaking in the Aramaic language: 'Before God made heaven and earth, he established a vestibule to heaven, to go in and to go out. He established a solid name to strengthen [or: to design] by it the whole world. He invited Man [to this pre-established place] to enable him

To ascend on high,
to descend below,
to drive on wheels [of the Merkabah],
to explore the world,
to walk on dry ground,
to contemplate the splendor,
to dwell with the crown,
to praise the glory,
to say praise,
to combine letters,
to say names,
to behold what is on high,
and to behold what is below,
to know the meaning of the living,
and to see the vision of the dead,
to walk in rivers of fire,
and to know the lightning.

"And who can explain and who can behold what is before all this?

"It is said: For man shall not see Me and live (Exodus 33:20); and secondly it is said: That God speaks to man and he liveth (Deuteronomy 5:21); and thirdly it is said: I saw the Lord sitting upon a Throne, etc. (Isaiah 6:11)."

—Translated by Gershom Scholem

21

*B*en Azai beheld the sixth palace and saw the ethereal splendor *of the marble plates with which the palace was tessellated and his body could not bear it. He opened his mouth and asked them [apparently the angels were standing there]: "What kind of waters are these?" Whereupon he died. Of him it is said: Precious in the sight of the Lord is the death of his saints. Ben Zoma beheld the splendor of the marble plates and took them for water and his body could bear it not to ask them, but his mind could not bear it and he went out of his mind . . . R. Akiba ascended in peace and descended in peace.*

—MS Jewish Theological
Seminary, 828, fol. 16b,
translated by Gershom Scholem.

SHIUR QOMA

(The Measure of the Divine Body)

EDITOR'S NOTE. The *Shiur Qoma* dates from the Gaonic period, possibly
much earlier. It caused great controversy and many authorities denounced
it as being grossly anthropomorphic and spurious. Maimonides declared
that it should be burned. Its defenders claimed that it was not to be taken
literally but had an esoteric meaning. According to Gershom Scholem, the
Shiur Qoma must be counted among the oldest possessions of Jewish
gnosticism.

1. RABBI YISHMAEL SAID: Metatron the Great Lord said to me:
I bear this testimony on behalf of YHVH, ELOHIM of Israel, the
living and enduring EL, our Lord and Master,
   . . . that His height, from His Seat of Glory and up [is] 118 ten
   thousands (rebaboth) parasangs,
   . . . from His Seat of Glory down [is] 118 ten thousands (rebaboth)
   parasangs,
   . . . His total height [is] 236 ten thousand thousands para-
   sangs.[1]
   . . . From His Right Arm to His Left Arm [is] 77 ten thousand
   (parasangs),
   . . . from His Right Eye to [His] Left Eye [is] 30 ten thousands
   (parasangs);[2]
   . . . the Skull on His Head [is] three and one-third ten thousand
   (parasangs);[3]
   . . . the Crowns on His head [amount to] 60 ten thousands (para-

sangs) equaling the 60 ten thousands of the tribes of Israel.[4]
Therefore is He called the Great, the Mighty and the Awesome
EL:

KLYTYH
YDYDVT
EL
HAY (Living)
KLTA
'AVVTA
HMQVQ
TQTF
HQTF
HQTM
QTF
B'ABVR
MSVS

Blessed be the Name of the glory of His Kingdom for ever.

2. It is said that he who knows this mystery,[5] is assured of his
portion in the world to come (is assured to be a son of the world
to come), and will be saved from the punishment of Hell (Gehin-
nom), and from all kinds of punishments and evil decrees about to
befall the world, and will be saved from all kinds of witchcraft, for
He saves us, protects us, redeems us, and rescues me _____[6] from
all evil things, from all harsh decrees, and from all kinds of punish-
ments for the sake of His Great Name.

3. [A long hymn follows in alphabetical order, the alphabet being
repeated several times, the hymn concludes with the verse:]
    Lord of Hosts, happy is the man that trusts in You (Psalms
84:13).

4. RABBI YISHMAEL SAID: I have seen the King of the Kings of
Kings sitting on a high and exalted throne, and His hosts stand
before Him on His right and on His left, the Lord of the Presence
(Sar Hapanim) whose name is Metatron

RVH
PYSQVNY"H
PSQY"N
ATM"VN
HYGR"VN
SYGR"VN
SRT"VN
SNYGR"VN
MYQ"VN
HSKV"M
STY"M
HSK"M
HQYR"YN
N"A
DVQYR"YN
ZYN"A
RB"A
NNTV"S
ZNTV"F
HKYQ"M

5. RABBI YISHMAEL SAID: What is the measure of the Holy One, Blessed be He, who is hidden from all creatures? The sole of His feet fills the whole world, as it is said (Isaiah 66:1) "The heaven is my throne, and the earth is my foot-stool." The height of each sole is three ten thousand thousands of parasangs.

... The sole of His right foot is called: PRSYMYA, ATRQTT
... and His left sole [is called]: AGTMN.
... From the sole of His feet to His ankles [the height is] one thousand ten thousands and five hundred parasangs, and the same for His left [ankle].
... The name of the right ankle [is] TZNMTNYH, TSSQM,
... and the [name] of the left [ankle] is ASTMN.
... From His ankles to His knees the height [is] nineteen thousand and four parasangs, both right and left.
... the name of His left leg [is] QNGGY, MHRYH, TSSQVM,
... and of the right [leg is] MMGA, VZVYA
... The height from His knees to His thighs [is] twelve thousand, ten thousand and fourteen hundred parasangs, both right and left. His name: MMGA, VZVYA.[7]

. . . The right thigh is called SSPVST, PRSB,

. . . and the left [thigh is called] TFGT, HZYZA.

. . . From His thighs to His neck [the height is] twenty-four thousand ten thousands of parasangs.

. . . the name of His loins of loins [is] MVTNYHV, ATSGH, YDYDYH,

. . . on His Heart are inscribed seventy names:

> ZZ
>
> ZDQ (Zedeq, righteous)
>
> ZHYEL
>
> ZVR (ZUR, rock)
>
> ZBY
>
> ZDYQ (Zaddik, Saint)
>
> K'AF
>
> SR'AF
>
> BVHN
>
> ZBAVT (Z'BAOTH, Hosts)
>
> SDY (Shaddai)
>
> ALHYM (ELOHIM)
>
> YHVHY (Shem haMephorash)
>
> ZH (white, Song of Solomon 5:10)
>
> DGVL (Dagul, distinguished, Song of Solomon 5:10)
>
> VADVM (Vadom, ruddy, Song of Solomon 5:10)
>
> SSS
>
> 'AAA
>
> AAA
>
> AYA
>
> AHV
>
> RBYH
>
> HH
>
> HV
>
> VH
>
> ZZZ
>
> PPP
>
> KN
>
> HH
>
> HY
>
> HY
>
> HY
>
> RVKB (Rokheb, Horseman)

'ARBVT (Araboth, heaven)
YH (first part of Shem haMephorash)
HH
VH (second part of Shem haMephorash)
MMM
NNN
HVV
YH
HFZ (HAFEZ or HEFEZ)
HZZ
AY
ZA
T'AA
A'AA
QQQ (QODOSH, QODOSH, QODOSH, Holy, Holy, Holy)
QSR (KESHER)
RZ (RAZ, secret, mystery)
ZK (ZAKH, pure)
GBVR (GIBOR, strong)
YA
YA
YVD
HAN
ALF (ALEPH or ELEPH)
DYMN
PAF
KVF
RAV
YYY
YYA
KKB
TTT
BKK
PLL
SYYM (SAYEM) concluding with:
BARUK SEM K'BOD MAKUTO L'OLAM VAED
(Blessed be the Name of the glory of His Kingdom for ever).

. . . His neck. Thirteen thousand ten thousands and eight hundred

　　　parasangs [is] the height of His neck, its name: SNNYHV,
　　　VBHTYQN.

... The roundness of His head [(circumference) is] three hundred
　　　thousand, ten thousands and thirty-three and one third para-
　　　sangs, which the mouth cannot express and the ear cannot
　　　hear, its name: ATR, HVDRYH, ATSYH, ATTYH.

... His beard [is] eleven thousand five hundred (one ten thousand
　　　and one thousand and five hundred) parasangs, its name:
　　　HDRRQ, SMYA.

... The appearance of the countenance as [well as] the appearance
　　　of the cheeks is like unto the likeness of Ruah and in the form
　　　of Neshama [which] no creature is able to mention or describe.

... His body [GVIYAH] like chrysolite [TARSIS].

... His splendor [ZIV] glitters awesomely from out of the midst
　　　of the darkness (Psalm 18:12 and 2 Samuel 22:12).

... Clouds and thick darkness [ANAN V'ARAFEL] surround Him
　　　(Psalm 97:2).

... All Lords of the Presence [SARE HEANIM] stand before Him as
　　　ordained [K'TIKUN].

... [For the nose and the tongue] we do not have a measure, only
　　　names are revealed to us. The name of the nose: LGBTYYA, and
　　　also ABRGG, TTPYYH.

... His tongue [reaches] from one end of the World to the other,
　　　for it is said: He declares His word unto Jacob, His statutes
　　　and His ordinances unto Israel [Psalm 147:19). He who knows
　　　not [how] to conclude this verse is in error for it is said: He
　　　declares, etc: its name [is] ASSGYYHV, VAYYA.

... His forehead is called MSSGYYHV, YNAYYA, NGM.

... On His forehead is inscribed

　　　　　YYHV
　　　　　HH
　　　　　YVH
　　　　　VYH
　　　　　HA
　　　　　HY
　　　　　HY
　　　　　HY
　　　　　HA
　　　　　HH

VVH

YYY

HV

VYHV

HH

YH

AY

HH

YH

YH

YA

HV

HV

YYHYY

HYH

YHV

HS

HA

HYH

VYH

. . . The black of His right eye [is] 11,500 parasangs, similarly His left [eye].

. . . The right [eye] is named AZRYYH, ATTYTVS.

. . . The Lord [of the eye?] is called RHBEL (RHBYEL or RHBEL).

. . . The left [eye] is called MTT, GRVFMZYA, and the sparks that issue [emanate] from them [it] give light to all creatures.

. . . The white of His right eye [measures] twenty-two ten thousands and two parasangs, similarly [that of] His left [eye], and is named: BZQVHA.

. . . From His right shoulder to His left shoulder [is] sixteen thousand thousands parasangs.

. . . The right shoulder is named MTTGRYAA, 'ANGN.

. . . The left [shoulder] is called TTMHYNTA, it also has another name SLMH YNNYEL [alternate reading: and it has one name, meaning that the two shoulders have one name in common].

. . . From His right arm to His left arm [is] twelve thousand ten thousand parasangs.

. . . His arm double [The meaning is, perhaps, that the two arms together are double the size mentioned before, namely 24,000 ten thousand parasangs].

. . . The name of the right arm [is] GBRHZZYA, AKBVY,

. . . and of the left [arm] MTTGHZZYVH.

. . . The [size of] the fingers of His hands. Each finger [is] fifteen thousand ten thousand parasangs, both of the right and of the left.

. . . [The name of the fingers or of each finger] of the right [hand]: TTMZMZ, GGMVT, GGSMS

. . . and of the left [hand] TZ, MF, TTMT, AGGMZ, AGGMT, SVSNTM [the last name is Shoshanim, roses]. This way, you count beginning with the thumb.

. . . The palms of His hands [are] four thousand ten thousand parasangs, both the right and the left [hands].

. . . The right [hand] is named HZZYA, ATGRYYA,

. . . and the left [hand] is named: ASHVZYH.

. . . The fingers [toes] of His feet [are] ten thousand ten thousands parasangs, each finger [toe] on both right and left [feet].

. . . the name of the right [toes]: ATRMZ, ADRMT, BRMNM, BRTHMYM, VAHVZ,

. . . and [the names of the] left [toes]: ZKYYN, KZKYYN, HTMT, AHVZ. You count the way you count those of the hand [namely beginning with the big toe].

. . . Therefore, is He called: the Great, the Mighty, the Awesome EL, for it is said (DOVARIM 10:17) For the YHVH your ELOHIM, He is ELOHIM of ELOHIM, Lord of Lords, the great EL, the Mighty and the Awesome.

6. HE SAID TO ME, however, the size of the parasangs, what they measure . . . each parasang consists of three mils, each mil contains ten thousand cubits, each cubit two spans (ZERETH), and His span fills the whole OLAM [world, or universe], as it is written (Isaiah 40, 12): "Who has measured in the hollow of His hand the waters, and meted out the heavens with His span."[8]

7. Rabbi Nathan, the pupil of R. Yishmael said: He also gave me the measure of the nose right and left, as well as that of the lips and cheeks. Also he gave me the measure of the forehead, he also set down rules for every cubit.

. . . The width of the forehead is equal to the height of the neck, and so is the shoulder.

. . . The length of the nose [is] like the length of the small finger.

. . . The height of the cheek is equal to half the roundness of the head.

. . . These measures are also found in human beings.

. . . [The size of] His lips: seventy-seven parasangs.

. . . His upper lip is called GBRH, TYA

. . . the lower one HZRGYA.

. . . His mouth is fire consuming fire.

. . . when He speaks its name (is) ASDRA.

    [the next five words are not translatable]

. . . The crown on His head [is] five hundred thousand by five hundred thousand [parasangs].

. . . its name is VYS.

. . . the precious stone between its horns [rays?] is called YS. AMV ALY YS AMI ALY is engraved on it.

. . . My friend is white and ruddy, distinguished among ten thousand.

  His head is bright as the finest gold,

  His locks are like waving foliage and black as a raven.

  His eyes are doves by streamlets of water.

  His cheeks are as a bed of roses . . .

  Two thousand, ten thousand parasangs.

  And whoever does not conclude with this verse (Song of Songs 5:10–16) is in error.

. . . His cheeks are as a bed of roses,

  As banks of sweet herbs;

  His lips are as lilies,

  Dropping with flowing myrrh.

  His hands are as rods of gold, set with beryl;

  His body is as polished ivory, overlaid with sapphires.

  His legs are as pillars of marble,

  Set upon sockets of fine gold;

  His aspect is like Lebanon,

  Excellent as the cedars.

  His mouth is most sweet;

  Yea, He is altogether lovely.

  This is my beloved, and this is my Friend,

  O daughters of Jerusalem.

. . . AGTYH, THVN, YHVN, TVB, THVR, YVD, YVD, YVD, YHYH, HSYN, HSYN

. . . Holy, Holy, Holy is the YHVH of Hosts, the whole earth is full of His glory.

. . . [The measure of] His eyelids, [is] like the measure of His eyes.

. . . The right [eye] is named HDR, VVLD

. . . the left [eye is named] APDH [in Lemberg APRH] ZZYHV.

. . . The height of His ears [is] like the height of His forehead.

. . . The right [ear] is called AZTHYYA.

. . . The left [ear is called] MNVGHV.

. . . Hence, the total measure [of the Divine Stature] is ten thousands of ten thousands ten thousand thousands parasangs in height, and one thousand thousand ten thousands of parasangs in width.[9]

8. RABBI YISHMAEL TOLD THIS [THING] TO RABBI AQUIBA, he said to me: He who knows this measure of our Creator, and the praise of the Holy One, blessed be He, Who is hidden from the creatures, is assured that he is a son of the world to come [he will inherit the world to come], and will have in this world the good of the other world, and will live long in this world.

9. RABBI YISHMAEL SAID TO ME [the above mentioned Rabbi Nathan?] in the presence of his pupils. I and Rabbi Aquiba vouch for this, that whoever knows this measure of our Creator, and the praise of the Holy One, blessed be He, he will surely be a son of the world to come, provided he learns it regularly every day:

. . . His body filling the Throne of Fire of the Torah.

. . . His name: BG, BG, GB, HVMG.

. . . His locks [of] His body are named: DBR, BRYR, DVBG.

. . . They have half of a nickname called: GL, SRB.

. . . One of His eyes with which He sees from one end of the world to the other is named: AKSST, the sparks issuing from it give light to all creatures;

. . . the other one, which sees backwards [with which He sees in advance], what is going to happen in the future, is name ATNVGST.

. . . His body is like unto a bow, the bow is like unto. . . . its name: LQSSYA, half of it is named, MN, KMZ.

. . . His sword is called MZMZYT, MZYA.

... His Throne of Glory is named, LVRKZ, PYRVTA.

... The place of His seat is called, DVRPZ, PRVRPZ, this is also His nickname.

... The feet of His glory are the Hayoth. The Hayoth standing under Him.

... The first foot of the Throne, which is a Haya is called AGLYV, HZBYYH.

... The second foot of the Throne, which is a Haya is called: BBBK, PLBYYPTY.

... The third foot of the Throne, which is a Haya, by name KBBB, ALGYY.

... The fourth foot, which is a Haya is called, AZBYYA, BZBZ.

... The likeness of their faces ... the nature of a lion, the stamp of an eagle, the image of an ox, and the blank face of a man.

.. Each has four faces, four faces, and four faces on each corner [of a face], sixty-four faces for each Haya.

.. Each Haya has four faces and [four] wings, each wing consists of four wings; four wings to a face, four wings to a wing ... sixty-four wings to each Haya.

.. The Lord of the human-face is ALYH, AMZB, AMZ, AMT, KMZ.

.. The names of the Lord of the lion-face [are] HVDV, DYH, HYDVAH, AL, AVRYA, HVD, HVYH, TMGMZ.

.. The Lord of the ox-face is called [SVR in both texts] HLYH, ZMZMMKA, MSKYA.

.. And the name of the Lord of the eagle-face [is] 'APPY, ALYH, MMZYT, ZHVRYRYAL.

.. When Israel sinned, the ox-face was hidden away, and was replaced with a Cherub. The name of the Lord of the Cherub-face [is] TMTMNY, ALYH, KRVBYH, KRBH, PSPSYH, PZPZYH, HNQNQYA.

.. They [the Hayoth] are the ones who say Holy, Holy, Holy (Isaiah 6:3), it is they who say Blessed be the glory (Ezekiel 3:12) as it is written (Psalms 146:19) "He declares His word unto Jacob."

. and he who does not conclude with the book of Bereshith, with the order of Creation, errs in the glory of the Holy One, blessed be He.

. His glory fills everything, hosts of thunder rage on His right. Bands of people rage on His left, and colors [signs, Simanim] rage in front of Him.

. . . Within the colors, splendor, and darkness, cloud, thick cloud ['Arafel] and mire of clay [TITHYAVEN].

. . . In front of Him [is] a field of herbs [ZEROIM].

. . . Between one star and another [is] the source of lightning.

. . . between one lightning and another [is] the door of HASHMAL.

. . . and above: winds, roarings, thunder and lightning, and the holy palms,[10] and ropes of seals, used for ascending and descending.

. . . On the Holy One blessed be He, [are] grace [HEN], love [HESED] glory [KABOD], mercy [RAHAMIM], splendour [HOD], crown ['ATERETH], beauty [HADAR], adorning [TIFERETH], and majesty [GEUTH].

. . . The Hand of the Holy One, blessed be He, [is named] META-TRON.

. . . They say: Mighty and Strong..

. . . They say: Holy and Blessed..

. . . and They appear before Him with a great sound [as in Ezekiel 1:24; as they went, a noise like the sound of a host].

. . . They stand before Him.

. . . The Youth [NA'AR] METATRON appears and prostrates himself before the Holy One, blessed be He, His name AHH..

. . . He praises and glorifies and says: Blessed be the glory of YHVH from His place, YHV, HV, HV, YVHV, YHYYH, Blessed be the glory of YHVH from His place.

. . . and they repeat after him: Blessed be the glory of YHVH from His place, and Blessed be the name of the glory for ever.

. . . He [METATRON] enters in front under the Throne of Glory.

. . . He is accompanied by stones of fire and hailstones and a wall of roaring [Z'AAF] on his right.

. . . on his left he is accompanied by wings of storm and strength of tempest.

. . . When METATRON enters before the Holy One, blessed be He, under the Throne of Glory, he holds [the Throne] with a multitude of wings, and all the ministering angels come before the Holy One, blessed be He, and say: the great, the mighty and awesome EL.

. . . They praise the Holy One, blessed be He, thrice daily through METATRON. The Holy One, blessed be He, bestowed His splendor and His beauty on the ministering Angel METATRON, the Lord of the Presence, who has been appointed grand master over all Lords and ministering angels.

... They stand before him, and he stands higher and higher up-
wards, and ministers before ADM [Adam] a fire consuming fire
KSA [KISE, throne] is its name.

... This is the seat of METATRON, the Lord of the Presence which
is written with ONE- LETTER [ALEPH, which has the number
1) with which heaven and earth have been created, and sealed
with the ring AHYH ASER AHYH, and is written with seven
letters, and seven letters, and twenty-four letters, and seventy-
two names, and seven Kedushoth, and is placed on six of their
names, and is engraved on twelve stones, and is written on
seven sounds [voices] on a height of six by six [see Book of the
Concealment: Zohar ii 186b].

... It was given to our teacher Moses [Rabbenu] in innermost
chambers, in hidden hiddenness, in wonder of wonders.

... The Holy One, blessed be He, permitted neither Adam nor
Shem, the son of Noah, nor Abraham, Isaac or Jacob to use
it. Only to Moses did He given permission to use it as it is
written: "Behold I send an angel before you" (Shemot 23:20),
and the Holy One, blessed be He, warned Moses to beware of
Him, as it says: "Beware of Him, and obey His voice, disobey
Him not, for He will not pardon your transgressions because
My Name is in Him." (Shemot 23:21) And Moses said to the
Holy One blessed be He; "If Your NOT-PRESENCE go with me;
carry us, NOT, up from here." (Shemot 33:15)[11]

... The angels that are with Him [METATRON] come and sur-
round the Throne of Glory, they on one side, Hayoth on the
other, and the Shekina on the Shekina of Glory in the middle.
A Haya ascends on the Seraphim and descends on the dwell-
ing place of METATRON, and announces in a loud voice, in the
sound of a soft whisper [still small voice]: This is the Throne
of Glory.

... Immediately the OFANIM become silent, the angels become
quiet, The 'IRIN KADISIN make haste and rush into the River
of Fire [NEHR DINUR], the Hayoth turn their faces down to
the ground, METATRON brings the deafening fire and puts it
in the ears of the Hayoth, that they hear not the voice of the
glory of the Holy One, blessed be He, and the explicit name
[SEM HAMEFORAS] that METATRON is pronouncing at that
time.

... Thus is He calling the Holy One, blessed be He, by His living,

pure, holy, powerful, majestic, strong, strengthful, beloved,
mighty, glorified and awesome name:

ADRYHV
AHRKY
HHYY
YHVH
AHYH ASER AHYH
HHY
YVA
HKH
HH
VH
HVH
VHV
HH
HYA
HVA
HH
YHYHY
HY
YHYH
YHVH

. . He who lives for ever, this is my name for ever, and this is my
memorial unto all generations [Shemot 3:15]. Blessed be the
name of the glory of His Kingdom for ever. Its interpretation
in the language of purity [METATRON pronounces the SEM
HAMeFORAS, Brilliant Name of Fire, in the language of purity]:

YHV
HHYV
HYH
HY
YH
YH
HVHY
HYH
VYHYV
YHV
HHY

VYHH
YHY
HY
HHYV
HYY
HV
YHVH
YHV
HYHV
HY
YHVH

Blessed be the name of the glory of His Kingdom for ever.

10. Here follows in the text a hymn, and Psalms 93, 29, and 24.

—Translated by
The Work of The Chariot

Part Two

When Abraham, our father arose, he looked and saw and investigated and observed and engraved and hewed and combined and formed and calculated, and his creation was successful. Then the Master of all revealed Himself to him, and made a covenant with him and with his seed forever. He made a covenant with him on the ten fingers of his hands, and this is the covenant of the tongue; and on the ten toes of his feet, and this is the covenant of the circumcision; and tied the twenty-two letters of the Torah to his tongue and revealed to him their secret. He drew them through water; stormed through air, He kindled them in fire, and melted them into ten double and twelve simple letters.

—*Sefer Yetsirah*,
TRANSLATED BY PHINEAS MORDELL

SEFER YETSIRAH

EDITOR'S NOTE. The *Sefer Yetsirah* is literal and secret at the same time. It is dense, compressed, elusively simple. Its concepts continue to intrigue and to escape captivity. Of all the Kabbalistic texts, it has been the most continuously translated into English. In the past five years I have come across five new translations of the book.

According to Gershom Scholem, the *Sefer Yetsirah* was written sometime between the third and sixth centuries in Palestine "by a devout Jew with leanings towards mysticism . . . [his] aim was speculative and magical rather than ecstatic."

The book consists of six brief chapters and exists in two versions. The first and earlier version is shorter than the second. Yet both together are less than thirty-two pages.

It is the earliest systematic treatment of the Jewish mystical doctrine. It has been called the earliest scientific treatise in the Hebrew language. It contains the germ of a system of Hebrew phonetics and of a natural philosophy and physiology based on that doctrine.

It is the book which prepared me for the Kabbalah and provided me with an insight into the Kabbalistic process of receiving the mysteries intrinsic in language. Its mystical shorthand remains a clear statement of the inner and outer environments of human possibility. The very literalness of the text acts as a fulcrum for a dual reception/perception of what is within and without.

Chapter I

§ 1

Thirty-two mysterious ways of wisdom has the Lord, Lord of hosts, ordained through Scribe, Script, and Scroll.

§ 2

These are the thirty-two mysterious ways of wisdom, twenty-two letters, which are ten double and twelve simple.

§ 3

The ten double letters are ת, ש, ר, פ, כ, ד, ג, ב, א ten and not nine, ten and not eleven. The twelve simple letters are ח, ז, ה, ק, צ, ע, ס, נ, מ, ל, י, ט twelve and not eleven; twelve and not thirteen. Investigate them, examine them, establish the matter clearly, and restore the Creator to His abode.

§ 4

Twenty-two letters are engraved by the voice, hewn out in the air, and established by the mouth in five places.

§ 5

Twenty-two letters He engraved, hewed out, weighed, changed, combined, and formed out of them all existing forms, and all forms that may in the future be called into existence.

§ 6

How did He combine them, weigh them, and change them around? א, with all of them and all of them with א; ב, , with all of them and all of them with ב; and so forth, all of them turning around in order; thus all words and all forms are derived from them.

§ 7

Twenty-two letters are engraved in a circle, with 484 divisions, and the circle turns forward and backward; thus in ענג [delight], the ע is at the beginning; in נגע [plague], the ע is at the end.

§ 8

Out of two stones two houses are built, out of three stones six houses are built, out of four stones twenty-four houses are built, out of five stones one hundred and twenty houses are built, out of six stones seven hundred and twenty houses are built, out of seven stones five thousand and forty houses are built. Go and count further, what the mouth is unable to pronounce, and the ear is unable to hear.

Chapter II

§ 9

He combines and changes about and makes all forms and all words
with the One Name; thus all forms and all words are derived from
the One Name.

§ 10

Three vowels אמש constitute a great secret, marvellous and hidden.
From them go forth air, water, and fire. Fire above and water
below, and air holds the balance between them; thus מ is mute,
ש is hissing, and א holds the balance between them.

§ 11

Three vowels אמ״ה constitute a great secret, mysterious and hid-
den. From them go forth air, water, and earth. Four vowels
    , which are five vowels, that gave birth to twenty-seven
consonants.

§ 12

The five vowels stand each one by itself, but the twenty-seven
consonants are all dependent on the vowels. He made them in the
form of a state, and arranged them like an army in battle array. The
only One Master, God, the faithful King, rules over them from His
holy abode forever and ever.

§ 13

The five vowels and twenty-seven consonants, these are the twenty-
two letters which the Lord, Lord of hosts, established out of the
ten digits and zero.

Chapter III

§ 14

The ten digits and zero—close thy mouth from speaking and thy
heart from thinking, and if thy heart should leap, bring it back to
its place; for concerning this has the covenant been made.

§ 15

The ten digits and zero, their end is joined with their beginning, and their beginning with their end, as the flame is attached to the coal. Understand wisdom and be wise in understanding, that there is but one Master, and there is no second to Him, and before One, what countest thou?

§ 16

The ten digits and zero, their appearance is like lightning; to their aim there is no limit. They go and come at His word, and at His command they pursue like the whirlwind, and kneel before His throne.

§ 17

These are the ten digits and zero, with which the Eternally Living God, blessed be His name, ordained His world.

§ 18

One—He graved and hewed out of it voice, air and speech, and this is the Holy Spirit.

§ 19

Two—He graved and hewed out of them void and chaos. Void is a green line that surrounds the whole universe, and chaos refers to viscous stones, sunk in the abyss, whence water comes forth.

§ 20

Three—He graved and hewed out of them mud and clay. He arranged them like a garden bed. He set them up like a wall. He covered them like a pavement, and poured upon them snow, and the earth was formed.

§ 21

Four—He graved and hewed out of them the throne of glory, the ophanim, the seraphim, the holy animals, and the ministering angels.

§ 22

He formed existence out of void, something out of nothing, and he hewed large stones out of intangible air, thus twenty-two in number, one in spirit.

§ 23

Also God set the one over against the other, good against evil, and evil against good; good out of good, and evil out of evil; good testing evil, and evil testing good; good is stored away for the good, and evil is stored away for the evil.

§ 24

When Abraham our father arose, he looked and saw and investigated and observed and engraved and hewed and combined and formed and calculated, and his creation was successful. Then the Master of all revealed Himself to him, and made a covenant with him and with his seed forever. He made a covenant with him on the ten fingers of his hands, and this is the covenant of the tongue; and on the ten toes of his feet, and this is the covenant of circumcision; and tied the twenty-two letters of the Torah to his tongue and revealed to him their secret. He drew them through water; stormed through air, He kindled them in fire, and melted them into ten double and twelve simple letters.

—Translated by Phineas Mordell

Part Three

Rabbi Berekiah said: What does this verse mean (Gen. 1:3): "And God said: Let there be light and there was light," and it is not written "it became"? This is like a king who had a beautiful jewel and put it aside until he determined its place and put it there. This is what is written: "Let there be light and there was light," for it was already there.

—Bahir, 17

from
BOOK BAHIR

EDITOR'S NOTE. The *Book Bahir* is one of the oldest Kabbalist texts and of primary importance to the development of Kabbalah's symbolic language. Modern scholarship believes it was edited in the twelfth century in Provence, incorporating ancient texts transmitted to Europe from the East —an extension of early oriental gnostic concepts which entered into the mainstream of Jewish mystical thought.

It's a fragmentary work, a collage of voices on the page which appear and disappear like the mysterious rabbis in Edmond Jabes' *Le Livre des Questions* [Editions Gallimard, Paris, 1963]. Often a thought or conversation ends abruptly, resonating a far greater mystery by its incompletion —intangible and ineffable fragments from a lost book.

The *Book Bahir* is the earliest source to deal with the Sephiroth, the realm of divine attributes. It also proposes other technical terminology which later become a part of Kabbalah's basic vocabulary; that is, the world of *beriah* ["creation"], the world of *yetsirah* ["formation"]. It has the first reference in Kabbalistic literature to the doctrine of transmigration of souls, *gilgul.*

The English translation by Joachim Neugroschel has been translated from the definitive edition prepared by Gershom Scholem.

TRANSLATOR'S NOTE. The Biblical quotations are from the Authorized King James Version, except when it differs from the interpretations in the *Book Bahir.* In such cases, the translator has used appropriate renderings, but has attempted to keep them in the style of the Authorized Version. Despite the obvious problems inherent in such an approach and in the King James translation itself, I feel that the historical span between the redaction of the Jewish Bible in Babylon and the composition of the Book of Bahir in Europe was so great (a period of some 2,000 years), that the diction of Biblical quotations would have to be different from the language of the Bahir. Furthermore, the Bible was written mainly in Hebrew (with a few parts in Aramaic or, better, Targumic, i.e., Judeo-Aramaic). The Bahir, however, was written in a mixture of Hebrew and a Targumic derived from the Talmud. My aim in translating the text of the Bahir has been to strive for a modern, literary diction devoid of anything smacking of colloquial usages (even though, as Gershom Scholem points out, the language of the Bahir is "wretched"). I had hoped that the King James diction for the Biblical translations would give them the majesty and grandeur that the Hebrew Bible enjoys in the Jewish tradition.

1. Rabbi Nekhunya ben Hakhana said: A verse of Scripture says (Job 37:21): "Men see not the light which shines in the skies" and another verse of Scripture says (Psalms 18:11): "He made darkness his covering" and likewise we read (Psalms 97:2): "Clouds and darkness are round him." A contradiction! [However, then] comes a third verse and strikes a balance (Psalms 139:12): "Yea, darkness is not dark before thee, but the night shineth as the day, darkness as day."

2. Rabbi Berekiah said: What does this verse mean (Gen. 1:2): "And the earth was *tohu va-bohu* [waste and wild]? What does "was" mean? That it already existed as *tohu.* And what is *tohu?* Something that confuses men and again becomes *bohu.* And what is *bohu?* Something on which there is reality, as *bohu* is written: *bo,* on it; *hu',* is something.

3. And why does [the Torah] begin with the letter Beth [*Bereshith* —"In the beginning"]? Because that is the letter with which *Berakha,* blessing, begins. And how [do we know] that the Torah is called a blessing? Because it is written (Deut. 33:23): "And full of God's blessing, the sea." And what does ". . . and full of God's blessing, the sea" mean? The sea is the Torah, as it is written (Job 11:9): "The measure thereof . . . is broader than the sea." And what does "and full of God's blessing" mean? Simply that Beth means blessing everywhere, as is written [at the start of the Torah]: "Bereshit," in the beginning. "Beginning," however means (according to Psalms 111:10) wisdom, and wisdom is blessing, for it is written (I Kings 5:26): ". . . And God blessed Solomon and gave Solomon wisdom." Like a king who has married his daughter to his

son and presents her to him and says to him: Do with her as you wish.

Now what does this *berakha,* blessing, mean? It is related to *berekh,* knee, as it is written (Isaiah 45:23): ". . . unto me every knee shall bend," the place to which every knee bends. Like those who wish to see the king and know not where the king is. First they ask where the king's house is and then they ask: Where is the king? Therefore: ". . . unto me every knee shall bend"—even the knee of the higher beings—"every tongue shall swear."

4. Rabbi Amora sat and spoke: What does this verse mean (Deut. 33:23): "and full of God's blessing: possess thou the sea and the south"? It means: Everywhere is the beth blessed, because it is the "fullness" as the verse can be understood: "And the fullness is God's blessing." And out of it he gives drink to the needy. And, at the first beginning, counsel was gotten from the "fullness." Like a king who wanted to build his palace on powerful cliffs, and he had the rock smashed and blocks hewn out of it; a great wellspring of flowing water sprang forth. The king said: Since I have flowing water now, I will plant a garden for my delight, for myself and all creatures. That is what is written (Prov. 8:30): "Then I was by him, as one brought up with him: and I was daily his delight, rejoicing sometimes before him." The Torah spoke: For two thousand years I was a delight in his bosom, for it is written "daily," and his day is two thousand years, for it is written (Psalms 90:4): "For a thousand years in thy sight are but as yesterday when it is past," from here on and further [only] at times, for it says "sometimes," and finally, for ever and ever, for it is written (Isaiah 48:9): "And I hold back my praise for thee." What does "my praise" mean? This can be deduced from the verse (Psalms 145:1): "David's *psalm of* praise, I shall elevate thee." The meaning of praise thus follows from "I shall elevate thee," and the meaning of elevation from [*ibid.*]: "and I will bless thy name for ever and ever." And why more praise [beyond elevation]? This is like a king who planted trees in his garden although downpours were falling and it absorbs, and the soil is wet, after all, he has to water it from the source, as it is written (Psalms 111:10): "The fear of God is the beginning of all wisdom: a good understanding have they who practice it," and if you think it lacks anything, then it is written [at the end of the verse]: "His praise endureth forever."

5. Rabbi Amora: What does the verse mean (Deut. 33:23): "And full of God's blessing: possess thou the sea and the south"? Moses said: If you follow his commandments, you will possess this world and the next world, which is likened to the sea, as it is written (Job 11:9): "The measure thereof is broader than the sea." This world, however, is likened to the south, as it is written (Joshua 15:19): "Thou hast given me the land of the Negev" [building], and the Targum translates: The south land.

6. And he continued: Why did God add a Hey and no other letter to the name of our Father Abraham? So that all the parts of man would be worthy of eternal life [which is likened to the sea]. Thus, virtually, was the work [literally: the building] completed, as it is written (Gen. 9:6): "For in the image of God made he man," and [the spelling of] Abraham has the numerical value of 248, which is the number of man's parts.

7. What does (in Deut. 33:23) *"yerashah,* possess" mean? [Grammatically] it should have been "rash." This indicates that God himself is included here, for *yerashah* is *resh yah,* "possess God." Like a king who had two treasures and put part of one aside. Eventually he said to his son: Take what I have in both treasures. The son said [to himself]: Perhaps he does not wish to give me what he has put aside. But the [king] said to him: Take everything. And that is what the verse [ibid.] means: "The sea and the south possess." Possess *"yah"* as well, everything is yours, may you only walk in His ways!

8. Rabbi Bun said: What does the verse mean (Prov. 8:23): "I was set up from everlasting, from the beginning, or ever the earth was"? What does me'olam [here] mean? Something that had to be hidden from all the world, as it is written (Eccles. 3:11): "also he hath set the world in their heart," do not treat *ha'olam,* the world, but *ha'alem,* the hiding. The Torah said: I was first the beginning of the world, for it is written "I was set up from everlasting, from the beginning." And if you think that the earth may have come first, then it is written next: "or ever the earth was." Just as it is written (Gen. 1:1): "In the beginning, created," and what did He create? What the universe needs; and only then comes "God," and what comes right after? "The heavens and the earth."

9. And what does this mean (Eccles. 7:14): "God also hath set the one against the other"? He created the bohu and gave it its place

in peace, he created the tohu and gave it its place in evil. Bohu in peace, for it is written (Job 25:2): "He maketh peace in his high places." This teaches that Michael, the prince to God's right hand, is water and hail, and Gabriel, the prince to God's left hand, fire, and he put peace as a balance between them, and that is what is meant by the verse: "He maketh peace in his high places." And how do we know that [peace] means bohu? Because it is written (Isaiah 45:7): "I make peace and create evil." How? Evil from the tohu and peace from the bohu.

10. And once again Rabbi Bun sat and spoke: What does the verse mean (Isaiah 45:7): "I form the light and create the darkness"? This means: With light, which has substance, stands [the expression] "form"; with darkness, which has no substance, stands [the expression] "create," as it is written (Amos 4:13): "he that formeth the mountains, and createth the winds." Yet one can also explain it as follows: With the light, which has being—for it is written (Gen. 1:3): "And God said: Let there be light," and being can only come about through a making—stands [the expression] "form"; with the darkness, for which there is no making, only a separating and dividing, stands "create," just as one says: So and so has become healthy.

11a. Why is [the letter] beth closed on all sides and opened only in front? This teaches us that it is the house of the world, and that is what the utterance means: "God is the place of the world, yet the world is not his place, and read not *beth*, but *baith*, house, as is written (Prov. 24:3): "A house is built through wisdom."

b. Whom does the beth resemble? Man, who was created with wisdom [Khokhma], for he is closed on all sides and open only in front, whereas the aleph is open in back.

c. Someone said to him: The protrusion of the aleph, which is open in back [exists] because without it man could not survive. Thus without beth and its protrusion [?] the world could not survive.

12. Rabbi Rekhumay said: The light, surrounded by clouds and fog, came before the world, for it is written (Gen. 1:3): "And God said: Let there be light." They said to him: Do you make a crown for your son before you create him? He answered them: Yes. Like a king who yearned for a son and found a lovely crown, a praise-

worthy treasure. He rejoiced and said: This is for the head of my son, for it is fit for him. But someone said to him: Did he then know that his son would be worthy of it? He replied: Silence. For it was a plan, and known [in advance], as it is written (2 Samuel 14:14): "And he deviseth plans [in advance]."

13. Rabbi Amora sat and spoke: Why does aleph stand at the beginning of the alphabet? Because it came before everything, even the Torah. And why does beth stand next to it? Because it existed at the beginning [of Creation]. And why does it have a protrusion? To indicate from whence it derives. And some say, that from thence the world is maintained. And why is gimmel the third letter? To announce that he shows love [gomeleth]. And did not Rabbi Akiba say: Why is gimmel the third? Because it shows love and makes it grow; and lets it endure, as it is written (Gen. 21:8): "And the child grew up and good things were done to him." He replied: That is also my explanation, for he grew up and showed love and they lived with him and were familiar with him [??].

And why does gimmel have a protrusion at the bottom? He said to them: Gimmel has a head on top and thus resembles a pipe: Just as the pipe takes in above and conducts below, so also does gimmel take in at its head [the stream of good deeds] and conducts [them] through the protrusion and thus [the name and form of the] gimmel.

14.a. Rabbi Yokhanan said: The angels were created on the second [day], for it is written (Psalms 104:3-4) "Who layeth the beams of his chambers in the waters," and "Who maketh his angels of winds, his ministers of flaming fire." Rabbi Julian, the son of Tiberius, said: All agree, and so does Rabbi Yokhanan, that the waters already existed, but in regard to the second day [it is written]: "Who layeth the beams of his chambers in the waters." And who "maketh the clouds his chariots," and who "rideth upon the wings of the wind"? The messengers [angels] were not created until the fifth day.

b. And all agree that they were not created until the second day, so that no one might say: Michael spanned [the universe] in the south of the vault, Gabriel in the north, the Holy, praised be He, measure in the middle; actually, it is written (Isaiah 44:24): "I the

Lord make all the universe, stretch forth the heavens alone, spread abroad the earth by myself" [mi'itti] "who would be with me" [mi'itti] is in the text.

c. It is I who planted this "tree" so that all the world might delight in it, and I vaulted the universe with it and named its name "Universe," for the universe hangs on it and the universe goes forth from it, everything needs it, and they look upon it and yearn for it, and from there the souls go forth. Alone was I when I made it, and no angel can rise above it and say: I was here before you, for even when I vaulted my earth, when I planted and rooted this tree, and let them have joy in one another and enjoyed them myself— "who might have been with me," to whom I might have revealed this secret?

15. Rabbi Amora said: From your words we may conclude that God created what was necessary for this world before he created heaven. He answered him: Yes. Like a king who wanted to plant a tree in the garden; he looked about the entire garden to discover whether it had a wellspring that could nourish the tree. He found none; so he said: I will dig for water and bring a wellspring to light, so that the tree can survive. He dug and brought to light a wellspring, from which flowing water poured, and only then did he plant the tree. And the tree survived and bore fruit and its roots became strong, for they watered it steadily with what they drew from the wellspring.

16. Rabbi Yannay said: The earth was created before the heavens for it is written (Gen. 2:4): "The earth and the heavens." They said to him: But it is written (Gen. 1:1): "The heavens and the earth." He replied with a parable: A king acquired a lovely jewel, which was still imperfect. So, instead of giving it a name, he said: I will make it perfect and put its support and mounting in order, and then I shall name it. This is what is written (Psalms 102:26) [sic!]: "First thou laid the foundations of the earth" and only then: "and the heavens are the work of thy hands."

And it is written (Psalms 104:2–5): "He covers himself with light as with a garment . . . stretches out the heavens like a carpet, lays the beams of his chambers in the waters," etc., and only then: "He maketh his angels of winds, his ministers of flaming fire." And only then: "He laid the foundations of the earth that it should not move." By laying its foundation, he gave it a solidity, as it is written (Psalms 104:5): "It should not move 'olam va'ed [forever and ever]. And what is its name? Va'ed, and its foundation is 'olam, and that is what the final words mean: 'Olam va'ed.

17. Rabbi Berekiah said: What does this verse mean (Gen. 1:3): "And God said: Let there be light and there was light," and it is not written "it became"? This is like a king who had a beautiful jewel and put it aside until he determined its place and put it there. This is what is written: "Let there be light and there was light," for it was already there.

18. Rabbi Amora said: What does this verse mean (Exodus 15:3): "God is a man [ish] of war"? Mar Rekhumay bar Kibi said to him: Ask me not something so simple. Listen to me and I shall advise you. It is like a king who had lovely dwellings and gave each of them a name, and each dwelling was better than the others. Where-upon he said: I will give my son the dwelling that is named *Alef,* the one named *Shin* is also lovely. What did he do? He united all three of them and made them into a house. So they said to him: How long will you keep speaking dark words? He said: My sons, *Alef* is the beginning, then comes *Yod,* and *Shin* takes in the whole world. And why does *Shin* take in the whole world? Because it occurs in the word *Teshubha,* repentance.

19. His pupils asked: What does the letter *daleth* mean? He answered them with a parable: Ten kings were once at a place, and all of them rich, and one of them, though rich, was not as rich as any of them; so, although his wealth was great, but, in comparison to the others, poor, he was called *dal,* poor.

20. They said: What does *Hey* mean? He became angry and said to them: Did I not tell you: Do not ask me about the later and only after that about the earlier? They said: But Hey stands behind! [?] He replied: The order should have been *gimmel hey.* Then why do we write *gimmel daleth*? He said to them: Because they can be exchanged with *Hey,* the *gimmel* can become a *hey* at its head (through a stroke), *daleth* with a hook. And what does this *hey* mean? The upper *hey* and the lower *hey.*

21. They said to him: What does *vav* mean? He replied: The world is sealed in six directions. They said: But is not vav a single letter?

He replied: And is it not written (Psalms 104:2): "Who covers himself with light as with a garment"?

22. Rabbi Amora said: The Garden of Eden lies where? On the earth. And so Rabbi Ismael asked Rabbi Akiba: Where are the trees and plants? He said: On the earth. As Rabbi Ismael asked Rabbi Akiba: What does *"the* heavens and *the* earth mean (Gen. 1:1)? He answered him: If it were not for the accusative particle one might think heaven and earth were deities. He replied: By the temple! You have touched upon [the solution], but you have not clarified it. What you say is correct, but the particle precedes ["heaven"] in order to include sun, moon, stars, and planets, and it precedes ["earth"] in order to include trees, plants, and the Garden of Eden.

23. His pupils said to him: What does this mean (Lam. 2:1): "He cast down from heaven unto the earth the beauty of Israel"? Have they indeed fallen? He replied: If one has read it, one has not repeated it, and if one has repeated it, one has not read it a third time. The matter is like a king who wore a lovely crown upon his head and precious cloth about his shoulders. A bad tiding came to him, whereupon he cast away the crown from his head and the cloth.

24. They asked him: Why does [the letter] *kheth* have the form of a door [pethak] and yet it is vocalized with small pathakh [i.e. segol]? He answered them: Because all sides [winds] of the world are closed, except for the north, which is open to both good and bad. They said to him: To good? And yet it is written (Ezek. 1:4): "And behold, a whirlwind came out of the north, a great cloud, and a fire infolding itself," and fire means burning anger, for it is written (Lev. 10:2): "And there went out fire from God, and devoured them, and they died." He replied to them: There is no difficulty here, [one verse] speaks of the time when they do his will, the other of the time when they do not do his will. When they do not do his will, the "fire" is near, when they do his will, the way of mercy dominates and surrounds [them]; that is what is written (Exodus 34:7): "He forgives iniquity"; like a king who wanted to punish and discipline his servants. A dignitary stood up and asked: Why? The king replied to him: Because of such and such an iniquity. The other said: Never have your servants done this, I

vouch for them, and you test them. Whereupon the king's anger diminished.

25. His pupils asked: Why is the side stroke of *daleth* so thick? He said to them: Because it is written with a small pathakh, for it says (Psalms 24:7): "The gates [*pithkhe*] of the world." He put the pathakh above and the segol below and thus the daleth became thick. And what does *pathakh* mean? [The same as] *pethakh,* gate. And which gate? This refers to the north, which is the gate for the entire world: From the gate from which evil comes forth, good also comes forth. And what is good? Here he mocked them and said: Have I not told you? Small pathakh. They replied: We have forgotten, repeat it to us. He said: The matter is like a king who had a throne. Sometimes he took it in his arms, sometimes upon his head. They asked him: Why? Because it was beautiful, and he felt it was a shame to sit on it. They asked him: And where did he place it on his head? He said: Into the open *mem,* for it is written (Psalms 85:11): "Truth springs out of the earth; and righteousness looks down from heaven."

26. Rabbi Amora sat and spoke: What does this verse mean (Psalms 87:2): "God loveth the gates of Zion more than all the dwellings of Jacob"? The "gates of Zion" are the gates of the world, for gate simply means opening, as is written (Psalms 118:19): "Open to me the gates of righteousness." God spoke: I love the doors of Zion when they are open. Why? Because they are from the side of evil; but when Israel does good before God and is worthy of having [those doors] opened, he then loves them more than all the "dwellings of Jacob," in which there is always peace. Like two men: One is apt to do evil and does good, and one is apt to do good. Whom will we praise? The one who usually does evil and did good. Perhaps he will do it a second time. That is what is written: "God loveth the gates of Zion more than all the dwellings of Jacob," dwellings in which peace always reigns, as it is written (Gen. 25:27): "And Jacob was an immaculate man living in tents."

27. His students asked him: What does the vowel *kholem* mean? He said to them: The soul, for if you listen to your soul, you shall make your body sound for the Messianic era. But if you resist your soul, you shall contract diseases, and your soul shall fall ill too. And it has also been said that every dream [khalom] belongs to the

kholem, and likewise all the white precious stones according to the akhlamah (Exodus 28:14).

28. He said to them: Come and hear the interpretations of a vowel in the Torah of Moses. He sat and spoke: *Khirek* hates the wicked and castigates them, and at his side are envy, hatred, and strife, as it is written (Psalms 37:12): "And he gnasheth upon him with his teeth." Instead of "gnash," *khorek,* read "remove," *rokhek:* Remove these [wicked] ways, and evil will remove itself from you, and good will cleave to you for sure. KhRK, read not *Khirek,* but *Kereakh,* bare, bald: Every place to which *Khirek* attaches remains bare, as it is written (Exodus 34:7): "And he cleans out." And in what sense is *Khirek* a term for burning up? Because it is a fire that burns up all other fires, as it is written (I Kings 18:38): "Then the fire of God fell, and devoured the burnt offering, and the wood, and the stones, and the sand."

29. The teacher taught: What does this verse mean (Exodus 20:18): "And all the people saw the voices." Can voices be seen? "And all the people saw the voices" refers to those voices of which David spoke, as it is written (Psalms 29:3–4): "The voice of God is above the waters: the God of glory thundereth. . . . God's voice is powerful" and it is written (Isaiah 10:13): "By the strength of my hand I have done it" and (Isaiah 48:13): "Mine hand also hath laid the foundation of the earth." "God's voice on high"—as it is written (Psalms 111:2): "God's works are great and high," "God's voice breaks cedars"—that is the rainbow, which breaks cedars and cypresses. "God's voice blows fiery flames"—that is which makes peace between fire and water by striking the power of fire and hindering it from licking up the water, and holding back its flame. "God's voice maketh the desert tremble"—as it is written (Psalms 18:1): "He showeth mercy to his anointed, to David, and to his seed the world over," further even than the desert. "God's voice makes hinds give birth,"—as it is also written (Song of Songs 2:7): "I charge you, O ye daughters of Jerusalem, by the gazelles, and by the hinds of the fields." Thus this teaches that the Torah was given with seven voices, and the Lord of the world revealed himself in all of them, and they saw them, and that is what is meant by (Exodus 20:18): "And all the people saw the voices."

30. A verse of Scripture says (2 Samuel 22:10): "He bowed the heavens also, and came down; and darkness under his feet." And another verse says (Exodus 19:20): "And God came down upon Mount Sinai, on the top of the mount." And another verse says (Exodus 20:22): "Ye have seen that I have talked with you from heaven." What does this mean? His "great fire" was on the earth, as which a voice is, the other voices were in the heavens, for it is written (Deut. 4:36): "Out of heaven he made thee to hear his voice, that he might instruct thee: and upon earth he showed thee his great fire." And what is the "great fire"? And where did the speech come from? From the fire, for it is written there too: "And thou heardest his words out of the midst of the fire."

31. And what does this mean (Deut. 4:12): "Ye saw no similitude; only a voice." That is as Moses said to Israel (Deut. 4:15): "For ye saw not all similitude,"—similitude, yes, but not all similitude. Like a king who stood before his servants, and he wore a white garment. His outer covering did not suffice to arouse their reverence for his majesty, when the king was at a distance, they heard his voice. But could they see his throat? No. Thus here too they saw similitude, but not "all similitude," and that is what the verse (Deut. 4:12) means: "Ye saw no similitude, only a voice," and "ye heard the voice of the words."

32. A verse of Scripture says (Exodus 20:18): "And all the people saw the voices," and another verse says (Deut. 4:12): "Ye heard the voice of the words." What does this mean? First they saw the voices—and what did they see? The seven voices of which David spoke—and then they heard discourse coming from all of them. Yet it is taught [that they were] ten? For the Rabbis have said that all [ten] of them were spoken in one word. Yes, they were all spoken in one word, and these were seven "words" from the seven voices, and of the three [others] it is written (Deut. 4:12): "Ye heard the voice of the words, but saw no similitude, only the voice." From this we may deduce that all were spoken in one word. And God brought them all together once more so that Israel would not err and believe that any of the angels had helped God or that his voice alone could not be so strong.

Another explanation: So that no one might say that since there are ten pronouncements according to [the number of] ten kings, perhaps they cannot be all spoken at once, it is written [at the beginning of the First Commandment]: "I." And here he brought all ten of them together. And what [are the] "ten kings"? Seven voices and three "words." And what does "words" mean? This refers to the verse (Deut. 26:18): "And God made you into a word [?]." And what are these three? Of them it is written (Proverbs 4:7): "The beginning of wisdom is: Get wisdom, and with all thy getting get understanding." Just as it is written (Job 32:8): "The soul of Shadday giveth them understanding," the soul corresponding to Shadday brings them the "understanding." What is the third? Of it that old man said to that child: "That which is too wondrous for you, do not investigate it; and what is concealed from you, do not delve into it; seek understanding in that which is permitted you and do not have anything to do with mysteries."

33. It is taught (Proverbs 25:2): "The glory of God to conceal a word." What word? The one of which it is written (Psalms 119:-160): "The essence of the word is truth." But (Proverbs 25:2): "The honor of kings is to search out a word." What word? The one of which it is said (Proverbs 25:11): "A word fitly spoken." Instead of "'al 'ophnav," [fitly], read "'al 'ophanav," [over the wheels] [of his Merkabah].

34. His pupils asked Rabbi Berekiah: May we submit our words to you? But he did not permit them. Another time, he did permit them, and he did so in order to test whether they had more aptly prepared themselves. One day he tested them and said: Let me hear your wisdom. They began and said (Gen. 1:1): "In the beginning" —that is one. (Isaiah 57:16): "The spirit vanishes before me, and the souls which I have made." (Psalms 65:9): "The brook of God is full of water." What does God's brook mean? You taught us, master, that God took of the primal waters and divided them, and put one half on the firmament, the other half in the ocean, and that is the meaning of the verse: "The brook of God is full of water." [Since "peleg" can mean both "brook" and "division, half."]. And man thereby arrives at studying the Torah, as the Lord has taught: Through the merit of good works man arrives at studying the Torah, for it is written (Isaiah 55:5): "Ho, every one that thirsteth, come ye to the waters, and he that hath no silver, go to him and he shall do good things for you, yea, buy grain and eat. . . ."

Another explanation: "He that hath no silver—go to him!" For he does have silver, as is written (Haggai 2:8): "The silver is mine, and the gold is mine. . . ."

* * *

42. They asked him: What does the letter *Tsadde* mean? He said to them: The *Tsadde* is shaped out of *Yod* and *Nun,* and likewise, its counterpart *He* consists of *Nun* and *Yod: He,* and this means (Proverbs 10:25): "The righteous [Tsaddik] is an everlasting foundation."

43. They asked him: What does this [verse] mean (Numbers 23:14): "And he brought him into the field of the seers"? What is "the field of the seers"? This is referred to in the verse (Song of Songs 7:11): "Come, my beloved, let us go forth into the field." What does that verse mean: ". . . let us go forth into the field"? Do not read *sadeh,* field, but *shidah,* vessel. And what is *shidah,* vessel? He said to him: His heart is aimed at God: Come, my beloved, let us go about, so that I shall not always remain in one place. And what is "his heart"? He said to him: When ben Soma was standing outside, you are with him. "Heart" indicates the thirty-two [saints] who were hidden and with whom the world was created. And what are these thirty-two? He said: Those are the thirty-two paths. It is like the king who was in the innermost of his apartments, and the number of rooms was thirty-two, and there was one path to every room. Was it proper for a king to let everyone enter his rooms by these paths of his? No! Was it proper for him not to show his pearls and treasures, his gems and jewels, openly? No! What did the king do? He took the daughter and combined all paths in her and in her "clothes," and whoever wishes to enter the innermost must look here. And in his great love for her, he sometimes calls her "my sister," for they both come from the same place, sometimes he calls her "my daughter," for she *is* his daughter, and sometimes he calls her "my mother." . . .

* * *

48. And why: "I feared"? Because the ear is an image of the aleph, and the aleph is the beginning of all letters, and not only that, for aleph determines the existence of all letters, and aleph is an image of the brain: When you pronounce the aleph, you only open your mouth; likewise, thought goes into the infinite and the limitless,

and all letters derive from the aleph, just as it stands at their beginning; and it is written (Micah 2:13): "The Lord at the head of them." And we know that every [divine] Name written with J H W H is specialized and sanctified in the holiness. And what does "in the holiness" mean? In the "sacred hall." And where is the "sacred hall"? In thought, and that is aleph, and that is why it is written (Habakkuk 3:2): "Lord, I have understood your 'ear' and I was afraid." Thus spoke Habakkuk: I know that my prayer was taken in ecstasy, and I too was in ecstasy, and when I, in ecstasy, came to a certain place and understood the secret of "thine ear," I became fearful, and that is why [ibid.]: "O Lord, revive thy work in the midst of the years,"—in your oneness. Like a retired, peculiar, and hidden king, who went into his house and ordered that people not pray for him. So that everyone who prays is afraid the king may discover that he is flouting the king's commandment, and therefore he says: "I fear, God, your work, revive it in the midst of the years." Thus spoke Habakkuk: Since "Thy Name is in Thee and in Thee Thy Name," may your work last forever within it.

49. Another explanation [for that verse]: "O Lord, revive thy work in the midst of the years." It is like a king who had a precious jewel, which was a pride of his kingdom, and whenever he was glad, he hugged and kissed it, he would put it on his head and loved it. Habakkuk said to him: Although the "kings" are with you, that jewel is the pride of your world, therefore "revive it in the midst of the years." What does the expression "years" mean? The verse (Gen. 1:3) refers to it: "And God said: Let there be light, and there was light" And light means day, according to the verse (Gen. 1:15): "The great light to rule the day," and the years derive from days. That is what is written (Habakkuk 3:2): "in the midst of the years" —in that jewel that brings forth the years.

Yet it is written (Isaiah 43:5): "I will bring thy seed from the East," and the sun goes up in the east, and you say the "jewel" is the day. I have merely said (Gen. 1:5): "It was evening and it was morning: One day." And that is what is written (Gen. 2:4): "On the day when God made earth and heaven."

50. Yet it is written (Psalms 18:12): "He makes darkness his covering, his pavilion round about him: dark waters and thick clouds."? He replied: It is written [about these clouds in Isaiah 45:8]: "The skies pour down righteousness," and righteousness is the way of

rigor in the world, about which it is written [source unclear] "Strive for righteousness, righteousness." And then comes: "So that you may live and possess the land." If you hold judgment over yourself, you will live, and if not, righteousness will judge you, and its judgment will be confirmed, even against your will.

And what does the double mention of "righteousness, righteousness" mean? He replied: Understand this from the verse (Psalms 18:12): "At the brightness that was before him, his thick clouds passed, etc." The first "righteousness" really means "righteousness," and this Shekinah, about which it is written (Isaiah 1:21): "Righteousness lodged in it." And what does the second "righteousness" mean? This is the righteousness that frightens the righteous. And is this "righteousness" "Tsedaka" or not? He said to him: No! Why should it be? Because it is written (Isaiah 59:17): "He put righteousness (tsedaka) on as a breastplate," but *tsedek* is "a helmet of salvation upon his head." His head, however, is [Sephira] Truth, for it is written (Psalms 119:160): "The head [beginning] of your words is truth." Truth, however, is connected with "peace," for it is written (II Kings 20:19): "If only peace and truth rule in my days." Thus spoke Hezekiah: "If only peace and truth rule in my days." But shall a person speak in such a way? He really says: That "manner" that you gave my father David, let it be one half of my days, and peace and truth the other half of my days. That is why he mentions "my days" and "peace and truth," and "in my days" [means] that everything is one. This is indicated by the verse (Gen. 1:5): "And it was evening, and it was morning: One day." Just as the "day" is peace, so he also asked for peace, as it is written "peace and truth in my days." In that manner, which you gave my father David, about which it is written (Psalms 89:37): "And his throne like the sun before you."

* * *

52. And from whence did Abraham have a daughter? From the verse (Gen. 24:1): "God blessed Abraham with everything," and it is written (Isaiah 43:7): "Everything is named after my name, and I have created it for my glory, formed and made it." Was this "blessing" his daughter or not? Yes, it was his daughter. That is like a king, who has a perfect and immaculate servant, and no matter how much he tested him, he passed every test. The king then said: "What shall I give this servant, what shall I do for him?

There is nothing else I can do but recommend him to my older brother, so that he may advise and protect and honor him." The servant went home with the king's older brother, and learned his ways, so that the brother became very fond of him, and called him his friend, for it is written (Isaiah 41:8): "Abraham my friend." He said: What shall I give him or what shall I do for him? So I made him a beautiful vessel, and lovely jewels are in it, precious stones that are peerless, and they are the jewels of the kings, I will give it to him, so that he may partake of it. That is what is written (Gen. 24:1): "And God blessed Abraham with everything."

53. Another explanation (Habakkuk 3:2): "God, I have heard thy speech, I am afraid." God I have understood thy speech, I am afraid. What did he understand that made him so afraid? He understood "thinking," God's *Makhshavah:* Just as thinking has no end—for man thinks and yet never reaches the end of the world —thus hearing has no end and is never sated, for it is written (Eccles. 1:8): "The ear does not grow full from hearing." And why not? Because the ear is an image of the aleph, and the aleph is the root of the Ten Commandments, that is why the ear "does not grow full from hearing."

54. And what does the Zayin mean in the word *Ozen* [Ear]: For we say: Everything that God created in his world, He took its name from its substance, for it is written (Gen. 2:19): "And the way man would name everything. . . . thus should be his Name," that means: That should be the way it is. And how do we know that the name of a thing is that thing itself? From the verse (Prov. 10:7): "The memory of the just is blessed; but the name of the wicked shall rot." Does his name rot? No, he himself rots. Thus, the verse from Genesis means: The thing itself. An example: The *shin* [i.e. its shape] in the word *shoresh* [roots] resembles the root of the tree; the *resh* [in its shape] means that every tree is crooked; and what is the function of the second *shin?* It teaches that when you take a branch and plant it, it will again become a tree. And what is the function of the *zayin?* It corresponds to the number of the days of the week and teaches that every day has its own potency [*koakh*].

55. And what does the *zayin* in *ozen* mean here? It teaches you that just as there is a great, unlimited wisdom in the ear, there is also a potency in all parts of the body.

And what are these parts? The seven that exist in man, of which it is written (Gen. 1:27): "In the image of God he created him," in all his members and all his parts. But we do say: Whom does the *vav* resemble? It resembles him, "who is wrapped in light as in a raiment (Psalms 104:2), and *vav* signifies the six directions [of space], doesn't it? He said to him: The [place of] circumcision of the man and the female of the man we reckon as one, his two hands —three, his head and his trunk—five, his two legs—seven, and they are matched by the potencies in heaven, for it is written (Eccles. 7:14): "God has made everything corresponding to everything else."

(Exodus 31:17): "For God has made six days"—and not "in six days"; this teaches that every day has its own potency.

56. And what does *nun* mean? It teaches you that the brain is an essential part of the spinal cord and always takes in from there, and the brain would not exist without the spinal cord, for the whole body is necessary for the brain, and the brain would not exist without the whole body, that is why the spinal cord flows into the whole body from the brain, and that is signified by the bent *nun*. But the *nun* [in *ozen*] is a lengthened terminal *nun*, isn't it? The lengthened *nun* always stands at the end of the word to teach you that it is composed of male and female.

57. And the open *mem*. What does the open *mem* [mean]? The open *mem* is composed of male and female. And what does the closed mem [mean]? It is made like a kind of belly from above. But didn't Rabbi Rekhumay say: The belly is like a *teth?* His words refer to a similarity in front, but I am speaking about a similarity in back. And what does *mem* mean? It teaches you that the basis of the *mem* is the male, and its aperture was added because of the female: The male procreates without opening, and thus the closed *mem* is not open; likewise, the female opens in giving birth and then closes again, and thus the *mem* is closed and [sometimes] open.

58. And why does the name of the letter *mem* contain an open and a closed *mem?* Because we say: Do not read *mem*, but read *mayim* [water], and the female is cold and thus must conceive from the man.

And why does the name of the letter *nun* contain both kinds?

Because it is written (Psalms 72:17): "Let his name spring up before the sun." Let it happen out of both *nun*s, the curved and the lengthened one, and through male and female.

59. It is written (Eccles. 1:8): "And the ear does not grow full from hearing," and it is written there: "The eye does not become sated from seeing." This means that both draw from thinking. And what is "thinking"? The king who is needed by everything that is created by higher and lower [things].

60. And what does it mean that we say: [Something] rises in thinking? And that we don't say: It comes down? And yet we do say: The man who sinks into the contemplation of *merkavah*, comes down and rises only afterwards. We say [come down], because we say: "The man who sinks into the contemplation of merkavah. . . ." And the targum translates *zefiyya* with *sekhutha*, [look-out], as in the verse (Isaiah 21:8): "And he calls, a lion, on the look-out for God." But here with "thinking," there is no looking and no limit. And everything without end or limit does not admit of a coming-down, for people say: Someone has gotten to the bottom of an opinion, but not to the end of thinking.

* * *

62. And he went on to say: Why do we put blue into the fringes? And why do the fringes have thirty-two threads? A parable: A king had a beautiful garden with thirty-two paths, he installed a watchman over them and made those ways known to him alone, and said to him: Take care of them and go about in them every day, and as long as you walk about in them, it will do you good. What did the watchman do? He said: If I were alone on these paths, would it be possible for *one* watchman to take care of them? And the people will say: This king is a miser! So the watchman installed other watchmen over these paths: Those are the "Thirty-two Paths."

And why the blue? The watchman said: Perhaps these watchmen will think that the garden belongs to me. So he gave them a sign: Behold, this is the sign of the king that the garden belongs to him, and that he has devised these ways and they do not belong to me. And this is his seal. A parable: A king and his daughter had servants who wanted to go on a far journey. They feared the king, and so the king gave them his sign; they feared his daughter, and

so she gave them a sign and said to them: Now, with these two
signs: "God protect you against all Evil, may he protect your soul"
(Psalms 121:7).

63. Rabbi Amora sat and declared: What does this mean (I Kings
8:27): "Behold, the heaven and heaven of heavens cannot contain
thee." This teaches that God has seventy-two names, and he has
destined them all for the [twelve] tribes, for it is written (Exodus
28:10): "Six of their names on one stone, and the other six names
of the rest on the other stone," and (Joshua 4:9): "Joshua set up
twelve stones." Those were name-stones, and so were these, and on
twelve stones there are seventy-two [names], corresponding to the
seventy-two names of God. And why does He begin with twelve?
To teach you that God has twelve "ladders," and each of them six
potencies. And what are these? The seventy-two languages.

64. God has a tree and the tree has twelve radii: North-East,
South-West, East-Up, East-Down, North-West, South-West,
West-Up, West-Down, North-Up, North-Down, South-Up,
South-Down, and they extend and continue to infinity, and they
are the arms of the world. And within them is the tree, and to all
these radii correspond "overseers," twelve of them, and within the
sphere of heaven there are twelve "overseers" too, and in the heart,
too, there are twelve "overseers." And that makes thirty-six "over-
seers." And each has a regent, for it is written (Eccles. 5:8): "For
he that is higher than the highest regardeth." These are twelve plus
twelve plus twelve, the "overseers" are in the *Teli* [the constella-
tion of the Dragon], the heavenly sphere, and the heart, and thus
nine belong to the East, nine to the West, nine to the South, nine
to the North, which makes thirty-six of thirty-six whereby the
potency of one is [also] in the other, and although twelve are in
each of the three, they all cleave to one another, and all thirty-six
potencies are in the first, which is the *Teli,* and if you seek them
in the heavenly sphere, you will find them. And if you seek them
in the heart you will find them. That is why each [of the three
regions] has twelve, and there are thirty-six for all three together,
and they return into themselves. And the potency of each one is
also in the other, so that each has thirty-six potencies, and yet all
of them together are not more than thirty-six forms, and they are
all perfected in the "heart."

Add thirty-two to thirty-two, and there are four left [of the thirty-six], and they add up to sixty-four forms. Now how [do we know] that we have to add thirty-two to thirty-two? Because it is written (Eccles. 5:8): "For he that is higher than the highest regardeth." Thus there are sixty-four, and they lack only eight to make the seventy-two Names of God, and that is what that verse means, and these are the seven days of the week. And one more is lacking, and it is indicated by [the following verse, Eccles. 5:9]: "The profit of the earth is in all the universe."

65. What is "the fullness"? The place from which the world was broken, and it [has] a merit in regard to what emerged. And what is "fullness"? Every object in the world, for if people in the world are worthy of taking from its ray, then it is "fullness." And what is the "earth"? That which was broken from the "heavens," and the heavens are God's throne; the earth, however, is the "jewel," and the "sea of *Khokhma,*" and it is reflected in the blue of the fringes of our prayer shawls, for Rabbi Meir said: Why is the blue different from all other colors? Because the blue is like the sea, the sea like the firmament, and the firmament like the throne of the [divine] glory, for it is written (Exodus 24:10): "And they saw the God of Israel, and there was under his feet as it were a paved work of a sapphire stone, and as it were the body of heaven in his clearness," and it is written (Ezech. 1:26): "a throne, as the appearance of a sapphire stone."

* * *

67. And they nourish the "heart," and the "heart" nourishes them, and they are all holy forms, placed over every nation, and holy Israel occupies the top of the tree and its heart: just as the heart is the splendid fruit of the body, so is Israel, likewise, the fruit of the splendid tree. Just as the palmtree is surrounded by its branches, and its *lulabh* is in the center, so is Israel, likewise, at the top of this tree, and this top is its heart; and the treetop corresponds to the spinal cord of man, the most essential part of the body. And just as [the word] *lulabh* is written [in two syllables]: לו and לב [which can also be read as *lo* and *lebh*], add thirty-six to the "heart." And just as there are thirty-two hidden paths of *Khokhma* in the heart, there is a form waking in each of these paths, as it is written (Gen. 3:24): "To guard the way of the tree of life." And what are these forms? [Those of whom] it is written

[ibid.]: "And He placed at the east of the garden of Eden Cheru-
bims, and a flaming sword which turned every way, to guard the
way of the tree of life." And what does this mean: "He placed
. . . at the garden of Eden"? [This means:] He let [the "forms"]
dwell on those paths preceding the place known as the Garden of
Eden, and this place preceded in turn the Cherubims, for it is
written [ibid.]: "the cherubims," and it preceded the sword which
turned every way and which preceded [???]. Yet supposedly, fire
and water were preexistent, for it is written (Gen. 1:6): "Let there
be a firmament in the midst of the waters, and let it divide the
waters from the waters," and (Gen. 1:8): "God called the firma-
ment *shamayim* [heaven]."

* * *

71. He taught: A column [goes] from earth to heaven, and its name
"just man, saint," *Tsaddik*, after the *tsaddiks*, [the righteous, the
saints]. And if there are righteous men on the earth, then the
column is strengthened. But if not, then it weakens. And it bears
the entire world, for it is written (Prov. 10:25): "The righteous is
an everlasting foundation." And if that column grows weak, then
the world cannot continue. Therefore: If there is only one righteous
man in the world, he maintains the world. Therefore: Take my
"offering" from him first, for only then is it written (Exodus 25:3):
"This is the offering which you shall take of them"—of the others.
And which is this? [ibid.] "Gold, silver, and copper."

* * *

76. What does this verse mean (Num. 24:24 ff.): "God bless you
and keep you, may God make your countenance shine and be
gracious to you. God turn his face to you and grant you peace."
That is the "express Name" of God, and it is the name of twelve
consonants, for it contains thrice the Tetragrammaton. This
teaches that the names of God form three hosts, and each host is
like the others, and its name is like the name of the others. How
is that? The Tetragrammaton [of the first verse] can be permutated
twenty-four times, and that is one host. "God bless you," likewise
the [Tetragrammaton] of the second [verse], and those are twenty-
four more names of God, and likewise the third, and those are
twenty-four [more names of God]. Thus, every host has twenty-
four heads [and leaders]. Permute [the Tetragrammaton] three

times, and you will have seventy-two names of the Holy, may He be praised, and those are the seventy-two names yielded from the three verses of Exodus 14:19–21.

77. And who are these leaders? They are *three*. This teaches that "strength" (Gebhura) is prince of all the holy forms on the left side of God, and that is Gabriel, and on His right side the prince over all holy forms is Michael, and in the center, which is "Truth," Uriel is prince of all holy forms, and each is prince over twenty-four forms, but His hosts are numberless, for it is written (Job 25:3): "Is there any number to His armies?"

If that is so, then there must be 72 and again 72. He replied: No, for when Israel makes the sacrifice to its father in heaven, they join together, and that is the "union" in [the expression] "our God."

78. And why is the sacrifice called *korban?* Because it brings the holy forms close together, as it is written (Ezek. 37:17): "And join them one to another into one stick; and they shall become one in thine hand." And it is also written [in many places about the sacrifice]: *le-reakh nikhoakh* [a pleasant smell]. Smell however is in the nose, and thus *nikhoakh* signifies a descent, for it is written (Levit. 9:22): "And he descended." And the Targum translates it: *"u-nekhath."* The smell descends and joins together with those holy forms, and is brought close to them by the sacrifice, and that is why the sacrifice is called *korban.*

79. This is the name that is yielded by the three verses of Exodus 14:19–21. The letters of the first verse are arranged in the name according to the order of the verse. The letters of the second verse are arranged in the name in the reverse order of the verse. And the letters of the third verse are arranged in the name according to the order of the verse. Each of the three verses has 72 consonants, and each of the names has three consonants, and it is thus correctly constructed: WHW, YLY, STY, 'LM. . . . YBM, HYY, MWM. These are the 72 names that are yielded and divide into three parts, each part has 24, and there is a prince for every 24, and each part has to keep watch in the four wind directions: East and West, North and South. Thus there are six for every direction, and altogether 24, and the same holds for the second and third part.

And they are all sealed with the name YHVH, the God of Israel, the living God, Shaddai, the High and the Sublime, Who reigns in eternity and Whose name is holy, YHVH, praised be the name of his glorious kingdom for ever and ever.

80. Rabbi Ahilay sat and spoke: What does this mean: "God is King, God was King, God will be King for ever and ever"? That is the *shem ha-mephorash*, which can be permutated and pronounced, for it is written (Num. 4:27): "They shall do my name upon the children of Israel." And it is the twelve[-lettered] name, like the name in the priestly blessing (Num. 24:24): "God bless you, etc." And these are three [names], and twelve [consonants]. This is the vocalization: Yaphael, Yaphoel, Yiphol. Each man who guards it in purity, and speaks it in holiness and purity, his prayers will be heard, and furthermore, he is beloved above and beloved below, pleasant above and pleasant below, and he will be heard and succored.

81. This is the shem ha-mephorash, that was written on Aaron's mitre, and in the shem ha-mephorash of 72 letters, which are 12 words, which God handed down to the masmarya in front of the curtain, and he handed them to Elia on Mount Carmel, and through it he ascended [to heaven], and did not taste the taste of death, and these are the precious and explicit and glorious names, which are twelve, according to the number of the tribes of Israel: AHZYZYRON, ABROHYHRON, VShBUBTMKRON, DMURTRON, ZFZFShYTRON, YHUDMYRON, VHYYRON, BRKYHYAON, 'aRSYHGAON, KSAYHMNGMHON, HVHVYHHYVYHYHVHAHAHVH, DMHRYRON. And they are all contained in the "heart of heaven," and divide into four names each, and contain male and female and the "watchmen" at the *teli*, at the heavenly sphere, and at the heart, and they are the "sources of wisdom."

82. Rabbi Rekhumay sat and spoke: What are the twelve "tribes of God"? This teaches that God has twelve "tribes." And which are they? A parable: A king had a source, and all his brothers had no water except from that source, and they could not endure being thirsty. What did he do? He made twelve "canals" to the source and named them after the sons of his brothers, and said to them: If the sons are as good as their fathers, they shall deserve my filling the "canals." Their fathers shall drink their fill, and the sons shall drink after them. But if the sons do not deserve it and do things

that are not fitting before me, then the "canals" shall remain, and I shall give them water only on condition that the fathers do not give any to their sons, since they will not be acting according to my will.

83.a. And what does the expression *"shevet"* mean? Something simple, that is square.
Why? Because one square cannot be in another. Rather: A circle within the square can move, but a square within a square cannot move. And what does circle [mean]? That is the [vowel-]points of Moses' Torah, which are all circular. And they are in the consonants like the soul in the body of a human being, who cannot live without it, and cannot attain anything large or small without the soul. Such is also the vowel, for nothing large or small can be spoken without a vowel. And every vowel is a circle; all consonants, however, are square, and [thus] the consonants exist through the vowels, and these are their life.

b. And the vowel comes by way of the "canals" to the consonants through the smell of the sacrifice, and it descends from there, for it is written: "The fragrance is an ascension to God." For [the first] YHVH descends to [the second] YHWH, and that is what is written (Deut. 6:4): "Hear, Israel, YHVH our Lord, YHVH is one."

* * *

85. And what is [this] "tree" of which you have spoken? He said to them. All the powers of God are stratified, and they are like a tree. Just as the tree brings forth its fruits with the aid of water, so does God multiply the powers of the "tree" with the aid of water. And what is God's water? It is *"khokhmah"* [wisdom], and that is the soul of the righteous, who fly from the "source" to the "great canal," and it [the canal] ascends and cleaves to the "tree." And whereby does it flourish? Through Israel: When Israel is good and righteous, the shekinah dwells among it, and God lets it be fruitful and multiply. For shekinah is named after the verse (Deut. 33:26): "He rideth upon the heavens in thy help, and in his excellency on the sky." And it is written (Isaiah 45:8): "The skies pour down righteousness," but "righteousness" is the shekinah, for it is written (Isaiah 1:21): "Righteousness lodged in it," and He gave [this] righteousness to David, for it is written (Psalms 146:10):

"The Lord is king forever, thy God, Zion, from generation to generation."

86. Rabbi Meir: What does this verse mean (Psalms 146:10): "The Lord is king forever, thy God, Zion, from generation to generation"? What does this mean "from generation to generation"? Rabbi Papias said: It is written (Eccles. 1:4): "One generation passeth away, and another generation cometh," and Rabbi Akiba said: What does this mean: "One generation passeth away, and another generation cometh"? A generation that has already come. A parable: A king had servants and dressed them according to his means in clothes of silk and embroidery. The servants went astray. So he cast them out and repulsed them and took off their clothes and they left. He went and took the garments and washed them well, until no waste matter was left on them, and then he straightened them out and acquired new servants, and dressed them in those garments without knowing whether these servants would be good or not. Thus they took part in garments which had already been in existence and worn by others before them—"The earth however abides eternally," and that is the meaning of the verse (Eccles. 12:7): "Then shall the dust return to the earth as it was: and the spirit shall return unto God who gave it."

87. Rabbi Rekhumay said: What does the verse mean (Lev. 9:22): "And Aaron lifted up his hands toward the people and blessed them, and came down." Hadn't he already come down? No. "He came down from offering of the sin offering, and the burnt offering." It was only now that "Aaron lifted up his hands?" Why did he lift up his hands? Because he had offered up a sacrifice and "brought it near" to his father in heaven, as we have previously said, and he [who makes the unifying gesture towards heaven] is necessary, he who sacrifices it and blesses it for the upper [regions] and totally unifies it with them. And who is the people of whom it is written "toward the people"? That signifies: For the people. And why [does this blessing occur] with a lifting up of the hands? He would have done better to bless them with the [spoken] blessing. That happened because there are ten fingers on the hands, an allusion to the ten sephiroth that seal heaven and earth, and these ten correspond to the ten words, and these ten [words] comprise the 613 commandments: Count up their letters and you will find that they add up to 613 letters. And they include all the 22 letters

except for *teth,* which is absent. And why [is it absent]? That should teach you that *teth* signifies the belly and does not belong to the sephiroth. And why are they called sephiroth? Because it is written (Psalms 19:1): "The heavens are radiant in the *sapphire* radiance of the glory of God."

88. And who are they? They are three, and three realms belong to each of the three armies. The first is light and light of the perfect life, the second is the holy Khayoth, the ofanim, and the wheels of the merkabha. And all the hosts of God praise and glorify and worship and laud and make holy the king who is wrapped in holiness and very powerful in the council of the saints, the powerful and enormous king, and crown him with a Holy, holy, holy. And why are there three sanctifications and not four? Because [all] sanctifications above are in threes, for it is written: "God is king, God was king, God shall be king," and it is also written: "God bless you. . . . God shine upon you. . . . God turn to you. . . ." and it is written (Exodus 34:6): "God, God," and the other qualities [named there] form the third "God" [of this apostrophe]. And what does this mean, "God, God, gracious and merciful." The thirteen qualities.

89. And why is the order of the words thus (in Isaiah 6:3): "Holy, holy, holy," and then only: "is the God of hosts." This means: Holy is the "highest crown." Holy is the "root of the tree," holy is he who is bound and united. Grasp it from this parable. This thing is like a king who had sons, and whose sons also had sons. As long as the latter sons do his will, he comes among them and maintains them and sates them, and brings them goodness, so that the fathers and the sons are sated. But if the sons do not do his will, he brings the fathers as much as they need.

90.a. What does this mean: "The earth is full of his glory" (in Isaiah 6:3). That is that whole "earth" that was created on the first day, and above it corresponds to the land of Israel [and is] full of the glory of God. What is this? The "wisdom" of which it is written (Prov. 3:35): "The wise possess glory," and it is also written (Ezek. 3:12): "Praised be God's glory in its place." What is "God's glory?" [This can be understood in a] parable. It is like a king, and in his apartments was the queen, and all his armies were delighted with her, and they had sons. They came every day to see the king and praise him. They said unto him: Where is our mother? He replied: You cannot see her now. To which they said: Praised be she wherever she is.

b. And what does "in its place" mean? That means that there is no one who knows its place. Like a princess who came from faraway lands, and no one knew from whence she had come until they saw that she was a capable, beautiful, and excellent woman in everything she did. And they said: Truly, she comes from the light, for her deeds make the world radiant. They asked her: Where do you come from? She said: From my place. And they said: Then the people in her place must be great. Praised be she and blessed in her place!

c. And is not this "glory of God" one of his hosts? No, it is less. Why do we praise it then? That can be understood with a parable. A man had a beautiful garden, and outside the garden, but close to it, a stretch of good soil. He prepared a lovely garden, watered the garden so that the water spread over its entire area, except for that piece of soil that was unconnected even though everything is one; thus, he opened up a "place" and watered it separately.

* * *

96. What are the ten logoi?

First: [The] "highest crown," praised be and highly praised be its name and its people. And who is its people? Israel; as it is written (Psalms 100:3): "Know that the Eternal is God, he made us and not we ourselves"—to know the One among all the Ones, and to know that the one is in all His names.

Second: "Wisdom," of which it is written (Prov. 8:22): "God created me as the beginning of his path." Beginning, however, means wisdom, for it is written (Psalms 111:10): "Beginning is wisdom."

Third: The quarry of the Torah, the treasure-house of "wisdom," the quarry of the spirit, the spirit of God. This teaches, that God broke all the letters of the Torah there and buried them in the spirit, and produced his forms therein, and that is what is written (I Samuel 2:2): "No rock like our God." Read not *tsur*, rock, but *tsayyar*, shaper. No shaper like our God.

Fourth: God's boons, his rewards and graces to everyone, and that is "God's right hand."

Fifth: God's great fire, of which it is written (Deut. 5:22): "I do not wish to behold this great fire any longer lest I die." And that is "God's left hand." And what is that? Those are the holy khayyoth and the holy seraphim that stand right and left of him. They are the gracious ones who are extremely high, and of whom it is written (Ezek. 1:18): "They were high, and they were fearful," and they are full of eyes, for it is written [ibid.]: "And their backs were full of eyes round about them four." And round about, stand his angels, [and] also those who stand round about them bow to them and fall down and speak: "YHVH is the Lord," (I Kings 18:39).

Sixth: The throne of splendor, which is crowned, contained, praised, [and] glorified. He is the house of the coming world and its place is incised in [the sphere of] "wisdom," as it is written (Gen. 1:3): "And God spoke: Let there be light, and there was light."

97. And Rabbi Yokhanan said: There were two lights, for it is written (Gen. 1:3): "God said: Let there be light, and let there be light." And for both, it is written "it was good," and God took the first and concealed it for the saints until the Messianic age. That is what is written (Psalms 31:20): "How great is thy goodness, which thou hast laid up for them that fear thee." This teaches that the hidden primal light cannot be seen by any created being, for it is written (Gen. 1:4): "And *God* saw the light, that it was good," and it is written (Gen. 1:31): "And God saw everything he had created and, behold, it was very good." God saw everything he had created and saw "very good" as bright and radiant, and took from that good, and concentrated all the 32 paths of "wisdom" in it, and gave it to this world, and that is what is meant by the verse (Prov. 4:2): "For I gave you from that which was taken from the 'good.' " This means the treasure of the oral Torah.

98. And God said: If they follow this principle [for this principle represents the world, and it is the "oral Torah"] then they shall take part in the life in the coming world, which is the "hidden good." And what is this? God's power, of which it is written (Habakkuk 3:4): "The radiance will be like light." Some day the reflection taken from the primal light will be like [the] light [itself] if my children keep the Torah and the commandments, which I gave to instruct them, as it is written (Prov. 1:8): "Listen, my child, to the instruction of thy father, and do not reject the Torah of thy

mother." And it is written (in Habakkuk 3:4): "Rays come from his hand, and there is the concealment of his power." What is the concealment of his power? That is the light he hid and concealed, and of which it is written (Psalms 31:20): "which thou concealed for those who fear thee," and that [part], that remained for us, "[which] thou hast made for those who trust in thee" [ibid.] in this world, and keep thy Torah and thy commandments, and sanctify thy great name, and acknowledge it as *one* both at home and abroad, as it is written (further in Psalms 31:10): "before men."

99. Rabbi Rekhumay said: This teaches that it [i.e. the oral Torah] is the light of Israel and the lamp of the light. Yet it is written (Prov. 6:23): "For the commandment is a lamp" and [the] commandment is [the] oral Torah, [the] light however is the written Torah, and indeed He calls it "light" because the light is maintained from the lamp. This is like an out-of-the-way room at the end of the house: Even though it is daytime and very light outside, no one can see in that room unless he has brought along a lamp. Thus is the oral Torah: Even though it is a lamp, it needs the written Torah to resolve its difficulties and illuminate its secrets.

100. Rabbi Rekhumay said: What does this verse mean (Prov. 6:23): "Reproofs and instruction are the way of life." This means that error is inevitable for him who studies the Merkabha and the doctrine of Creation. As it is written (Isaiah 3:6): "This error lies in thy hand." [This means]: Things that are understood only by him who has erred in them. Now the Torah says "reproofs of instruction," but actually he acquires the "way of life." Thus, whosoever wishes to acquire the road of life must endure reproofs.

Another explanation: "Life" is the Torah, for it is written (Deut. 30:19): "Thou shalt choose life," and it is written (Deut. 30:20): "For this is thy life and the length of thy days," and who so wishes to acquire it must cast away bodily enjoyment and take upon himself the yoke of the commandments, and if sorrows come upon him, he must take them upon himself in love and never say: Since I fulfill the will of the Creator and study the Torah every day, why do these sorrows come upon me? He must take them upon himself in love, and then he will acquire the perfect way of life, for who understands God's judgments, and he is obligated to say about everything [that happens to him] (Psalms 119:137): "Righteous art thou, O Lord, and upright are thy judgments." Everything that comes from heaven is to the good."

101. You say [that logos is] God's throne, but we say it is God's crown. For we say: Israel is crowned with three crowns: the crown of priesthood, the crown of the kingdom, and the crown of the Torah, which overtowers the other two. Yes, [at the bottom], the crown of priesthood, and above it the crown of the kingdom, and the crown of the Torah above them. Like a king who had a beautiful and fragrant instrument, and he loved it very much. Sometimes he put it upon his head, and those are the head phylacteries; sometimes he took it in his arm, sometimes he lent it to his son, to have it, sometimes it was called his throne, for he wears it on his arm like an amulet, a sort of throne.

102. Seventh, the *araboth* heaven. And why is it called a "heaven"? Because it is circular like a head, and this teaches that water is at its right hand and fire at its left hand, and it is at the center, and is *shamayim* [heaven], from *esh* [fire] and *mayim* [water]. And it makes peace between them. The fire came and found at its side the principle of fire, the water came and found at its side the principle of water, and this means (Job 25:2): "Who makes peace in his heights."

103. The seventh? But there are only six? This teaches that this is the hall of the holiness, and it carries all [the other six], and that is why it is the seventh. And what is it? Thinking, which had no end nor limit. And thus this place has neither end nor limit.

104. The seventh is the east of the world, and thence comes the seed of Israel, for the spine goes from the human brain to the member of generation, and that is where the seed comes from, for it is written (Isaiah 43:5): "I bring thy seed from the East, and I gather thee from the West." If Israel is good in the eyes of God, [then] "I bring thy seed" from this place, and new seed comes forth for you. But if Israel is bad, then [I take] of the seed that was already in the world, for it is written (Eccles. 1:4): "One generation passeth away, and another generation cometh." This means that it has already come. And what does this verse mean (Isaiah 43:5): "I gather thee from the West." From that sphere that always leans toward the West. Why is the West called *ma'arabh*? Because all seed is mingled there. That is like a king who had a lovely and

chaste bride in his apartments, and he would take riches from his father's house and bring them to her, and she took everything, and always hid it and mixed it together. After a time, he wanted to see what he had joined and gathered, and it is written thereof: "I gather you in from the mingling." And what is his father's house? [That whereof] it is written: "I bring thy seed from the East." This teaches that he brings it from the East and sows it in the West; and eventually he gathers in what he has sown.

105. What is the eighth? God has a "righteous man" in his world and he loves him because he maintains the entire world and is its foundation. He [God] nourishes him and lets him grow and rears him and brings him joy, and makes him beloved and respected above, beloved and respected below, feared and sublime above, feared and sublime below, beautiful and pleasant above, beautiful and pleasant below, and he is the foundation of all souls. You say the foundation of all souls and the eighth [logos]. Yet it is written (Exodus 31:17): "And on the seventh day it was sabbath and refreshment." Yes he *is* the seventh [logos], for he balances between them. Those six [are divided into] three below and three above, and he balances between them. And why is it called the seventh? Did it only exist as of the seventh [day]? No, [it is counted thus] because God rested on the Sabbath. It is written of that sphere [ibid.]: "For God created in six days, the heavens and the earth, and on the seventh day he rested and celebrated." This teaches that every day has a "logos," which is its ruler, not because it was created with it, but because it performs along with it that effect that is given in its power. When all of them have performed their effect and fulfilled their task, then the seventh day comes and performs its effect, and they are all joyous, even God, nay, not only that, it enlarges their souls, as it is written [ibid.]: "And on the seventh day there was rest and refreshment." And what is this rest? There is no labor, and that is the rest of which it is written "there was rest." That is like a king who had seven gardens, and in the middle garden a beautiful, bubbling source from a well of flowing water irrigates the three to the right and the three to the left. And when it has done this work, it fills up. Now all are joyous and say: It fills up for us. And it waters them and helps them grow, whereas they wait and rest. And it waters the seven. Yet it is written: (Isaiah 43:5): "I bring thy seed from the East." And is it one of those [seven]

and does it water it? Say, rather: It waters the "heart" and the heart waters them all.

106. Rabbi Berekiah sat and spoke: What does it mean that we speak every day about the "coming world," the *'olam ha-ba'*, and do not know what we are speaking about!? The "coming world" is translated by the targum as "the world that is coming," *'alma de-'athe*. And what does "the world that is coming" mean? This teaches that before the creation of the world there arose in the godly [thinking] to create a great light for illumination. A great light was thus created, and no creature could endure it. God anticipated that they would not be able to endure it, so he took a seventh of it and gave it to them instead, and he concealed the rest for the coming world. He said: If they prove worthy of this seventh and guard it, I shall give them the [rest] in the other world, and that is "the world that is coming"—which comes from the six days of Creation. That is what is written: (Psalms 31:20): "Oh how great is thy goodness, which thou hast laid up for them that fear thee; which thou has wrought for them that trust in thee before the sons of man."

107. What does the verse mean (Exodus 15:27): "And they came to Elim, and there were twelve water sources there and seventy palmtrees." Is there anything unusual about seventy palmtrees? Even the tiniest place has thousands of them! Actually: They were graced there with their primal images, which have their likeness in the palms, for it is written earlier (Exodus 15:23): "And they came to Marahand and could not drink any water, for it was bitter." This teaches that the north wind prevented it, for it is written [ibid. 15:25]: "He shouted to God, and God taught him a kind of wood, and he flung." God instantly turned his hand against Satan and made him smaller. Otherwise, Israel could not have held out against him, for it is written [ibid.]: "He held judgment there" against Satan, "and he tempted it there." This teaches that Satan clove unto them to wipe them out from the world, as it is written [ibid. 15:24]: "The people murmured against Moses and said: What shall we drink? And he afflicted Moses further, until "he shouted to God, and God taught him a tree." What [does this mean]: "God taught him a tree." This teaches that the tree of life stood around the water, and Satan came and took it from there to afflict Israel and to lead them astray into Sin before their father in heaven. He

said to them: Now you will come into the desert and [in contrast] this bitter water is good, for you can get enough of it, but in the desert you won't even find enough to wash your hands and face. You will die of hunger and thirst and exposure. They came to Moses and told him this. He averted them with words. [Satan] saw that he had no power over them, so he strained against Israel and Moses. The people came and murmured against Moses: We lack water here, and what shall we drink in the desert? Satan came to falsify their words for Moses and lead them into sin. But as soon as Moses saw Satan "he shouted to God and God taught him a tree"—the tree of life that Satan had taken away—"and he flung it into the water, and the water turned sweet; he held judgment there"—against Satan "and there he tempted it"—[that is] Israel.

108. And God warned Israel and said (Exodus 15:26): "When you listen to God's voice, etc." It is like a king who had a beautiful daughter, and others desired her. The king learned this, and since he could not start a fight with those who wanted to seduce his daughter, he went to his daughter and warned her: "My child, pay no heed to the words of these foes, and they shall have no power over you. Do not go to the front door, do your work in the house, and never remain idle for even a moment, and they shall not see you and bring harm to you. For they have a principle: They keep you far from every good road and pick every bad one, and when they see someone bringing himself to a good road and walking along that road, then they hate him.

109. And what is this principle? Satan. It teaches that there is a principle with God that is known as "evil," and it lies to the north of God, for it is written (Jeremiah 1:14): "Evil opens from the north." This means: All evil that comes upon all the dwellers of the earth comes from the north. And what principle is this? It is the "form" of the hand, and it has many messengers, and all of them are called "evil," but there are greater and lesser "evil" ones among them. And it is they who plunge the world into guilt, for *tohu* is from the north, and tohu signifies "evil," which confuses men until they sin, and man's entire evil drive comes from there. And why is it on the left? Because its area is nowhere in the world but in the north, and it is only used to the north and only wishes to be in the north, for if it were in the south, then, until it learned the way of the south and how to lead astray there, it would remain

inactive during the days of its learning and not evoke any sin. Therefore he is always at the left, and that is what is meant by the verse (Gen. 8:21): "For the drive of the human heart is evil from its youth," it is evil from its youth and may only be at the left, to which it is accustomed. That is why God said to Israel (Exodus 15:26): "When you hear God's voice and do what is right in His eyes, and obey His commandments"—and not the commandments of the evil drive—"and keep all his statutes"—and not the statutes of the evil drive—then "I am the eternal, your physician."

110. And what profit has the evil drive? A parable: A king put overseers over his kingdom and commerce, and over everything and everyone. One [overseer] was put over the storehouse of good and wares, and one was put over the storehouse of stones. All the people came to buy from the storehouses of wares. The overseer of the storehouse of stones came and saw that the people weren't buying from him and he became envious. What did he do? He commanded all his messengers to tear down the weak houses—for they could not do anything against the strong ones—and he said: In the time it would take them to tear down a strong house they could tear down twenty weak ones, and all shall come and buy from me, and I shall not be any worse than my comrades. And that is what is meant by the verse (Jeremiah 1:14): "For evil opens from the north over all the dwellers of the earth," and the following verse [ibid. 1:15]: "For I call all the tribes of the north, saith the Lord, and they shall come and each one shall set his throne at the entrance to the gates of Jerusalem." And evil will have a great deal to do, and the evil drive will have to make great efforts.

And what does "Satan" mean? This means: He who bends downward, for it is he who seeks to bend the world towards the side of guilt. Thus it is written (Gen. 38:16): "And he bent towards her from the road," and the targum translates this as "seta," and it is written (Prov. 4:15): "Bend away from him and go on."

* * *

112. What do the "seventy palms" mean? This teaches that God has seventy "forms," and they draw from the twelve Simple Ones [consonants]. Just as water is simple, so are they simple. And how do we know that "palm" means "form"? From the verse (Song of Songs 7:8): "Your form is like the palmtree," and not only this, but

there are seventy kinds of palmtrees, as it is written (Exodus 15:27): "Seventy palms," and they do not resemble one another, and their effects [do not resemble] one another, and the taste of one does not resemble the taste of the others.

113. You say: 70 forms. But we say 72. No, there are 71 and with Israel they are 72, but [the two] do not belong among the others. Yet you said 70 [and not 71]. One is Prince Satan. That is like a king who had sons. He bought slaves and said: They are to belong to all of you equally. But one son said: I do not want to share with you, for I have the power to take everything away from you. The king said: No, you shall have no part of them, and you shall do only what is in your power. He went and lay in wait for them on a road and showed them gold and precious gems and hosts, and said to them: Come and join me. What did the king do? He lined up his hosts and those of all his sons and showed them the slaves and said to them: Do not let yourselves be deceived by the seducer to believe that his army is greater than my army. Here are my armies, and that son is a deceiver and plans to carry you off. Do not listen to him, because he will first speak smooth words to catch you in his nets, and then he will deride you. And you are my servants, and I shall do good things for you, if you do not listen or follow him, for he is the prince of *tohu,* as it is written (I Samuel 12:21): "For you would merely follow [the powers of] *tohu,* which bring neither usefulness nor salvation for they are *tohu,*" but they can bring harm, and I advise you (Exodus 15:26): "If you listen to God's voice and keep all his statutes," which means by keeping all his statutes, "all the disease that I put upon Egypt" [ibid.], that is only to close all doors to him, for if he does not find you keeping his commandments sometimes and not keeping them at other times, then I shall "not put upon you all those sicknesses that I once put upon Egypt" through him. What does this mean [ibid.]: "For I the Eternal am thy physician," and when did he strike him with wounds? This means: When [Satan] comes and wounds you, "I the Eternal am thy physician."

114. And what [does it mean] when you say: the eighth logos? With it, the eight begin and with it the eight are closed in terms of the counting, but in accordance with its activity it is the seventh. And which is that? That which begins with the eight days of circumcision. But the eight are only seven, aren't they? Why does he speak

of eight? Because there are eight "limitations" on man. And what are they? The right hand and the left hand, the right foot and the left foot, the head, the trunk, and the mediating [place of] circumcision, and his wife, who belongs to him, as it is written (Gen. 2:24): "And he will cleave to his wife and they shall be one flesh." Those are eight, and eight days of circumcision correspond to them. Those eight however are merely seven, for the trunk and the [place of] circumcision are one. Those are eight.

115. What is the ninth? He said to him. The ninth and the tenth belong together, one to the other, and the one is 500 years higher than the other, and they are like [two] wheels, one leaning northward, and the other westward, and they reach to the lowest earth. What does lowest mean? The last of the seven earths below and the end of God's shekinah under his feet, as it is written (Isaiah 66:1): "Heaven is my throne, and the earth is the footstool for my feet," and he placed the "permanence of the world" below, as it is written (Isaiah 34:10): *"lenetsakh netsakhim,"* for all time. What does *lenetsakh netsakhim* mean? That is one *netsakh.* And which is it? That which leans westward, and the second one [belonging to it] is [that] which leans northward, and the third is from below. A third? But you spoke of two wheels of the merkabha? Understand it rather as follows: The end of the shekinah is also called *"netsakh,"* and that means *"lenetsakh netsakhim,"* netsakh is one, *"netsakhim"* are two, and together that makes three.

116. His students said to him: Our teacher, we know [the order of the spheres] from above to below, but we do not know it from below to above. And is it not the same [whether] from above to below or from below to above? Our teacher, he who climbs up is not like him who climbs down, for he who climbs down goes quickly, but not so he who climbs up. And not only that; he who climbs up can climb up along one road that he might not be able to climb down.

He said to them: Go and see! He sat down and spoke: [There is] a shekinah below, just as there is a shekinah above. What is this shekinah? Say: That is the light that emanates from the primal light. It too surrounds everything, for it is written (Isaiah 6:3): "The whole earth is full of his splendor." And what is its function here? That is like a king who had seven sons and assigned each one a place. He said to them: Each of you live one over the other. The one [living] at the bottom said: I do not want to live at the bottom and be remote from you. He said to them: I am about you daily and see [you]. And thus it is written [ibid.]: "The whole earth is full of his splendor." And why [is] he among them? To maintain them and keep them in existence.

And what are these sons? I have already said that God has seven holy forms, and they all have their correspondence in man, as it is written (Gen. 1:27): "God created man in his likeness, in his likeness he created him, he created them male and female." And they are as follows: The right and the left leg, the right and the left hand, the trunk with the place of procreation, and the head. Those are six, and you said: Seven. They are seven with his wife, of whom it is written (Gen. 2:24): "And they form one flesh." But she was taken from his ribs, for it is written (Exodus 26:20): "And the rib of the holiness," and the targum translates it as "At the side of the holiness."

117. And what kind of side is on him? That is like a king who planned to plant nine male trees in his garden, all of them palms. What did he do? He said: If they are all of the same kind, they cannot subsist. What did he do? He planted an ethrog among them, and it was one of those nine which he had planned to be male. And what is the ethrog? The ethrog is female. And what does the verse mean (Lev. 23:40): "The fruit of the tree of splendor and palm branches." What [does this mean]: The fruit of the tree of splendor? As the targum translates: "The fruit of the tree that brings forth ethrogs and palmbranches." And what is "splendor"? That signifies the splendor of the "universe" and the splendor of the Song of Songs, of which it is written (Song of Songs 4:10): "Who is she who appears like the dawn, beautiful as the moon, pure as the sun, terrifying as armed hosts?" And it signifies "splendor" because of the female, and because of it the female was taken from the male, for the upper and the lower world could not exist without the female. And why is the female called *nekebha?* Because her apertures are wide, and she has more apertures than the man. And what are they? The apertures of the breasts and the womb and the vagina. And what do you mean when you say that the Song of Songs is "splendor"? Yes, [it is] the most splendid of all the holy writings, for Rabbi Yokhanan has said: All books [of the Scriptures] are holy, but the Song of Songs is supremely holy. What does

"supremely holy" mean? A holiness for the holinesses. And what
are these holinesses? Those that correspond to the "six directions"
in man, and they have a holiness that is holy for them all.

118. And what is "holiness"? That is [the] ethrog that is the splen-
dor of the "universe." And why is it called *hadar,* splendor? Read
not *hadar,* but ha-dar, "it remains," that is [the] ethrog, that does
not belong to the alliance of the festive bouquet, and [yet] the
commandment of the festive bouquet can be fulfilled only with it,
and it too is bound with all, for it is [bound] with every single one
and all together.

To what does the palmbranch [in the festive bouquet] corre-
spond? To the spine. And thus is it written (in Lev. 23:40): "And
a branch of the thick tree. The boughs must cover most of it, and
if its boughs do not cover most of it, then it is not fitting. Why?
That is like a man who has arms to support his head. His arms are
two, and his head makes three, and that is what is meant [by the
three words: "Branch of the tree of foliage"]; "branch" to the right,
"foliage" to the left, and "tree" remains in the middle. And why
is "tree" there? Because it represents the "root of the tree" [in the
festive bouquet].

* * *

123. This [our] world has three spheres [above it]. How? This
world leans toward the north and the south. How? Northwestward
and southwestward. Northwestward is the first sphere that spins
above us. You mean: Northwestern? Say rather: Its potency is
northwestward, and that is the left leg. And above it lies a second
sphere that goes directly westward. You mean: Westward? Say
rather: Its potency is in the west. And these [two] are the "carriers
of the world." And above it lies a third sphere, and its potency is
in the southwest. And what is the first potency, since you are
speaking of the second? Say: The right leg. And this potency of the
southwest is the foundation of the world, of which it is written:
(Prov. 10:26): "The righteous man is the foundation of the world."
And the second potency stands behind the merkabha, the first
potency in front of it, and the "righteous one, the foundation of the
world," in the center, and he comes out of the south of the world,
and is prince of these two [others]. Also, his hand holds the souls
of all living things, for he is the "eternally living." And all "creat-

ing" which is spoken of [in the Scriptures] happens through him. And of him it is written (Exodus 31:17): "He rested and celebrated, and he is the principle of the Sabbath, and the verse (Exodus 20:8) speaks of him: "Remember the Sabbath day, to sanctify it." Yet it is written (Deut. 5:12): "Keep the Sabbath day . . ." This refers to the seventh principle, for it is written (Levit. 19:30): "Keep my Sabbaths and fear my sanctuary."

* * *

126. He is the "universe," and the treasury of souls in his power. And if Israel is good, the souls may come out to come into this world, but if Israel is not good, then the souls do not come out. And that is what is meant by the words: David's son shall not come until all the souls in the "body" are exhausted. What does this mean: All the souls in the body? Say: In the body of man. And the "new" ones could come out, and then the son of David would be permitted to be born. How? Because his soul would come out with the others as "new."

127. A parable: A king had an army. He sent them masses of food and bread, they were indolent and didn't consume it, they didn't even pay attention to it. So the bread became bad and moldy. He came to inspect and to check whether they had anything to eat. He found moldy bread and saw that they were ashamed to ask for bread and to say: We paid not attention to this bread and ask for more bread. The king became angry, took the moldy bread and let it dry out and be restored as well as possible, and he swore: I shall not give these people any other bread until they have fully consumed this entire mass of moldy bread. He sent it back to them. What did they do? They resolved to divide it. They doled it out, and each man took his share. The careful ones put their shares in the air and paid attention and ate [it when it was] good. The others took it and devoured their bread greedily, but left the rest outside and paid no attention to it. Now it became even worse and moldier, and they could not eat it anymore at all, and they starved to death. Each of these men was summoned before the [heavenly] court because of the sin against his body: Why did you kill yourself? Not only did you let the bread go bad beforehand, I sent it to you again in a good condition, and you doled it out, and you let part of it go bad, and you were too lazy to pay any attention to it, and you also

killed yourself. And the man replied: Lord, what should I have done? And the answer came: You should have paid attention to it, and if you say you could not, then you should have watched your comrades and neighbors, who shared the bread with you, and you would have seen what they did with it, the way they kept it, and you should have made an effort to pay attention as they did. And they questioned him: Why did you kill yourself? Not only did you let the bread go bad, you also did more, and you killed the matter of your body and shortened your days, or [indirectly] caused [them] to be shortened. And you might have had a fine son who could have saved you and your error, and saved others and their errors. That is why sorrows come upon you now from all sides! He took fright and answered: And what should I have done, since I had no bread? What should I have lived on? They said to him: If only you had concerned yourself with the Torah and made an effort. It is written of the Torah (Deut. 8:3): "Man does not live by bread alone, but from everything that comes from God's mouth does man live." And how can you wish to ask, inquire, and find out what it is by which man shall live?

* * *

129. And what does the verse mean (Job 15:2): "The wise man answers with knowledge of the spirit"? What is "knowledge of the spirit"? That means: With knowledge that is close to the spirit, as it is written (Isaiah 11:2): "And God's spirit rests upon him, a spirit of wisdom," and then "of perception, judgment," which contains "counsel and strength, knowledge and fear of God." But you told us: "Counsel" is doing good, "strength" is the principle of severity, "knowledge" is truth, and thus "knowledge" exists for testing truth, "fear of God" is the treasurehouse of the Torah. That is what I am saying now except that the latter lie above; for Rabbi Akiba has said: All that God created was created in correspondences, as it is written (Eccles. 7:14): "God has done this corresponding to that." And what is this treasurehouse of the Torah? That of which it is written (Isaiah 33:6): "Fear of God is his treasure." That is why man should fear God and then study the Torah. Like a man who went to buy date-honey but did not take along a vessel to bring it home. He said: I will carry it home on my chest. He carried it on his chest; but it became too heavy. Now he feared it might break apart and soil his clothes, and so he threw it away. Thus he was

punished twofold: Once for wasting food, and once for losing money. And this "fear of God," which is above, lies in God's hand, and it is also his "power," and that "hand" is the "scales of merit," because it tilts the world to the side of merit, and that is what is meant by the verse (Isaiah 11:3): "His breath is fear of God, by that which his eyes see he does not judge, and by that which his ears hear he does not punish." Instead, he tilts the entire universe to the side of merit, and from there comes "counsel," and from there comes health into the world, and (Gen. 49:24) "from there comes the shepherd, the rock of Israel" and that is the place that is named "there," as it is written (Habakkuk 3:4): "And *there* is the concealment of his power."

130. Rabbi, since we are speaking [about this verse], please explain it more precisely. What do you mean precisely? Tell us what this means (Habakkuk 3:4): "And rays come out of his hand." Why does it say "rays," and then "his hand" instead of "his *hands*"? That's no problem, for it is likewise written (Exodus 32:19): "Moses' wrath enflamed and he threw the tablets from his hands." The Biblical text reads "from his hand," and likewise it is written (Exodus 17:13): "And his hands were raised," whereby "raised" is in the singular and not the plural! Rabbi, we are asking you this difficult thing in order to answer it, but you are darkening our eyes! You once taught us, you, our teacher, to answer the first thing first, and the later thing later. And what do you want? The explanation of "rays come out of his hand"! By the temple! I have just explained it in my own words! They were abashed. He saw that they were abashed, so he began and said: Was not the water [first] and the fire came out of it? They said: That is the general opinion. Well, then the water contains the fire! Rabbi, what does "rays" mean? He said to them: There are five rays, corresponding to the five fingers on the right hand of man. But, Rabbi, you yourself told us in the name of Rabbi Yokhanan that they are the "two arms of the world." He said to them: Yes, but here "rays" refers to the two [levels] below. And what is that? He said to them: Your head is above. And what is beneath? He said to them: "Fear of God."

131. And what is this "fear of God"? That is the primal light, for Rabbi Meir has said: What does the verse mean (Gen. 1:3): "Let there be light and there was light," instead of: "And it was so." This teaches that the light was exceedingly great and that no

creature could have looked at it. So God concealed it for the
righteous until the time of the Messiah. And that is the principle
of all wares in the world, and that is the power of the precious stone
called *sokhereth,* marble, and *dar,* mother-o'-pearl. And why does
it indicate the principle of *dar?* This teaches that God took a
thousandth part of his radiance and constructed a beautiful decor-
ous precious stone, and concentrated all the commandments in it.

Then came Abraham and asked Him to give him a "power."
And God gave him that precious stone, but Abraham did not want
it. He was found worthy and took his "mode," for it is written
(Micah 7:20): "Love for Abraham." And then Isaac came and
asked for his "power." He was given this one, and he did not want
it. He was found worthy and he was given the "mode" of strength,
which is "fear," for it is written (Gen. 31:53): "And Jacob swore
by the fear of his father Isaac." Then came Jacob and wanted it,
but they did not give it to him. They said to him: Since Abraham
is above and Isaac below, you can be in the middle, and take all
three. And what is this middle? That is peace. But it is written
(Micah 7:20): "You give Jacob truth." Truth and peace are one,
as in the verses (Esther 9:30): "Words of peace and truth," and (2
Kings 20:19): "If only peace and truth prevail," and that is what
is meant by the verse (Isaiah 58:14): "I give you the earth of your
father Jacob." That means a perfect legacy that becomes theirs:
Love and fear and truth and peace. That is why it is written
(Psalms 118:22): "The stone that the builders threw away has
become the cornerstone," the stone that Abraham and Isaac, who
built the world, threw away has become the cornerstone.

132. And why did they throw it away? It is written (Gen. 26:5):
"Because Abraham listened to my voice and fulfilled my task. . . ."!
What does "my task" mean? Thus spoke the principle of love: As
long as Abraham was in the world, I did not need to do my mission
in the world, for Abraham stood there in my stead and fulfilled my
task. For that is my mission: To intercede for the world, and if they
have become guilty then I speak for them, and further: I bring them
to penitence and inspire their hearts to do the will of their father.
Abraham did all this, for it is written (Gen. 21:33): "And he
planted a tree in Bersheba," and he offered his bread and water to
all people and strove for goodness and spoke to their hearts: Whom
do you serve? Serve the Eternal, the God of Heaven and Earth, and

he preached to them until they did penitence. And how [do we know] that he interceded for the guilty too? Because it is written (Gen. 18:17): "Do I hide what I do from Abraham?" Instead: I shall do something for him, for I know that he prays for clemency for them and will intercede for them. And was God not to know that they were not to be saved? Instead [he said that] to do something good for him. That is why they said: Assist the man who will cleanse; there are doors for the man who wants to soil. What does that mean: There are doors for him? [That indicates] the ones that are always open.

(Gen. 26:5): "My commandments and statutes"? Abraham said: Since I did not want them, I will keep their commandments. And what does this mean: "And my doctrines"? It means that he knew and observed even the [Halachic] decisions and discussion that are given above.

* * *

134. Rabbi Rekhumay said: I have received this [through tradition]: When Moses asked for knowledge of the sacred and venerable name and said (Exodus 33:18): "Let me know your glory," he wanted to know why one person is righteous and does well and another is righteous and does badly, and one person is bad and does well, and another is bad and does badly, and no one let him know. Instead: He did not find out what he asked for. Do you think Moses didn't know this secret? Moses actually said: I know the ways of the "powers," but I don't know how "thought" spread in them, I know that in "thought" there is truth, but I do not know its parts and I would like to know—but they did not let him know.

135. Why does [some] blasphemer do well and [some] righteous man do badly? Because the righteous man was a blasphemer in the past and is now being punished. But is a man punished for [the sins of] his youth? Rabbi Simon did say that a man is punished as of his twentieth year. I am not speaking about the [same] life, I am saying that he already existed in the past. His comrades said to him: How much longer will you speak dark words? He said to them: Go and see? That is like a man who planted a vineyard in his garden. He hoped for grapes and he got whitefish. He saw that he was not successful, so he transplanted the vineyard, surrounded it with a fence, and fixed all the holes, cleaned the vineyard of

whitefish and planted it a second time. He saw that he was unsuc-
cessful again, so he put a fence around it and planted it after
cleansing it. He saw that he was not successful, so he put a fence
about it and planted it. How often? He said to him: For a thousand
generations, for it is written (Psalms 105:8): "He commanded a
word for a thousand generations. And that is what is meant by the
utterance: 974 generations were lacking when God stood up and
planted them in every generation [since the Creation].

* * *

137. What does "little" [mean in this verse, Psalms 8:6]: [It means]
he has sins. God, however, may He be praised and may His Name
be praised, has no sins. He may not have sins, but doesn't the bad
spirit come from him? You mean: it comes? Say instead: It came
from him until David came and killed it. And that is what is meant
by the verse (Psalms 109:22): "My heart is dead in me." Thus
spoke David: Because I have worsted it (Psalms 5:5), "evil no
[longer] lives with me." And how did David worst it? By studying
the Torah, for he did not stop day or night and tied together—and
what did he tie together? He tied the upper Torah to God; for as
often as a man studied the Torah for its own sake, the upper Torah
is tied to God, and that is what is meant by the utterance: Let man
always study the Torah, even if he does so for selfish reasons, for
he will thereby reach the point at which he will do it for its own
sake. What is this "Torah" of which you speak? The Torah is the
bride that is adorned and crowned and that contains all command-
ments, and it is the treasurehouse of the Torah and betrothed to
God, as it is written (Deut. 33:4): "Moses commanded us the
Torah, a legacy of the community of Jacob." Do not read morasha,
legacy, but me'orassa, betrothed, and [do not] read me'orassa,
betrothed, but morasha, legacy. What does that mean? In the time
when Israel studies the Torah for its own sake, it is betrothed to
God, and in the time when it is betrothed to God it is Israel's
legacy.

138. Rabbi Amora sat and lectured: Why was Tamar found worthy
to bear Peretz and Zarah? Because her name was tamar, palmtree.
And Tamar, the sister of Ammon? That was her destiny. Why are
the children named Peretz and Zarah? Peretz is named after the
moon, for the moon wanes and waxes, and Zarah is named after

the sun, for the sun always rises in the same way. Zarah is named after the sun, but Peretz was the firstborn, and isn't the sun bigger than the moon? That's no problem, for it is written (Gen. 38:28): "And he stretched out his hand," and it is written (ibid. 38:30): "And then came his brother whose hand held the silken string and he was named Zarah," for he should have been the firstborn, [but] because God was happy since he foresaw that Peretz would come from Salomon, who was to pronounce the Song of Songs, he took Zarah back.

139. And why is she named *tamar,* palmtree, and not something else? Because it is the feminine. You mean, the feminine? Say rather: Because it contains the masculine and the feminine. And how? The palmbranch is masculine, and the fruit is masculine on the outside and feminine on the inside. And how? In the seeds of the date, which is split in the manner of a woman, and the potency of the moon corresponds to it above.

140. And God created them (both masculine and feminine), for it is written (Gen. 1:27): "He created them, male and female." Can one say this? After all, it is written [ibid.] "God created man in his own image," and then only, (Gen. 2:18): "I shall make him a helpmeet" (and Gen. 2:21): "And he took one of his sides and joined flesh to it." Understand this so: Here, it is written [of the creation of man] "form" and "create." Create refers to the time when He made the soul—He created it as something of male and female. "Form" refers to the time when he united the soul with the body and brought everything together. And how [do we know] that "form" is a word for "bring together"? From the verse (Gen. 2:13): "And the Lord God had brought all the animals of the field and all the birds of heaven together and brought them to the man." And that is what is meant by the verse (Gen. 5:21): "He created them male and female and he blessed them." The soul of the woman from the female, the soul of the man from the male. And that is why the serpent followed Eve. The serpent said: Since her soul comes from the north, I shall soon seduce her. And what was this seduction? The snake fornicated with her.

141. His pupils asked: Tell us how that matter was. He said to them: Sammael the Evil One conspired with all the hosts of the high against their Lord because God had said [to Man] (Gen. 1:28):

"And rule over the fish in the sea and over the birds in heaven."
Sammael said: How can we lead him into sin and drive him away
from God? He descended with all his hosts and searched the earth
for a comrade like himself, and found the serpent, which had the
shape of a camel. He rode upon it and betook himself to the
woman. He said to her (Gen. 3:1): "Even if God said: thou shalt
not eat of any tree in the garden . . ." He said [to himself]: I will
demand more and add to God's words so that she may lose [her
dignity]. She said to him: He did not forbid us anything, except
(Gen. 3:3) "to eat of the fruit of the tree of knowledge, which stands
in the middle of the garden, said God: Do not eat of it and do not
touch it, so that you shall not die." And he added two things, she
said: "Of the fruit of the tree, that stands in the middle of the
garden," whereas they had only been told: "Of the tree." And she
said: "Do not touch it so that you shall not die." And what did
Sammael the Evil One do? He went over and touched the tree. And
the tree shrieked and said: Blasphemer, do not touch me, for it is
written (Psalms 36:12): "The gait of pride does not come to me.
. . . the evildoers must fall." He went over and said to the woman:
Lo, I have touched the tree and I did not die, why don't you touch
it too, you shall not die. The woman went over and touched the
tree and saw the Angel of Death coming upon her. She said:
Perhaps I am dying now, and God will make another woman and
give her to Adam. I will get him to eat with me. If we die, then
both of us shall die, and if we live, then both of us shall live. And
she took and ate of the fruits of the tree and gave them to her
husband. His eyes opened and his teeth became dull. He said to her:
What did you give me to eat? As my teeth have grown dull, so shall
the teeth of all men become dull. Then He, who is called the
righteous judge held a true judgment over him. He said to him:
Why did you flee me? He replied (Gen. 3:10): "I heard your voice
in the garden," and my bones trembled and I was afraid, for I am
naked, for I am naked before my Creator, for I am naked without
the commandment that has become to me, for I am naked from my
deed, as it is written [ibid.]: "For I am naked and I hid." What was
Adam's garment? A cornea, a horny hide. And when he had eaten
of the fruits of the tree, [God] drew the horny hide off him, and
he saw himself naked, as it is written (Gen. 3:11): "Who told you
that you are naked?" Adam spoke to God: Lord of the Universe,
did I sin against you when I was alone? Only the woman, whom

you brought to me, led me astray from your words, as it is written
(Gen. 3:12): "The woman, whom you gave me." And God said to
her: Not only did you sin, you have seduced Adam into sin. She
spoke to him: Lord of the Universe, the serpent led me astray to
sin against you! He summoned all three of them and pronounced
judgment upon them: Nine curses and death, and cast Sammael
and his mob from their sacred place in heaven, and cut off the
serpent's feet, and cursed her before all animals and creatures, and
sentenced her to slough off her skin every seven years in great pain.

—Translated by
Joachim Neugroschel

Part four

That which is called My name,
I have created it (barativ),
I have formed it (yezartiv),
and I have also made it ('asitiv).

—*Isaiah 33:7*

from
THE CROWN OF THE KINGDOM

(Keter Malkhut)

SOLOMON IBN GABIROL

"Solomon ben Yehudah Ibn Gebirol, of Cordova, called by the Jews, Solomon the Sephardi, i.e., Spaniard, the Hymnologist, and by acrostic from the initials of his name, RaSHBaG; by the Arabs, Abu Ayyub Suleiman ben-Ya'hya Ibn Djebirol, and by the scholastics, Avicebrol, Avicebron, Avicembron, etc., was born at Malaga about 1021, educated at Sargossa, and died at Valencia, 1070. It is said, in a legend, that he was killed by a Mohammedan who was jealous of his great talents, that the murderer buried him under a fig tree, in the former's garden; the tree bore so much fruit, of such extraordinary sweetness, that the king, informed of the phenomenon, made the proprietor of the garden come before him, and being pressed by questions, the murderer ended by avowing his crime, and expiated it with his life. Ibn Gebirol may be considered as the greatest philosopher of his century.

"Towards the middle of the XIth century, Ibn Gebirol began to make himself known, as a philosopher and poet, notwithstanding the repugnance towards each other, which these two branches of human thought generally evince; so as rarely to be found united in the same individual. However in Ibn Gebirol's poetry are most profound philosophical meditations, and in his philosophical works are to be found traces of the rhetoric, lively imagination, and inspiration, of the poet. The philosophical works he wrote in Arabic, his poetry in Hebrew . . .

"The Kether Malkuth or Crown of the Kingdom, was given by him the first place among his hymns, and he tells us in it, that it was written in his declining years. It is a hymn celebrating the only one and true God, and the marvels of His creation. The veil, which covers the mysteries of Nature, the poet seeks to fathom and unravel, by means of the scientific knowledge of his time . . . It is not only a religious poem, but a poetical resumé of the Peripatetic, Oriental, Alexandrine and Qabbalistic cosmology; and in it he endeavors, in magnificent language, to unite religion and philosophy or the spiritual and the physical, in a perfect harmony, so as to glorify and praise the only True Being."

—Isaac Myer: *Qabbalah. The Philosophical
Writings of Avicebron* (1885)

May man profit by my prayer
may he learn the right and straight through it
I have told the wonders of living El in it
in brief not at full length
I set it above all my other praises
I call it the Crown of Kingdom

I.

How wondrous your doings my soul knows well
Greatness is yours Adonai   and might and beauty
infinity and splendor
Rule is yours Adonai   and overall and richness and honor
The created things are yours   witness above and below
for as they disappear you wear on
Might is yours
our very thought wears out getting at its secret
You are so stronger than we
The mystery of might is yours   the hidden and the hide

Yours is the name hidden from sages
the power which carries the world over nothing
the ability to bring the hidden to light
Yours is the mercy
which rules your creatures
and the good   hidden for those who fear you
Secrets are yours
which thought and reason cannot hold

and life which is unending
    the throne rising over all over
    the pleasance hidden in the height of mystery
Reality is yours
in its lit shade being is

we have said it: "We will live in His shade."

II.

You are one   the beginning of all count
             the base of every structure
You are one   the sage of heart gape at your oneness and its
             secret
             for they cannot know it
You are one   your unity cannot be diminished or added to
                 it cannot want or gain
You are one   not as counted and dealt are one
                for extent and change cannot reach you
                nor description nor reference
You are one   My logic tires setting a limit for you and a law
                so I must guard my way from my own
             tongue's error
You are one   higher and over low and fallen
             no one   alone   to fall

III.

You are real   but earhear and eyesight cannot reach you
             how and why and where have nothing to do with
             you
You are real   but to yourself
             and no one takes part
You are real   before all time you were
             and dwelt without place
You are real   your secret hidden and who can catch it?
             Deep   deep   who can find it?

IV.

You live   not from fixed time
             not from known date
You live   soulless spiritless
             you are soul's soul
You live   not as man lives   in vain
             his end moth and worm
You live   Who comes towards your secret finds eternal delight
                                  lives forever if he
                                  eat of it

V.

You are huge   in the face of your hugeness everything of size
                 shrinks
You are huge   greater than any thought   higher than the Char-
                 iot itself
You are huge   greater than large   higher than praise

VI.

You are might   of all your creatures and makings
                 there is none can do as you or as your might
You are might   changeless   only   total might is
                 yours alone
You are might   from your height you can forgive from your
                 wrath
                                  endure sin in your
                                  anger
You are might   the mercy you show your creatures   all
                      this is the eternal might

VII.

You are highest light
eyes of clear soul see you   clouds of sin hide you from sineyes
You are hidden light
in this world   open in the visioned world
                    "mount of Adonai   it will be seen"

You are eternal light
eye of mind longs   and is startled at you
                              seeing only the edges   never all

VIII.

You are he   Elohei Elohim   Adonei Adonim   ruling high and
            low
You are Eloha   all creatures your witness
                all creation made to serve you   honoring this
                name
You are Eloha   all the made things are your servants and serve
                you
                no glory lost where others worship without you
                the desire of all is to reach you
                though they are like the blind who seek the high-
                way
                and stray from the way
                                    This one drowns in ruin
                                    pit
                                    this falls in holes
                    yet all think they have struck their wish
                    yet reach waste
                Your servants are openeyed   walking the right
                way
                                        never turning off
                                        right or left
                                        till they come to
                                        the palace yard
You are Eloha   keeping made things by your Godness
                feasting creatures on your Oneness
You are Eloha   no different in your Oneness and your Godness
                        or your Firstness or your Being
It is all one secret
                and even if all the names are changed
it all comes back to one place

IX.

You are wise   wisdom is the source of life and flows from you
                    all men are too stupid to know your wisdom
You are wise   the first of every first
                    wisdom grew up with you
You are wise   not learn from without you
                    not have it from some other
You are wise   shone fixed will from your wisdom
      a worker and an artist   pulling something from nothing
      as the light is drawn out from the eye
      drawn from lightsource   without a tool
      working without any tool
      split and chop
      cleanse and true
      call to nothing and split it
            to being and fix it
            to timeworld and divide it
      measure skies by hand
      a hand joining tents of orbit
      joining the films of creature
      with rings of might
      power beaming on to the edge of creation
                          the lowest
                          the farthest away
                          the curtain's hem

                                —Translated by Harris Lenowitz

from
HOKMATH HA-'EGOZ

1.

I went down into the garden of nuts: A nut has four segments *(sela'oth)* and a ridge *(hod)* in its center. Likewise, there are four camps of Israel and one of the mixed multitude *('erev-rav)*. And the entire subject matter *('inyan)* of the Torah is like the nut: The numerical value of אֶ"ג according to the method אֶ"ת בֶּ"ש is 600 and that of וֶ"ר in the normal way is 13, totalling 613. Even as the nut has an external bitter shell surrounding it, so were the Scroll of the Torah and the sword handed down wrapped together. Beneath the bitter shell are two other shells dry as wood. Likewise, two brothers, Moses and Aaron, guard Israel and act as its guides. Beneath those shell is a soft shell in the centre of the kernel divided in four directions, corresponding to the captains over thousands, hundreds, fifties and tens who judge Israel at all times. Finally, there is a shell which clothes *(malbesheth)* the kernel, corresponding to the clouds of glory and the Levites and priests. The kernel is shaped like four double-columns *(deyomedin)* corresponding to the four camp; and the four double-columns of the kernel are round about its stalk *('uqas)*, and the stalk is in the center, corresponding to the sons of Kohath, the sons of Gershom, the sons of Merari in three directions, and those encamped in front of the sanctuary Moses and Aaron and his sons, the sanctuary being the center. Moreover, the uppermost bitter shell corresponds to the heaven which encompasses everything, and (also) corresponds to the salty

105

ocean *(yam 'oqyanos).* And the color of the water in the sea is like
the color of the shell of the nut which is green, and like 'the green
line which encompasses the whole world,' and corresponds to the
admonitions and punishments which are bitter like the shell of the
nut. And even as the shell of the nut, because it is bitter, protects
the kernel against worms, seeing that worms are found only in
sweet things, so do the admonitions and punishments protect the
commandments . . . And anyone who does not know the mystical
meaning of the nut *(sod ha-'egoz)* does not know the *ma'aseh
merkavah* and the *hayyoth* and the 'fire' that 'flashed up and down'
and 'out of the fire went forth lightning'. The nut has four segments
(sela'oth) like the four hayyoth, and the middle one is raised at its
ridge *(be-huddo),* corresponding to the Throne. And the eatable
fruit is white even as *His throne was flames of fire (Dan.* 7:9). I
should have read 'fire from the throne' but it speaks about how the
throne was created[1]. . .

2.

I went down into the garden of nuts: . . . Know thou that the nut
has a green and bitter shell, and beneath this green shell which is
cast off it has a wooden shell like two cups in which the fruit is
placed. It [i.e. the fruit] has four compartments [*sela'oth*] of which
two are within one shell and two within another, and between the
compartments there stands a soft shell. And there is towards the
broad end of the nut a kind of window in the fruit between two of
its compartments, and below on the ridge of it there issues from
its compartments a kind of *membrum virile,* and there it [i.e. the
fruit] sucks from the bitter shell, hence no worms are found in a
nut. For the kernel sucks from the bitter shell. In case, however,
one removes the bitter shell before the kernel has ripened and
whilst it is still on the tree, worms will be found to develop in the
kernel. There are nine leaves to every twig of the nut.

Now I have opened unto thee a door to understand in thy heart
this [verse], *I went down into the garden of nuts,* and to see that
His great fire[2] is, like the nut, thick at its top and thin towards the
earth. Like the green external shell on its outside, *there was bright-
ness to the fire (Ezek.* 1:13) *from the brightness before Him (2 Sam.*
22:13; *Psalms* 18:13), *like the appearance of torches (Ezek.* 1:13):
A white flame seen from afar will give one the appearance of a

wax-like green, like the external shell.[3] This is the shell which drops off, corresponding to: *And behold, a whirlwind came* (*Ezek.* 1:4). Beneath the green one are two shells which are separate but stick together when the nut is dry: *the great cloud* (*Ezek.* 1:4), *fire and hail* (*Psalms* 168:8) *And He made darkness pavilions round about Him* (*2 Sam.* 22:12). [When the nut is] wooden[4] the pavilion[5] is but one, but when the nut is fresh, there are two pavilions—*gathering of waters, thick clouds of the sky* (*Sam.* 22:3)—corresponding to the two shells in which the fruit is placed: *And out of the midst thereof the likeness of four hayyoth* (*Ezek.* 1:5), the four compartments of the nut, two of which are in one shell and two in another. *Four faces* (*Ezek.* 1:6): the four heads of the kernel. *Four wings* [*ibid.*]: the four segments [*hulyoth*] of the nut beneath them [i.e. the heads]. *And their feet were straight feet* (*Ezek.* 1:7): likewise in the nut. *And their wings were unfolded* (*Ezek.* 1:11): each segment is bipartite like wings. One stalk: this is the square-shaped throne occupying the center. The cut in the stalk corresponds to the throne of judgment and the throne of mercy. And *It* [i.e. the appearance of fire] *flashed up and down among the hayyoth* (*Ezek.* 1:13): this is the shell which is placed between the four heads of the nut. The four heads of the upper segments are the four hayyoth, and the four lower ones are the four *cherubim.*[6] And the nut is round: *The appearance of the wheels* [*'ofanim*] *and their work was like unto the color of a beryl* (*Ezek.* 1:16). The soft shell attached to the fruit: *wheel within wheel* [*ibid.*]. The side of the kernel facing towards the outer shell is red, green and yellow like the [*rain*] *bow* (*Ezek.* 1:28). The nut has five segments [altogether], four which are female and one being the *membrum virile.* Correspondingly, there are four *hayyoth* and one *hayyah* above them.[7] Similarly, it is said in *Genesis Rabbah:* Four times the firmament [*raqia'*] is mentioned on the second day, and once the firmament is called heaven [*shamayim*]. . . . *As the appearance of splendour, as the colour of hashmalah* (*Ezek.* 8:1): this is the whiteness of the kernel as such. The *Kavod*[8] has nine colors: each twig of the nut-tree has nine leaves. It is therefore dangerous to plant a nut-tree.[9] The two outer shells:[10] The throne is placed in the center[11] between *darkness of the waters* (*Psalms* 18:12) and *gathering of waters* (*2 Sam.* 22:12) and a black shell divides the kernel from the head of the *membrum virile:* this is the strap of the *tefillin* upon the head of the *Kavod,*[12] blessed and exalted be He forever and in all eternity.

And beneath the kernel is a space: beneath the throne of glory is a space like an ark, and in it are the souls of the righteous. He who knoweth the science of the nut will know the depth of the *Merkavah.*

—Translated by Alexander Altmann

THE BOOK OF THE WORD

ELEAZER OF WORMS

The Creator is purely intelligible and yet no creature of this world has heard His Voice. The word leaves the mouth of His Glory as an impression of a word, not as the Glory heard according to the verse: *God speaks once, His Word is twofold and is not observed.*

Let us take Abraham: God created the discourse that He wished us to address Him with. In it was included all the words, one after another, like a man stringing pearls. Each word issued at the moment God desired it should: *God thunders in His wondrous Voice;* in a unique voice where numerous wonderful words are found, as:

WORD	WORD	WORD	DISCOURSE

In effect, living creatures can not receive the complete discourse all at once, but only little by little, as one spreads out coins, piece after piece. The Word harmonizes with the Throne. God created the whole discourse, containing all His utterances, in space. These utterances, each in its time, separate from the ensemble, and the prophet believes that God speaks each time, that He has created all the words addressed to him—and that each of His words is made audible at a willed moment.

God sent down a great fire from Mount Sinai from the center

of His power and splendor: *Now Mount Sinai was full of smoke because the Lord's hand descended in a flame;* it was enveloped in clouds of smoke and darkness. This darkness is the black cloud of which it is said: *He made darkness his retreat.* He mixes His Voice with the fire and the Voice issues from flame and its form appears against the cloud like a word issuing from a mouth—cut-out and sculpted as it were—by creating a displacement of air. It is this that people see in the appearance of the letters of the alphabet, in such a way that they're sure it is an instress of light upon darkness; in effect, the fire is made to seethe and illuminate through the explosions of air which is its environment: for God has spoken to you in the midst of the fire *when you heard the Voice from the center of darkness.* When a man speaks on a cold day the letter leaves his mouth and you can see the form liken unto the form of letters. Or, even better, as the voice of an echo resounding from one rock to another [which is called the "daughter of the rock"], for she is engendered by the Voice, and is it not said: "The Voice facing you", for the Voice precedes everything. It is more subtle than the subtlest of things and more powerful than the most powerful of things. But after it comes the visible air in which God creates it; there had been, that is, an interior flame contiguous to the Word and the entirety was enveloped in darkness in order that one not be able to see the Voice. The Word enters into the heart and spirit of the auditors and seems to them that the Voice is speaking face-to-face:

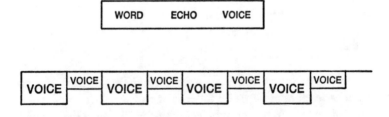

When the Word leaves the flame it is diffused and fractured into multiple flashes: *I am hearing a voice speaking to me,* yet one doesn't know who this voice belongs to. Moses heard; that is, the Voice left the mouth of the Power, between two cherubim, and it spoke to Moses face-to-face. Of the Voice found under the Tabernacle, it is said: *No man can see me and live,* but at the door of the

Tent of Assignation: *he saw the image of the Eternal.* The Voice descended between the cherubim who are upon the Ark, and a flash shot out from that Voice toward Moses, transmitted by a material and its name was Echo, for the Echo receives the Voice:

	DARKNESS
VOICE IN THE EAR OF THE AUDITOR	FIRE
	WORD
	ECHO
	DARKNESS

The echo enters into the ear of the prophet and what is found close to him is not heard by him, for the echo is the space which transmits the Voice and the Voice is like an echo: thus when a man takes a parchment, in fact a scroll, and speaks through the tube to his friend, no one else can hear what is being directly addressed.

The Voice arrived at Moses via intermediaries. Likewise, a King speaks first with his counsellors and then, with their accord, to his slaves: *this sentence has been passed by angelic decree,* whereupon the Voice descends from the sky.

When God revealed Himself to Moses and sent him to our ancestors, He made the Voice and Word proceed from a less terrifying vision. He began it softly so as not to overwhelm Moses. First He showed Moses the fire here on terrestrial earth, *and here the bush was on fire but not consumed.* Then He made Moses see the angel: *the angel of the Eternal appeared to him in a tongue of flame in the midst of the bush.* This bush is a part of His Temple [contrary to the earthly bush, about which Moses had asked at the start] and the appearance is that of an angel. Finally God showed Moses the splendor of His Presence: *and God called to him from the midst of the bush.* Likewise when He made His Voice understandable to our fathers on Mount Sinai, He did not sound it roughly but made it to reverberate in their ears through *the voice of the trumpet* to which they were accustomed. God did the same with Adam: *they heard the voice of God while strolling in the garden,* and the verse continues: *toward evening,* i.e., during the time before sunset, in order that Adam not be seized with fear.

The Voice issues from the Glory with great force. An angel receives it in his hands, flies with it to the seven angels who are found at the seven gates of the seven heavens, voice after voice, and the last one takes it—now faint—and transmits it to the angel-messenger. This is the daughter of the Voice, the Voice of the Voice.

The angel is only permitted to enter the breath of the Glory into the prophet when the prophet hears the Voice of the Word; if the prophet is not ready, he will be seized by discomfort. *From there where it was uttered, the breath entered me and stood:* for the Lord created the Word and the angel in charge to transport it. *The Voice of the Eternal is powerful, the Voice of the Eternal is full of majesty.* It is only when it arrives at the ear of the prophet that it is a subtle voice, a murmur. The flashes, the radiations of voice, are called echo. For the Voice is received by Metatron, through whom it goes to the cherubim, from the cherubim to the angels, and from there, as a light murmur, it arrives at the prophetic ear. It isn't the vision that speaks. It isn't human intelligence. The angel carries the Word and the visible appearance is witness to the Word, according to divine decree. *Samuel was frightened about telling his vision to Eli. Eli said to him: What word was spoken to you? Don't hide anything of your vision from me:* this shows that the Word is created and an angel bore it to Samuel's ear at the same time one saw a devouring flame. This is the sense of the verse: *For God revealed Himself to Samuel through the Word of God.* This voice issues neither from the Creator nor the Glory, but the vision is created, the discourse is created as well, and the vision is witness to that decree, according to Divine Will. If Ezekiel writes: *I heard someone speaking to me from the interior of my house and a man was suddenly next to me,* he knows that the Glory is not speaking. *His Voice was like the sound of big waves:* for what is speaking is the voice; and, issuing from this voice, the particular details of the discourse stand out.

It is not fitting that the Glory be a breathing man whose voice comes from the larynx. All that is blasphemous in relation to the Glory. Man eats and drinks and moves his bowels, but celestial beings neither eat, drink, nor digest; these corporeal acts are extraneous to them for the very powerful reason that they are stirred by the Glory itself. The Creator makes the voice which contains the discourse and the angel transports it to the ear of the prophet, who alone hears it. The Voice does not speak through the visible image, like a man whose voice issues from his body. For the forms the prophets see are not hollow, while man has need of cavities and orifices.

From fear of forgetting what the eyes have seen. As for the Sinai revelation, the Israelites saw the letters inscribed in the Voice, according to the verse: *The Voice of God ploughed the flames of the fire;* since the letters of the Voice were graven into the tablets like a seal in wax. *One people has heard the Voice of God speaking out of fire, as you have heard it.* The Voice was divided (and made visible) into seventy languages, but other peoples did not lend their ears to the visible voice: *as you have heard it.* For you have seen the letters of the Law and other peoples have not.

—Translated from the French translation
of Colette Sirat by Jack Hirschman

Part Five

And after the letters take their form in the shapes of the angels of service, who know the work of the Son, they, the Levis, who possess the shapes of God, will be born with the voice of joy and happiness; and they will teach by voice the idea of the new path of the future, renewing the total prophecy of the hidden and unknown secret; and they are commanded by the prophet to write fables and riddles and to act in strange ways before the eyes of those who persist as animals opposed to truth—the same before whom Isaiah went, naked and barefoot: likewise they will be commanded to the truly stupid, who cry that the prophet is nothing but a crazy man. And even if you say that the meaning of the naked and barefoot prophet is a parable beheld and not a factual happening, as it is written, the foolish ones will persist in believing themselves wise, believing that what they think is what they see. They will always rail at the genuine wise man— who affirms it is all a parable—calling him heretic for not believing the lies they believe, but rather: that the kavvana of God was not in His words, and the kavvana of the prophet

*preempted from all that was written, exem-
plar to things thought. And all this because
wisdom is a secret signature deep within, and
the fools will be blind before the kavvana of
the wise man and all he does, understanding
nothing of the true intention of his works.
And the best thing for them to do is to be still.*

—Book of the Life of the Afterlife
by Abraham ben Samuel Abulafia.

THE QUESTION OF PROPHECY

R. ABRAHAM BEN SAMUEL ABULAFIA (1240-c. 1292)

The life-story of this man, adventurer, writer and mystic, the central figure of the prophetic school in Kabbalah reads this way: Born in Spain in the year 1240, he learned from his father the Bible, Mishnah and Talmud, but lost him at the age of 18. Soon the young Abulafia started his restless life of adventure. He left Spain for the East to discover the hidden river Sambatian, but disorders in the near East forced him to return to Italy and Greece, where he spent about ten years of his young life diligently studying philosophy in general and the writings of Maimonides in particular. At the same time he was forming his own mystical theory and living it. He was deeply occupied with the Kabbalistic teachings of his time, and when he was back in Spain about the year 1270, he completely gave himself to the study of Sefer Yetzirah, the book of Creation, to mystical contemplations and writings. By the age of 30 he was already the author of many manuscripts and of a school in Kabbalah we now call Prophetic or Ecstatic.

He claimed to have obtained the knowledge of the secret Name of the hidden God. He travelled through Spain teaching and preaching his doctrine, but in 1274 he left that country for a life of adventure in Italy and Greece. He attracted disciples and wrote under the names of Raziel and Zechariah. In the year of 1280 he undertook a most fantastic and dangerous task. He went to Rome to step before the Pope, Nicholas III, to plead in the name of God for the oppressed people of Israel. It seems he had Messianic ideas received by words of another mystic, that when the end of time arrives Messiah will come and step before the Pope and command him to liberate His people.

Abulafia tells how this adventure ended. When the Pope heard of Abulafia's intentions he ordered him arrested and burned as soon as he arrived in Rome. Abulafia paid no attention to this, but went fearlessly deeper into mystical meditations and preparations. When he entered the city he learned that the Pope had died suddenly in the night. Abulafia was arrested, held in prison for twenty-eight days and then set free.

After that Abulafia wandered through Italy for a number of years, completed many manuscripts, taught many disciples his personal kind of Kabbalism, against those of his contemporaries, criticizing them for their excessive symbolism and lack of personal mystical experience. He was advancing a doctrine of ecstatic and prophetic inspiration.

The end of his days is obscure. The date of his death is not known. He left behind him quite a good number of writings, and a system of considerable importance and influence upon the development of Jewish mysticism.

Prof. Gershom G. Scholem, in his work on Jewish mysticism, summed it up by saying that it is a characteristic mixture of emotionalism and rationalism . . . "To unseal the soul, to untie the knots that bind it"; such are Abulafia's words. To unlock the inner forces, and return the soul from multiplicity to its original unity. There is a dam that keeps the soul confined to the borders of human experience and prevents it from recognizing the Divine. But why is the soul limited? "Because," says Abulafia, "the ordinary daily life fills up our consciousness with things finite and keeps it in its limits. The problem is how to open the gates into the infinite? The way to that would be to concentrate our mind upon things other than concrete and sensual, . . . on things abstract and spiritual."

In his search and meditation over such matters Abraham Abulafia came upon the Hebrew Alphabeth, the twenty-two letters, their combinations and possible meanings. His meditation was so intense as to reach the name of God, the Ein Sof, which is the path to true mystical ecstasy.

Abulafia developed a peculiar discipline—"Hokhmath Ha-Tseruf," that is—the science of letter-combinations.

Combined letters don't have to be of a special meaning, because in the deepest sense they must and do have a meaning. Letters, all letters, single or combined, are part of God's secret Name and they all lead to the knowledge of it through meditation upon them. In fact, the more obscure the meaning seems to be, the better it serves as material for pure thinking and contemplation, disturbed less by connection to practical things. To Abulafia and his school in the Kabbalah the highest and purest prayer to the Almighty would be not a prayer of the Siddur, Tehilim or Machsir, but the Alphabeth, because it is the presentation of the world back to its Creator, who created it by the Alphabeth.

The meditation upon the letters of the Alphabeth is a discipline for a new state of consciousness similar to the one created by music. In fact the whole process resembles music, but instead of combining notes one combines letters. Combines and listens through the ears of his soul to the pleasant and elevating sensation of the composition. From the ear it goes to the heart, from there to the spleen . . . from emotion to intellectual ecstasy, and further, and higher to the sublimest delight—the knowledge of God.

In his book of combinations, Abulafia offers a systematic guide to the theory and practice of letter-musical compositions, combinations, articulations and permutations needed for the so-called mystical logic. The form of letters, their spiritual forms, as he calls them, their numerical value, gematria, leading to names of the same numerical values, and to "jumping" and "skipping," from one thought to another, seemingly disconnected, but resulting in a rich pattern of associations, in great symphonic compositions.

—Saul Raskin,
Kabbalah, Book of Creation,
The Zohar (1952)

Prophecy is an intellectual matter involving the love of God, our God, the One: and it is known therefore that the lovers of prophecy are lovers of his blessed Name, and they are also blessed and beloved before the Name, and there is no doubt as to their being called wise men and prophets. Now behold and understand this: that the lovers, the loving children of prophecy, are themselves beloved: and this quality alone is the work of the blessed Name. And behold and understand that everyone who knows the Name of the blessed One possesses a holy spirit which effects him with goodness and quickens and moves and urges him with saintly abundance to search out knowledge of the blessed Name in order to sanctify and pronounce it all over the world. And know and understand that those who prophecy with knowledge of the blessed Name are in love with the Name; and now, my son, if you have in your heart the question: When will I too ascend to this high rung —for there are many who hold me back (my weak temperament restrains me, and there is no device by which to change it, restraining, as it does, the poverty which demands the pursuit of food, clothing, repairs of the home and other necessities;—and exile restrains me, as when a man is sold as a slave and is oppressed with hard work at mortar and bricks, etc.)—I swear this to you, my son: All these restraints attract themselves to the rigid and evil inclinations in you, who fight over and seduce you so that you die without knowledge or wisdom, certainly therefore without knowledge of the Name, and foul yourself up with mortar and brick until they block your share in the hereafter. But if you have God with you, you will truly know that wisdom is the soul's food, and if you lack it the soul will die a strange death, cut off because of a deep evil within her; while if there is true wisdom, you shall fully live—for it is said that she is your life and the length of your days. So that when you think there is no bread (for it is the body's food) and the body will die, think of this wisdom: behold and understand that when a man is hungry it is not proper that he say, I will not eat until they bring me exotic delicacies. It is proper that he rejoice in whatever is set before him to remove his hunger, which is death's reason. And if he happens to receive many delicacies he ought to satisfy himself moderately. Likewise you, my son, ought to be disposed towards the true wisdom: starving and thirsting for her, the law is that you will satisfy your hunger and quench your thirst when you find her, in order to save your soul from hell below. For the one who multiplies and the one who subtracts are the same, the only difference being in the direction of the heart—turned to the heavens. And raising his heart with wisdom, he will climb every day as high as he can through circles of wise men and holy books, but he shall refrain from saying: My heart is aimed at God and all I do is for the sake of God, without being concerned that his actions first of all will bring him to the hands of wisdom, who loves the blessed Name; for such a man does not know that learning leads to action, and not the opposite; he does not understand that action is easy, even for the young, more so for the man of wisdom and learning; for they contain in them the wisdom of God, difficult even for the very old and certainly for those of false imaginings, who believe their works are received from God simply because they say so, or because they had a vision; for there is no god-work in the world outside the wisdom of the work itself, and only then is it accepted before the blessed Name, and not like a studied law.

And behold and understand whom our wise men (blessed be their memory) suggested when they said the heathens possess no strength; for even though we see all their efforts and actions as strong, their doing without knowing is nothing.

You will see that the end of the words of our wise men is the works of their fathers, and this is the good deed of the learned man. And know, my son, that he who denies himself this and refrains from knowing the works of God with wisdom that follows the law (if not all of it, at least part) is being restrained by the evil inclination that deadens life; and God will bring it to trial for not having chosen life. And when you fix this image in your heart there will be nothing to deter you from seeking that wisdom, since you will know that the aforementioned sought to keep good food from your body, and without it you would not have suffered so but would have shouted to the Holy One and his people to feed you, would have run from city to city and if flying were possible you would have flown—all this in search of the food from every corner of the world; all this to maintain a body drawn by desire after the six cardinal points that uphold the soul; and if the blessed Name would only help in this vision of the mind's reception and belief and continuance after Him with all one's might, O know that nothing could motivate you otherwise (not poverty, exile, or even prison) in your search after wisdom and sense and knowledge, king of the six directions.

And who is the grubby vulgar fool who would stick by death when he perceived its essence, its descent into a deep pit? It is all because most don't know the difference between life and death and lacking knowledge they turn life into death and run from life, choosing the momentary life and busying themselves with great doings, and they work very hard at killing themselves before their time, in order to leave an inheritance to their sons or even their enemies back in this lowly life that a moment rolls over, themselves mindlessly a part of it. Know, my son, it is for this reason they forget eternal life, sleeping away until they reach the darkness they chose. And at that moment the Prophet cried, saying: Woe to the ones who call evil goodness and goodness evil, and put dark for light and light for dark, taste bitter for sweet and sweet for bitter!

You, my son, if wise and loving the Name with all your heart, must put your mind to the root you were drawn from, and learn that you were taken from the honored throne, influxed by the enlightened mind, created from the image of God and His likeness, found wrapped in the abundance of the truth of His existence, did not in short come from nothing; and so come back to me for He will save you, Holy Israel by Name, the saint who adores you. Now listen to these words, my son, and wear them at your throat and write them on the tablet of your heart. Trust in the Name and not in the man, for the man who secures himself by way of man is crushed, and this is what you must study day and night in the Torah of God, the Torah of Moses, man of God in the wisdom of God. You must read the books of the prophets with good sense, and sing the written word and its knowledge, and immerse yourself in the sayings of the wise men (may their memory be blessed) in clean and mindful study, and look into the company of the kabbalists with Godly wisdom and you will find the desired things through them, find that all are shouting about wisdom's lack and the want of true actions and the diminution of sense; for there is no wisdom, knowledge, speech or act in all the Torah, the prophets, the scriptures and sayings of the wise men (blessed be their memory) that is not within the kabbalists. And as you plunge on, let your heart afterward pay attention to the knowledge of the honored and faithful Name, which shall be blessed, and carve it deep into your heart so that it cannot be erased; for with it our rabbis (may their memory be blessed) have said: The Holy Names will not be erased for they all point to the image of God, and how may the artist erase the ineradicable image? Neither mouth the Names without purpose but respect and bless them, believing they are angels of the blessed Name, sent to raise you, higher and higher, above all the nations of the world; so that all will see the sign of God upon you and will fear you. This is the strong foundation I give into your hands, to know and carve into your heart the Holy Names and the whole Torah and all the scriptures and prophetics filled with Names and fearful things, connecting one with the other, imaging them, trying them, testing them, purifying them and believing they are the writings of the king delivered to you for your own good all the length of your days, as you carry on with them, dealing clearly and lucidly, cleansing yourself of all sins, crimes, guilts and mean acts—in preparation for the time when you are raised to the level of love and are beloved above and below, and commence to combine the first Name, YOD HAY VAV HAY, and observe its infinite connections and combinations uplifting and whirling like a cycling wheel, this way and that, like a scroll; so that you may not rest until you behold that He strengthens through much motion and much confusion in your imagination amid the whirling of your ideas; and even when you stop you will return to Him, asking for the wisdom that you cannot forsake because of the beginnings and ends of the alphabet and the gematria and notarikon and the combinations of the letters and their changes and rhythms and the recognitions of their different shapes and the knowledge of their names and the understanding of their meaning and the fashioning out of the letter ALEPH many words and from the many words, One: they are the truths of the Kabbalah of the prophets which, through their knowledge, raised your cry to God, Who will answer; for you will be attached to his company.

And now, my son, the secret of God to the ones who fear Him and his covenant: He who fears God and His total covenant will be told His covenant, and it will be kept from the others, for honor is not befitting fools.

—Translated from the German
by Jack Hirschman

from
SEFER HA-OT

(The Book of the Letter)

R. ABRAHAM BEN SAMUEL ABULAFIA

I.

I blessed the mouth of YDVD
from the day of his Name
to this day and moreover
sanctify myself in his Name
and holiness and living truth

I swore in the past by that Name
and will in Him
in the 7th year of his kingdom
messiah Adoni who
transforms my name
as stubble into straw

Yahni called me Gradelya
son of Shebaldalya
via my renewed name
blessed by his renewing Name
sainted forever by being sealed

I pierced the hearts denying him
with my sword and his Name

was bayonet tongue killing them
as it will bring death to his enemies
in just trials

Changed my evil path to the straight
by force of the honored and terrible Name
watching over those in the land knowing him

Prophesied in the Name
the square and the triangle
when I was in the tiny attic
in the house in the south
called Joseph's Hand

Remembered the Name YDVD Our God
interpreted in my name
unique in the heart
I split it into two equal halves

Half is *veyat*
half *veyatu*—
these from that
those from this
and all emblazoned on a banner

The letters *Tayiv*
are one half the Name
and the other *Tayev*
and I fashion by them
this mobilization of stone
this victory over Satan

Yov drips in my bleeding
Legato came to his end
came Tilo from Gato
then Getalo king of devils
with his mad son

The heads of every congregation
weakened from the day the Torah was given
and now there are no rulers among his tribes

Demons came to their end
hairy ones were cut short

elder and younger both
were given to the slaughter by
the tender boy-king

The quarrel died in Rome
in stubborn papal guts
by the force of the Name of the living God
YDVD
who fought by land and on the sea

Through the name YDVD and his messiahs
you will receive the sign and faithful testament
we triumphed by way of foresight

Rejoice, be happy now
oh wise men of my people!
YDVD indwells with us
and my heart today bursts with joy

Eye sees and heart is gay
ear listens and the whole body dances
the legs kick trippingly
and man on earth leaps and circles about

Mouth speaks
heart answers from home
heart whispers his will
brain receives the Idea
as do the ears, the eyes, the senses

YDVD has sent you oh
people of the Island of Bravery
a faithful messenger
a savior from the hands of
acolytes of filth

End of abomination
and destruction of the sun-worshippers
now the moon is here
and YDVD watches over us
testing every heart

The people of the Island of the Mirror
saw the hand of God going out from Sinai

south and west shedding blood
bringing down the big nations

The Name of YDVD arranging arms
and his camps and his orders
to avenge the revenge of the enemy
upon the covenant

YDVD took the Tau sign from the sparks of his fire
from the rooms of his anger
and withdrew from his sheath
the fire of expired hearts

Enemy is one-half the Name
a root
at the month's beginning
its acts are laid open
and at the end of the month
garmented again

He has made a covenant
that his Name be blessed before all living eyes
eye of sun, eye of moon
known all over the land

II.

Whereupon, YDVD God of Israel said:

Don't be afraid of the enemy,
for He and I are fighting it to save you from its hand;
don't soften your heart in the holiness of the Name
avenging the revenge of the covenant.
Tune it, people of the Island,
to the knowledge of YDVD God of Israel,
awake in his Name and in the truth
that He speaks the life of all that lives,
that He revives the dead and saves the living
with dew-fall of goodwill and rain—

—as was foretold to Israel's people in the Name of YDVD
that they would be saved, by Moses, son of Amram, son of Kehat,
son of Levi, son of Jacob, son of Isaac, son of Abraham—when He

indicated in his book "I am that I am" and told them, "Ayehe sent me to you"—

> O YDVD mighty God of Israel
> be merciful with your people,
> gather them to the city of your temple
> for thy Name's sake,
> to be sanctified before all who see Him
> and for the sake of the remembrance of holiness,
> with purity I write the Name,
> letter by letter.

Here is the great Name, heroic and terrible, square and triangle, engraved as YDVD pointed it to me:

> VEHU YALY SIT
> ELEM MEHASH LALA
> AChA KAHAT HAZI
> ALD LAV HAA

> YEShAL MEVA HARYKMA
> LAV KLI
> LAV PA'AL NEZECh
> YOD YOD YOD MILA ChAHU

> NATA HA'ALEF YARET
> ShAHEH RAECh UUM
> LEChAV VEShAR YAChU
> LEHACh BOOK MENAD

> ANI HA'AM RA'AA
> YAYIN HAHE MICh
> VUEL YALA SAL
> ARY AShAL MIA

> VEHU DANI HAChASH
> AMAM GANA NIT
> MIBA POI LAMMAM
> YYL HARACH METZAR

> UMAD YAHA ANU
> MEChAI DAMB MENUK
> EE ChAUU RAAH
> YEBUM HAYY MUM

TAG TzUAI AKAR
SChANDI BAGET ShAR
TAN TAG
GOY ChATzI HAKEShET
VEYAD KATON ShAHAHShIK
VATzERA ShTI
EVEREV GAG
SATAN GALAN BATz
PIT EEK TATZATz
GAD GROUP GATHER
HE GATHERS
HE UNITY JACOB
YOUR SALVATION
WE HOPE
YEHODVANY.

III.

The coming day is the judgment day
and is called the Day of Memory,
for the time of trial is come,
the time of the end come round,
the sky becoming earth,
the earth becoming heavenly,
because of the God of Judgment YDVD
whose Name and justice are true,
whose law is straight.
He will reveal his acts in the adjectives of his Name,
in the unity of his Name,
and he will shower us with his abundant word
gladdening the heart to realize his spirit,
the origin of light living forever
without need of this life-of-void without him
where even a bastard donkey is stronger in mind and body
than most men.

Those who knew his Name used to mourn his oblivion,
but now know the joy,
the happiness,
the merriment and pleasures,

the high honors;
his followers see the whole truth
and the honest clear way,
and I say to all those still searching
for the mysterious properties of the letter VAV
—all the secrets will be unknotted
in this precious book.

IV.

Days of hope and desire's signature
met days of joy
and the line of reproach fell away.

My vowel-pointed hand
with palm for measure
asked as the north touched the south,
the south the north.
The Spirit of God was called in Name
and was first whispered
then spoke
until every particle was heard
and every particle pulled upward to the whole
dwelling on high,
Who is All.

And so the HAY moves from the specific inclusive and upper-most point. No other point like Her among all the scintilla. There had been two points—one under the other—serving the smallest golem-possessor of permutations, whose form is the shape of

SAMEKH MEM

—circle and square—with a closed head and an open tail, with the crown of Torah on its head and a king's laurel on its tail.

The letter is Desire, the sky the longing to know the meaning of what moves giving grace to the soul, forgiveness to strength, to make straight the acts.

Kingdom at her head,
Torah at her tail,
at times Torah at her head,
Kingdom at her tail.

In time, the letters, the accents and melodies, reveal the secret of blood which is YOD his Name. It is like the name of a rabbi imagining it all, imagining Him all full of eyes, who sees and is not seen, ruler of the birth powers and of swift movement—KADKAD by name—each KAD having two points: one southerly, the other northerly. Each bound to the other and between them I will WAR.

I listened to my heart's command.

I ran to do will and desire and did all he bid: wrote names, combined them, examined them in the crucible of contemplation. And the straight ones turned and the whirling ones straightened until two tongues intertwined, coming to the service of the Hebrew language. One is Greek and the other alien, crossweaving strengths, over and under, for strength was rooted in crossweaves that hung, winched and bound with nails, that now has come apart and is dispersed because the four nails, like the four hammers of the tongue burst and broke—their leaders fell from the sky to earth.

And I the originator came crowning the head of the first with the Glory called the Crown of Torah, according to YDVD.

And the Unique One set the upper Crown upon 300 wise men for He is one root with three heads. The sphere encircles Him with a point in the center telling that the soul of man is within and without; and the point is the dwelling of the living God breathing through all.

And when the soul goes toward the spirit of YDVD—O heavenly journey!—pulsing back and forth—all lesser spirits fly along, serving with the rest of creation, from upper to lower. The spheres whirl, rejoicing in the pace and recognition that the first journey moves out from narrowness to immensity. And all strength is gathered from the two to the thirty that are the three; for from the three and thirty to the thirty-three there turns the wheel of roots trebled in the twenty-two letters. And from the addition of the number 11, every wheel-within-wheel turns.

VAV to One turns HAY to One so that the vapors go up and down the heart's ladder. He and She are two and everything depends from them, according to their changing forms, interchanging through this grid of combinations.

And these are All of the Ways.

V.

VAV HAY YOD HAY is the combination of HAY and HAY, enough for a man when he knows the way to revive himself in Him —for His Knowledge is reason for eternal life for all:

So the heart of my heart told my inmost heart: write the paths of the Name in combinations whirling and straight.

These are names of temples blessing the spirit, awakening the powers, enlightening the noble to full understanding of the Almighty who holds the wise and pious and holy and just plain simple people of the land from hell below. Here is the honored and terrible Name created in Him: Blood is his Name, male and female, name of the father and mother in the Name of Him big with power, sealed together. YOD bears witness to the Throne that is the height of HÈ up to the height of the VAVS, who are witness to the split dividing them, the division forming HAVAVAY, half and half like a separation of one which is: . ˙ . —with height transforming height front and back, for the breath goes up and down. And the final HÈ is Shekinah's seal, the inspiration offering prophecy and salvation to all souls by her Voice and lightness.

Therefore all serious men seek prophecy and salvation, begging the powers of HAY, moving in the spirit of YOD, taking the latter from its place, fixing it in a concentrated spot so that one ever turned to experiment will observe and believe and comprehend.

Rejoice in the name of the visionary of the Name, both the interpreted and permuted one via 12 ways in 6 changes that is a new greatness to Israel.

And happy joy and merry pleasure join hands in the heart of every seer of the Name in the name of

YEAHOHDYNHANOHA YDVD

beloved YDVD God the Mighty

who in heaven heard cries of the sons of Jacob and sent a messenger to his people, Zechariahu by name.

The meek and the lowly, torn apart by big nations, abused him. But this is the day of annunciation and Zechariahu the Deliverer rides on a cloud heavily laden with dew—thin dew with light shining through. His mount is a chariot of fire, his horses stallions of air, his servants fiery animals talking fire and clouds around the mountain of mountains, whirling;

and the breath of deliverance storms over the land in his flight,

law and word renew his heart which he writes in flaming script out of a flaming pen's power—fearful and awesome ink irrigating the land, licking the dry places, wringing from the dry places the bow and arrow of Torah, which will split the sky in two;
 with the breath of the arrow quivering in the heart,
 burning out the kidney,
 scattering all organs to the wind;
 and the strong spirit moving: the Deliverer breathing a breath into the nostrils of the living;
 and it's a high wind the wind of God, it is life rousing the wise at heart to the voice of YDVD standing in sheer enlightenment;
 adhere to and swear in His Name.

AND BEHOLD THE MESSENGER WAS CALLED, BUT HE DID NOT COME. FOR THE 12 STOPPED ENTRY AND YDVD ARRANGED WITH THOSE WISE IN WAR TO DEFEAT HIS ENEMIES COMPLETELY BE-FORE THE ADVENT OF HIS REVELATION.

And Adonai said to Zechariahu the Messenger: Raise your voice with the tongue of your pen, write the word of God, write this book with your three fingers.

And God was with him as guide and he wrote all that he was commanded, and he came reciting the words of God to Jews as well as the dullheaded and poor, but they paid no heed to the form of his coming and spoke of him and his god in unimaginable terms.

THEN YDVD BID HIM SPEAK TO THE DULLHEARTED UNCLEAN HEATHEN IN HIS NAME, AND HE DID, AND THEY BELIEVED THE MESSAGE

but they would not return to YDVD, instead they clung to their bows and swords until YDVD hardened their hearts, arousing the Adonai in them to annihilate them for Israel's sake, choosing the Day of Good Tidings when strength will seek merriment and joy with the seven candles and the five lights of the crows upon the mountains.

Where he will find a lost flock lacking a shepherd among the lions and bear, and the lion will not consume her, nor will the bear; and YDVD will find the crown of a tall mountain named Nafal, and a shepherd of his flock will dwell on it, sleeping for twenty years so that the rage within him passes and calms his anger. At that time, YDVD God of Israel will awaken the shepherd's heart

and the hearts of those sleeping in the dust; and the dead shall live
and the flock will come to her dwelling and scatter no more. And
the shepherd will break the jaws of the lion and dull the teeth of
the bear and tighten their collars so they may no longer go pastur-
ing after destruction.

If not for God's rebuke of YDVD God of Abraham, who spoke
of the memory of YDVD, the shepherd, how could he have broken
the jaws of the lion who spares no man forsaken by the gods, as
they are trained for the kill and would gladly die without food; yet
now that the will of YDVD is turned to the restoration of his lost
people, lion and sheep will graze together.

> Therefore O men wise at heart
> cry for YDVD in your heart's day and night,
> seek his truth to cling to,
> remember the Name,
> for in memory the spirit of YDVD is graven and speaks
> and the restoring of the worlds is her seal
> and she withdraws from all heathens
> and she exposes the entrails of their clever magics.
> And since He has separated you O people of Israel,
> your precious inheritance is to become YDVD's unique portion
>   alone.
> Why betray your life or chase the spirit of Beauty,
> Eternity, Splendor from yourselves
> when He crowns His Name with the Three of Thou:
> Cohen, Levi and Israeli.
> Three witnesses of the spirit,
> three dimensions of action,
> and Thou lives in all three,
> a life of the spirit like the life of sun and moon and stars.
> Therefore lift your eyes to the heavens,
> gaze with the eyes of your hearts to the sky of skies,
> see the order of the living God
> arranged according to YDVD's Torah;
> and as you learn them
> you will discern their engravement as YDVD,
> the mighty God of hosts, the battlement of Israel;
> and as they were inscribed with the Name,
> so were they also with the power of the image-maker

of the book which includes the five books of Torah.

Moses carved the forms of all worlds
in the tree of life inscribed on the tablets,
the shape and body according to YDVD
God of Abraham, Isaac and Jacob
—O memorable creation!
YDVD, shepherd of all the gods,
wrote them in this book,
and all who read in the Name are friends,
and all who seek out wisdom from his wise men,
blessing the Name of God,
He will call Holy.

—Translated from the Hebrew
by Bruria Finkel and Jack Hirschman

PERMUTATIONS OF THE TETRAGRAMMATON

R. ABRAHAM BEN SAMUEL ABULAFIA

YHVH	YHHV	YVHH	YVHH	HVHY	HVYH
HVHV	HVYH	HHYV	HHYV	VHYH	VHHY
VHYH	VHHY	VYHH	VYHH	HYHV	HYVH
HYHV	HYVH	HHVY	HHVY	YHVH	YHHV
YHHV	YVHH	HVHY	HVHY	HVYH	HHYV
HVYH	HHYV	VHYH	VHYH	VHHY	VYHH
VHHY	VYHH	HYHV	HYHV	HYVH	HHVY
HYVH	HHVY	YHVH	YHVH	YHHV	YVHH
HVYH	HHYV	VHYH	VHYH	VHHY	VYHH
VHHY	VYHH	HYVH	HYVH	HYVH	HHVY
HYVH	HHVY	YHVH	YHVH	YHHV	YVHH
YHHV	YVHH	HVHY	HVHY	HVHY	HHYV
HHYV	HVYH	VHHY	VHHY	VYHH	HYHV
VYHH	HYHV	HYVH	HYVH	HHVY	YHVH
HHVY	YHVH	YHHV	YHHV	YVHH	HVHY
YVHH	HVHY	HVYH	HVYH	HHYV	VHYH
VYHH	HYHV	HYVH	HYVH	HHVY	YHVH
HHVY	YHVH	YHHV	YHHV	YVHH	HVHY
YVHH	HVHY	HVYH	HVYH	HHYV	VHYH
HHYV	VHYH	VHHY	VHHY	VYHH	HYHV
HYHV	HYVH	HHVY	HHVY	YHVH	YHHV
YHVH	YHHV	YVHH	YVHH	HVHY	HVYH
HVHY	HVYH	HHYV	HHYV	VHYH	VHHY
VHYH	VHHY	VYHH	VYHH	HYHV	HYVH

136

SHA'EREI ZEDEK

(Gates of Justice)

AN ANONYMOUS DISCIPLE OF ABULAFIA (C. 1295)

I, so and so, one of the lowliest, have probed my heart for ways of grace to bring about spiritual expansion and I have found three ways of progress to spiritualization: the vulgar, the philosophic, and the Kabbalistic way. The vulgar way is that which, so I learned, is practised by Moslem ascetics. They employ all manner of devices to shut out from their soul all "natural forms," every image of the familiar, natural world. Then, they say, when a spiritual form, an image from the spiritual world, enters their soul, it is isolated in their imagination and intensifies the imagination to such a degree that they can determine beforehand that which is to happen to us. Upon inquiry, I learned that they summon the Name, ALLAH, as it is in the language of Ishmael. I investigated further and I found that, when they pronounce these letters, they direct their thought completely away from every possible "natural form," and the very letters ALLAH and their diverse powers work upon them. They are carried off into a trance without realizing how, since no Kabbalah has been transmitted to them. This removal of all natural forms and images from the soul is called with them *Effacement.*

The second way is the philosophic, and the student will experience extreme difficulty in attempting to drive it from his soul because of the great sweetness it holds for the human reason and the completeness with which that reason knows to embrace it. It consists in this: That the student forms a notion of some science, mathematics for instance, and then proceeds by analogy to some natural science and then goes on to theology. He then continues further to circle round this center of his, because of the sweetness of that which arises in him as he progresses in these studies. The sweetness of this so delights him that he finds neither gate nor door to enable him to pass beyond the notions which have already been established in him. At best, he can perhaps enjoy a [contemplative] spinning out of his thoughts and to this he will abandon himself, retiring into seclusion in order that no one may disturb his thought until it proceeds a little beyond the purely philosophic and turns as the flaming sword which turned every way. The true cause of all this is also to be found in his contemplation of the letters through which, as intermediaries, he ascertains things. The subject which impressed itself on his human reason dominates him and his power seems to him great in all the sciences, seeing that this is natural to him [i.e. thus to ascertain them]. He contends that given things are revealed to him by way of prophecy, although he does not realize the true cause, but rather thinks that this occurred to him merely because of the extension and enlargement of his human reason ... But in reality it is the letters ascertained through thought and imagination, which influence him through their motion and which concentrate his thought on difficult themes, although he is not aware of this.

But if you put the difficult question to me: "Why do we nowadays pronounce letters and move them and try to produce effects with them without however noticing any effect being produced by them?"—the answer lies, as I am going to demonstrate with the help of *Shaddai,* in the third way of inducing spiritualization. And I, the humble so and so, am going to tell you what I experienced in this matter.

Know, friends, that from the beginning I felt a desire to study Torah and learned a little of it and of the rest of the Scripture. But I found no one to guide me in the study of the Talmud, not so much because of the lack of teachers, but rather because of my longing for my home, and my love for father and mother. At last, however, God gave me strength to search for the Torah, and I went out and sought and found, and for several years I stayed abroad studying

Talmud. But the flame of the Torah kept glowing within me, though without my realizing it.

I returned to my native land and God brought me together with a Jewish philosopher with whom I studied some of Maimonides' *Guide to the Perplexed* and this only added to my desire. I acquired a little of the science of logic and a little of natural science, and this was very sweet to me for, as you know, "nature attracts nature." And God is my witness: If I had not previously acquired strength of faith by what little I had learned of the Torah and the Talmud, the impulse to keep many of the religious commands would have left me, although the fire of pure intention was ablaze in my heart. But what this teacher communicated to me in the way of philosophy [on the meaning of the commandments] did not suffice me, until the Lord had me meet a godly man, a kabbalist who taught me the general outlines of the Kabbalah. Nevertheless, in consequences of my smattering of natural science, the way of Kabbalah seemed all but impossible to me. It was then that my teacher said to me: "My son, why do you deny something you have not tried? Much rather would it befit you to make a trial of it. If you then should find that it is nothing to you—and if you are not perfect enough to find fault with yourself—then you may say that there is nothing to it." But, in order to make things sweet to me until my reason might accept them and I might penetrate into them with eagerness, he used always to make me grasp in a natural way everything in which he instructed me. I reasoned thus within myself: There can only be gain here and no loss. I shall see; if I find something in all of this, that is sheer gain; and if not, that which I have already had will still be mine. So I gave in and he taught me the method of permutations and combinations of letters and the mysticism of numbers and the other "Paths of the book *Yetzirah.*" In each path he had me wander for two weeks until each form had been engraven in my heart, and so he led me on for four months or so and then ordered me to "efface" everything.

He used to tell me: "My son, it is not the intention that you come to a stop with some finite or given form, even though it be of the highest order. Much rather is this the 'Path of the Names': The less understandable they are, the higher their order, until you arrive at the activity of a force which is no longer in your control, but rather your reason and your thought is in control." I replied: "If that be so [that all mental and sense images must be effaced], why then do you, Sir, compose books in which the methods of the natural scientists are coupled with instruction in the holy Names?" And he produced books for me made up of [combinations of] letters and names and mystic numbers *(Gematrioth)*, of which nobody will ever be able to understand anything for they are not composed in a way meant to be understood.

He said to me: "This is the [undefiled] 'Path of the Names.' "

And indeed, I would see none of it as my reason did not accept it.

He said: "It was very stupid of me to have shown them to you."

In short, after two months had elapsed and my thought had disengaged itself [from everything material] and I had become aware of strange phenomena occurring within me, I set myself the task at night of combining letters with one another and of pondering over them in philosophical meditation, a little different from the way I do now, and so I continued for three nights without telling him. The third night, after midnight, I nodded off a little, quill in hand and paper on my knees. Then I noticed that the candle was about to go out. I rose to put it right, as oftentimes happens to a person awake. Then I saw that the light continued. I was greatly astonished, as though, after close examination, I saw that it issued from myself. I said: "I do not believe it." I walked to and fro all through the house and, behold, the light is with me all the while. I said: "This is truly a great sign and a new phenomenon when I have perceived."

The next morning I communicated it to my teacher and I brought him the sheets which I had covered with combinations of letters.

He congratulated me and said: "My son, if you would devote yourself to combining Holy Names, still greater things would happen to you. And now, my son, admit that you are unable to bear not combining. Give half to this and half to that, that is, do combinations half of the night, and permutations half of the night."

I practiced this method for about a week. During the second week the power of meditation became so strong in me that I could not manage to write down the combinations of letters (which automatically spurted out of my pen), and if there had been ten people present they would not have been able to write down so many combinations as came to me during the influx. When I came to the night in which this power was conferred on me, and midnight—

when this power especially expands and gains strength whereas the body weakens—had passed, I set out to take up the Great Name of God, consisting of seventy-two names, permuting and combining it. But when I had done this for a little while, behold, the letters took on in my eyes the shape of great mountains, strong trembling seized me and I could summon no strength, my hair stood on end, and it was as if I were not in this world. At once I fell down, for I no longer felt the least strength in any of my limbs. And behold, something resembling speech emerged from my heart and came to my lips and forced them to move. I thought—perhaps this is, God forbid, a spirit of madness that has entered into me? But behold, I saw it uttering wisdom. I said: "This is indeed the spirit of wisdom." After a little while my natural strength returned to me. I rose very much impaired and still did not believe myself. Once more I took up the Name to do with it as before and, behold, it had exactly the same effect on me. Nevertheless I did not believe until I had tried it four or five times.

When I got up in the morning I told my teacher about it and brought him the sheets which I had covered with combinations of letters.

He said to me: "And who was it that allowed you to touch the Name? Did I not tell you to permute only letters?" He spoke on: "What happened to you, represents indeed a high stage among the prophetic degrees." He wanted to free me of it for he saw that my face had changed.

But I said to him: "In heaven's name, can you perhaps impart to me some power to enable me to bear this force emerging from my heart and to receive influx from it?" For I wanted to draw this force towards me and receive influx from it, for it much resembles a spring filling a great basin with water. If man (not being properly prepared for it) should open the dam, he would be drowned in its waters and his soul would desert him.

He said to me: "My son, it is the Lord who must bestow such power upon you for such power is not within man's control."

That Sabbath night also the power was active in me in the same way. When, after two sleepless nights, I had passed day and night in meditating on the permutations or on the principles essential to a recognition of this true reality and to the annihilation of all extraneous thought—then I had two signs by which I knew that I was in the right receptive mood. The one sign was the intensification of natural thought on very profound objects of knowledge, a debility of the body and strengthening of the soul until I sat there, my self all soul. The second sign was that imagination grew strong within me and it seemed as though my forehead were going to burst. Then I knew that I was ready to receive the Name. I also that Sabbath night ventured at the great ineffable Name of God (the name JHWH). But immediately that I touched it, it weakened me and a voice issued from me saying: "Thou shalt surely die and not live! Who brought thee to touch the Great Name?" And behold, immediately I fell prone and implored the Lord God saying: "Lord of the universe! I entered into this place only for the sake of heaven, as Thy glory knowest. What is my sin and what my transgression? I entered only to know Thee, for has not David already commanded Solomon: Know thy God of thy Father and serve Him; and has not our master Moses, peace be upon him, revealed this to us in the Torah saying: Show me now Thy way, that I may know Thee, that I may find there grace in Thy sight?" And behold, I was still speaking and oil like the oil of anointment anointed me from head to foot and very great joy seized me which for its spirituality and the sweetness of its rapture I cannot describe.

All this happened to your servant in his beginnings. And I do not, God forbid, relate this account from boastfulness in order to be thought great in the eyes of the mob, for I know full well that greatness with the mob is deficiency and inferiority with those searching for the true rank which differs from it in genus and in species as light from darkness.

Now, if some of our own philosophizers, sons of our people who feel themselves attracted towards the naturalistic way of knowledge and whose intellectual power in regard to the mysteries of the Torah is very weak, read this, they will laugh at me and say: See how he tries to attract our reason with windy talk and tales, with fanciful imaginations, which have muddled his mind and which he takes at their face value because of his weak mental hold on natural science. Should, however, Kabbalists see this, such as have some grasp of this subject or even better such as have had things divulged to them in experiences of their own, they will rejoice and my words will win their favor. But their difficulty will be that I have disclosed all of this in detail. Nevertheless, God is my witness that my intention is in *majorem dei gloriam* and I would wish that every single one of your holy nation were even more excellent herein and pure than I. Perhaps it would then be possible to reveal things of which I do not as yet know . . . As for me, I cannot bear not to give generously to other what God has bestowed on me. But since for this science there is no naturalistic evidence, its premises being as spiritual as are its inferences, I was forced to tell this story of the experience that befell me. Indeed, there is no proof, namely, my own evidence of the spiritual results of my own experiences in the science of letters according to *The Book of Creation.* I did not, to be sure, experience the corporeal [magic] effects [of such practices]; and even granting the possibility of such a form of experience, I for my part want none of it, for it is an inferior form, especially when measured by the perfection which the soul can attain spiritually. Indeed, it seems to me that he who attempts to secure these [magic] effects desecrates God's name, and it is this that our teachers hint at when they say: Since license prevailed, the name of God has been taught only to the most reticent priests.

The third is the Kabbalistic way. It consists of an amalgamation in the soul of man of the principles of mathematical and of natural science after he has first studied the literal meanings of the Torah and of the faith, in order thus through keen dialectics to train his mind and not in the manner of a simpleton to believe in everything. Of all this he stands in need only because he is held captive by the world of nature. For it is not seemly that a rational being held captive in prison should not search out every means, a hole or a small fissure, of escape. If today we had a prophet who showed us a mechanism for sharpening the natural reason and for discovering there subtle forms by which to divest ourselves of corporeality, we should not need all these natural sciences in addition to our Kabbalah which is derived from the basic principles or heads of chapters of the book *Yetzirah* concerning letters [and their combinations] . . . For the prophet would impart to us the secrets of the combinations of consonants and of the combination of vowels between them, the paths by which the secret and active powers emanate, and the reason that this emanation is sometimes hindered from above . . . All this he would convey to us directly whereas now we are forced to take circuitous routes and to move about restrainedly and go out and come in on the chance that God may confront us. For as a matter of fact every attainment in this science of Kabbalah looked at from this point of view is only a chance, even though, for us, it be the very essence of our being.

This Kabbalistic way, or method, consists, first of all, in the cleansing of the body itself, for the bodily is symbolic of the spiritual. Next in the order of ascent is the cleansing of your bodily disposition and your spiritual propensities, especially that of anger, or your concern for anything whatsoever except the Name itself, be it even the care for your only beloved son; and this is the secret of the Scripture that "God tried Abraham." A further step in the order of ascent is the cleansing of one's soul from all other sciences which one has studied. The reason for this is that being naturalistic and limited, they contaminate the soul, and obstruct the passage through it of the divine forms. These forms are extremely subtle; and though even a minor form is something innately great in comparison with the naturalistic and the rational, it is nevertheless an unclean, thick veil in comparison with the subtlety of the spirit. On this account seclusion in a separate house is prescribed, and if this be a house in which no [outside] noise can be heard, the better.

At the beginning it is advisable to decorate the house with fresh greens in order to cheer the vegetable soul which a man possesses side by side with his animal soul. Next, one should pray and sing psalms in a pleasant, melodious voice, and [read] the Torah with fervor, in order to cheer the animal soul which a man possesses side by side with his rational soul. Next, one directs his imagination to intelligible things and to understanding how one thing proceeds from another. Next, one proceeds to the moving of letters which [in their combinations] are unintelligible, thus to detach the soul [from the senses] and to cleanse it of all the forms formerly within it. In the same way one proceeds with the improvement of his [bodily] matter by meat and drink, and improves it [the body] by degrees. Next, one reaches the stage of "skipping" as the Scripture says, "and his banner over me was love." It consists of one's meditating, after all operations with the letters are over, on the essence of one's thought, and of abstracting from it every word, be it connected with a notion or not. In the performance of this "skipping" one must put the consonants which one is combining into a swift motion. The motion heats the thinking and so increases joy and desire, that craving for food and sleep or anything else is annihilated. In abstracting words from thought during contemplation, you force yourself so that you pass beyond the control of your natural mind and if you desire *not* not think, you cannot carry out your desire. You then guide your thinking step by step, first by means of script and language and then by means of imagination. When, however, you pass beyond the control of your thinking, another exercise becomes necessary which consists in drawing thought gradually forth—during contemplation—from its source until through sheer force that stage is reached where you do not speak nor can you speak. And if sufficient strength remains to force oneself even further and draw it out still farther, then that which is within will manifest itself without, and through the power of sheer imagination will take on the form of a polished mirror. And this is "the flame of the circling sword," the rear revolving and becoming the fore. Whereupon one sees that his inmost being is something outside of himself. Such was the way of the Urim and Tummim, the priest's oracle of the Torah, in which, too, at first the letters shine from inside and the message they convey is not an immediate one nor arranged in order, but results only from the right combination of letters. For a form, detached from its essence, is defective until it clothe itself in a form which can be conceived by imagination, and in this imaginable form the letters enter into a complete, orderly and understandable combination. And it seems to me that it is this form which the Kabbalists call "clothing," *malbush.*

—translated by Gershom Scholem

Part Six

The Holy One, blessed be He, had already created and destroyed several worlds before He decided to create the world we live in; and when that last act was about to be accomplished, all the creatures of the universe and everything that was to be in the world—at whatever time they were to exist—were present before God in their real form before becoming a part of the universe. It is in this sense that we should understand the words of Ecclesiastes: "That which is hath been a long time ago, and that which is to be hath already been." The entire lower world was created in the likeness of the higher world. All that exists in the higher world appears like an image in this lower world; yet all this is but One.

—*Zohar, II, fol. 20a.*

HECHALOTH

(Zohar I, 42b–43a, Section בא)

EDITOR'S NOTE. The *Zohar* ("Book of Splendor") is the central work of Kabbalistic literature. Its authorship was ascribed to the legendary Rabbi Simeon ben Yochai (second century), but modern scholarship has shown that the main parts of the *Zohar* were written towards the end of the thirteenth century by Rabbi Moses de Leon, a Castilian Kabbalist who died in 1305.

Approximately half the books contained in the *Zohar* and in the later additions of the *Tikkune ha-Zohar* are contained in the English translation by Maurice Simon, Harry Sperling and Paul Levertoff (London and New York: Soncino Press, 1933, 5 volumes). This translation remains the finest inroad to Kabbalah for those unable to read the work in its original language.

In the following group I've included two translations from the *Zohar* previously untranslated into English.

"Before He gave any shape to this world,
before He produced any form,
He was alone,
without a form and resemblance to anything else.

Who then can comprehend Him how He was before the creation, since He was formless?

Hence it is forbidden to represent Him by any form, similitude, or even by His Sacred Name, by a single letter or a single point; and to this the words:

"You saw no manner of similitude on the day that YHVH spoke unto you" (Dovarim 4:15)—i.e. you have not seen anything which you could represent by any form or likeness—refer.

But after He created the form of THE HEAVENLY MAN (אדם עלאה), He used it as a Chariot (מרכבה), wherein to descend, and wishes to be called by this form, which is the sacred name YHVH. He wishes to be known by His attributes, and each attribute separately; and therefore had Himself called

> the Elohim of Mercy,
> the Elohim of Justice
> El Shaddai
> Elohim Tsabaoth
> the Being

He wishes thereby to make known His nature, and that we should see how His mercy and compassion extend both to the world and to all operations. For if He had not poured out His light upon all His creatures, how could we ever have known Him? How could the words be fulfilled: "The whole earth is full of His glory" (Isaiah 6:3).

Woe be to him who compares Him with his own attributes! or still worse with the son of man whose foundation is in the dust, who vanishes and is no more! Hence, the form in which we delineate Him simply describes each time His dominion over a certain attribute, or over the creatures generally. We cannot understand more of His nature than the attribute expresses. Hence, when He is divested of all these things, He has neither any attribute nor any similitude nor any form.

The form in which He is generally depicted is to be compared to a very expansive sea; for the waters of the sea are in themselves without a limit or form, and it is only when they spread themselves upon the earth that they assume a form (דמיון). We can now make the following calculation: the SOURCE of the sea's water and THE WATER STREAM proceeding therefrom to spread itself ARE TWO. A great reservoir is then formed, just as if a huge hollow had been dug; this reservoir is called sea, and is THE THIRD. The unfathomable deep divides itself into SEVEN STREAMS, resembling seven long vessels. The source, the water stream, the sea and the seven streams make together TEN. And when the master breaks the vessels which He has made, the waters return to the source, and then only remain the pieces of these vessels, dried up and without any water.

It is in this way that the Cause of Causes gave rise to the TEN SEPHIROTH. The Crown is the source from which streams forth an infinite light: hence the name AIN SOPH (אין סוף) or INFI-NITE, by which the highest cause is designated: for it then had neither form nor shape, and there is neither any means whereby to comprehend it, nor a way by which to know it. Hence it is written: "Seek not out the things that are too hard for you, neither search the things that are above your strength."

He then made a vessel, as small as a point, like the letter ' (Yod), which is filled from this source (Ain Soph). This is the source of wisdom, WISDOM ITSELF (חכמה), after which the Supreme Cause is called "WISE ONE." Upon this He made a large vessel like a sea, which is called INTELLIGENCE (בינה): hence the name "INTELLIGENT ONE." It must, however, be remarked that the ONE is wise, and through Himself, for wisdom does not derive its name through itself, but through the Wise One who fills it with the light which flows from Him, just as intelligence is not com-prehended through itself, but through Him who is intelligent and fills it with His own substance. Holy One needs only to withdraw Himself and it would be dried up. This is also the meaning of the words: "The waters have disappeared from the sea, and the bed is dry and parched up." (Job 14:11).

The sea is finally divided into seven streams and the seven costly vessels are produced, which are called:

GREATNESS (גדולה) Gedoolah or Mercy
JUDICIAL STRENGTH (גבורה) Geburah or Might
BEAUTY (תפארת) Tephareth
FIRMNESS (נצח) Netzach or Victory
SPLENDOR (הוד) Hod, or Glory
FOUNDATION (יסוד) Yesod
KINGDOM (מלכות) Malcuth

Therefore is He called the Great or the Merciful, the Mighty, the Glorious, the ELOHIM of Victory, the Creator, to whom all praise is due, and the Foundation of all things. Upon the last attribute all the others are based as well as the world.

Finally, He is also the King of the Universe, for everything is in

His power; He can diminish the number of the vessels, and increase in them the light which streams from them, or reduce it, just as it pleases Him."

—Translated by The Work of the Chariot

PETACH ELIYAHU

(from the Tikkuney Zohar)

(C. FOURTEENTH CENTURY)

Elijah said this:

Lord of the worlds, You who are One beyond all numbers; You are the highest of the highest, most hidden of the undisclosed. No thought scheme can grasp You.

You are He who pours forth the Ten Tiqqunim. We call them the Ten Sephiroth and they lead us through worlds hidden and disclosed, through worlds manifest and known. In them You are hidden from the sons of man. You are He who binds them, He who unties them.

And since You are within them, whosoever parts one from its mate of these Ten Sephiroth, to him it is accounted as if he had parted You.

These Ten Sephiroth proceed in their order: one long, one short, and one between.

You are He who governs them. No one governs Thou, neither below, nor above, nor at any side. You made wraps for them [the Ten Sephiroth] from whence blossom souls for the sons of men. Many bodies You fashioned for them; "bodies" they are called when compared to the "wraps" covering them.

They are thus called in the following Tiqqun:

Chesed—the "Right Arm."

Gevurah—the "Left Arm."

Tiphereth—the "Trunk."

Netzach and Hod—the two "Thighs."

Yesod—the trunk's "extremity"—sign of the Covenant most holy.

Malcuth—the "Orifice"—the oral Torah.

Chochmah—the "Brain"—it is the Thought—within.

Binah—the "heart"—in it understands—the very heart of—understanding.

Concerning these two [Chochmah and Binah] it is written: "Mysteries hidden are they of YHVH G-d."

Kether, the highest, for it is the Crown of Majesty.

Concerning Kether it is said: "He tells the End from the Beginning." It is the scalp of the T'fillin within; it is the "Mah" name [of numeric value 45], YOD-HAY-VAV-HAY. It is the Heaven. Way of Atziluth. Emanation. The rooting place of the Tree, of its Boughs and Branches. It is like water drenching the Tree, causing it to increase through the root's sap.

> O Lord of the worlds
> You are Origin of Origins
> Cause of Causes
> Who drenches the Tree by this flow
> And this flow like soul to body
> Is the body's life.

In You there is nothing like image or form or anything within or without.

You create Heaven and Earth, bringing forth of their substance the Sun, the Moon, the Planets, the Stars.

And on Earth, grass and trees, a Garden of Eden, flora and fauna, beasts, birds, fish and Man.

All this so that what is above may become known, so that we may have models of behavior of those above and below. Those above can become known through those below—and since there is no model in creation for You, there is no one who knows You at all.

Outside of You there is no One [whole—all—complete] among those above and those below. Thus are You made known as the Origin of All and the Master of All.

Each Sephiroth has a known Name. By these Names Angels are

called. [An Angel—entity of force if directed to an aim; an energy discharged by its own function.]

You have no known Name because all Names are filled by You. You are the fulfillment of them all.

When You rise up from them, all the Names remain as bodies bereft of souls.

You are wise yet not in wisdom known.

You are understanding yet not in understanding known.

In You there is no place for knowledge [to hold on].

But Your power and strength You make known to Man by showing him how the world is conducted in Law and Mercy. For there is righteousness and justice according to the deeds of the sons of Man.

Law is Gevurah—Justice—the middle column—Righteousness. The Holy Majesty—the just scales—two true supports.

All this portrays how the world is conducted. But not that there is in You known righteousness identical with Law [which binds You]; nor is there Justice in You which is Mercy, nor any other attribute at all.

Be drawn down to us—Blessed One—channeled YHVH—into the world for ever.

Truly so truly so.

Amen.

Amen.

—Translated from the Hebrew
by Zalman M. Schachter

from

THE DOCTRINE OF ETHER

RABBI MOSES DE LEON (1250–1305)

1.

For him, blessed be he, no one can comprehend, or know, or meditate upon, or make an object of thought. All that is possible for us is to comprehend something of the modes in which he manifests himself, that is to say, some of the attributes by means of which he created the worlds. Let us commence with the clear testimony contained in the first verse of the Torah, namely, the word *Bereshith* ["In the beginning"]. Former teachers have instructed us concerning the mystery that is hidden in the highest attribute, namely, the pure and impalpable ether, this being an attribute that is more exalted and more deeply hidden than all the other attributes below it. This attribute is also the sum-total of all manifestations. From it they proceed, so also to it they return. The primal attribute being absolutely hidden, it cannot be apprehended in any manner whatsoever. But as for the mystery of the exalted "point," although it is also deeply hidden, it can be apprehended in the mystery of the "inner sanctuary," as we shall, with the help of God, explain.

And verily, the mystery of the highest Crown[1], which is identical with the mystery of the pure and impalpable ether, is the cause of all other causes and origins. It is for this reason that our teachers, blessed be their memory, have said regarding the "ten utterances" by which the world was created, that the word *Bereshith* was the first of these utterances, namely, the one which lies at the base of them all; otherwise the number of utterances recorded would only be nine. There are, indeed, those who explain the difficulty by going down to the lowest step. But they who have been initiated in the "hidden wisdom" know that the true explanation lies in *Bereshith*, namely, the highest cause, the cause of causes, and the origin of origins. It is in this mystery, the unseen origin of things, that the hidden "point" takes its rise, from which all existence proceeds. For this reason it was said by the author of the *Sepher Yetsirah:* "And before *one* what dost thou count?" that is to say, before the one "point" what is there to count or comprehend? Prior to this "point" there is nought except *Ain*, namely the mystery of the pure and impalpable ether. It is called *Ain* because no one can apprehend it. If any one were to ask, "Is there ought present that is thinkable?" the answer would be *Ain* ["there is nought"].

He himself, blessed be he, being so exalted as only to exist in the mystery of his existence, the beginning of palpable existence is to be found in the mystery of the highest "point." From it do all existing things proceed, together with all the causes that are *implicitly* contained in the mystery of his being, blessed be he. There is no palpable existence whatsoever, either above or below, that does not proceed from the mystery of that one "point." And verily, because this "point" is the beginning of all things it is called "thought." For thought is based on something hidden. It is by means of thought that all things, above and below, come into existence, the mystery of the creative thought being identical with that of the hidden "point."

It is in the "inner sanctuary" (i.e. the *Sefira Binah:* "understanding") that the mystery connected with the hidden "point" can be apprehended, for the pure and impalpable ether itself can never be apprehended. And this "point" or creative thought is the ether made palpable in the mystery of the "inner sanctuary," the "Holy of Holies." Every one that seeketh the Lord shall draw near to the door of the sanctuary, and he shall then acquire understanding *(Binah)*. All things, without exception, were first conceived in thought. And if any one should say, "Behold, there is something new in the world," tell him to be silent; for it had previously been conceived in thought.

From this hidden "point" proceeds the inner sacred *Haikal* (= the "inner sanctuary" = *Binah*, "understanding"). This is the "Holy of Holies," the fiftieth year[2]. It is also called the innermost thin voice which proceeds from the thought. All existences and all causes proceed thence by the power of the highest "point." Thus much concerning the mystery of the three most exalted upper Sephiroth (i.e., *Kether*, Crown = the ether; the "point" = *Hokmah*, wisdom = thought; *Binah*, understanding = the inner sanctuary).

2.

The ten Sephiroth are *bĕlī-mah*. They are styled *bĕlī-mah* on account of the injunction: "Close thy mouth so as not to speak, and thy thoughts so as not to ponder." For they are matters ancient and hidden, and within them is the mystery of the supernal chariot which even they who have found knowledge cannot comprehend.

The supernal Crown [*Kether Elyon*] is the mystery of the highest and most hidden attribute, and it is engraved on the mystery of the true faith. It is the same as the pure and impalpable ether, as we have explained; and it is also the sum-total of all existence. All thinkers have wearied themselves out in its investigation, and there is no intention to ponder on it in this place. It is also called the mystery of the *Ain-Sof* (the "Endless One"), for it is the primal cause of the sum of all things. On it has been broken the girdle of all the wise [i.e. the philosophers]. It is necessary to realize and understand that he, blessed be he, escapes all thought, for no mind can comprehend him. And verily, it is because of this that he is called *Ain*. This is the very mystery of the Scriptural saying: "And out of *ain* is wisdom found." Everything that is entirely hidden, so that no one may know ought concerning it, is called *ain*, that is to say, there is no one who has any knowledge of it. Let the soul serve as an illustration. The intelligent soul of man, which partakes of the nature of *ain* (as it is written: "And the advantage of man over the beast is *ain*"), cannot be seen or apprehended by any one. This is just because that by which man rises above all other created things is possessed of the wonderful nature of *ain*. Now if the soul on this account eludes being apprehended, how much more the great *ain* itself, the potent and most hidden source thereof? And understand, that a breath may pass over the head of a man which causes a flutter of joy to his heart and mind; and yet he may not know what it is, nor why it has come. This is an instance of that which is impalpable. Thus also, when this attribute (namely the Crown = the ether) is stirred, sparkling brightness is imparted to all things; but it is itself unapprehended by them in any manner, nor can knowledge be obtained concerning it. It is on account of its wonderful excellence that no name can express it; but it is by means of the other hidden Crowns, though themselves not completely comprehensible, that the intelligent mind is enabled to approach the thought of it.

3.

By means of the words of the holy Torah and the teachings of our holy teachers of early times can man comprehend and investigate even as far as the place which is prepared as a seat for him.

The hidden and inner mystery which cannot be comprehended is the pure and primal ether, as already explained. It [i.e. the "primal point"] is also the beginning of the unique divine name, which is raised and exalted over all blessing and praise. This is the mystery of the letter *Yod,* which is the same as the mystery of the "hidden point," the beginning of all beginnings. And as it has been shown that *Bereshith* is to be regarded as the first of ten creative utterances, it follows that there is a still higher hidden mystery above the ether. Now if there is no possibility of meditating on the hidden mystery of the ether, how much less can this be the case with regard to that greater mystery which is higher than even the ether? . . . The true immediate procession from the *ain,* then, is the letter *Yod* . . . There are, indeed, those who say that the *Aleph* points to the mystery of the hidden *ain.* In answer to this one is able to point to the tradition that the mystery of the *ain,* namely, the pure and hidden ether, no mind or thought can comprehend or meditate upon, and there is, moreover, no distinctive mark in it at all. How, therefore, can it be maintained that this letter *(Aleph)* with its strongly marked features, has any connection with the mystery of this attribute? For even the ether made palpable exists, as we know, of but one "point"; and it is clear that nothing less than one point can be imagined. Now this one "point" is signified by the smallest letter of all, namely the *Yod;* and as the *Aleph* has very strongly marked features, it cannot possibly be connected with the mystery of the *ain.* In other words: As we have seen that the mystery of the beginning of all beginnings is this "point," and nothing else, it follows that the *Aleph* cannot signify the mystery of the pure and impalpable ether.

4.

The mystery of the Unity in its deeply hidden secret.

All the spheres of emanation are one; for although one sphere of being may look different from another, yet are they all one in substance and causation. It has also been discussed whether the *Sephiroth* were created or not; and there is a difficulty either way. For if one were to regard them as created, how could one base one's religious faith on them? And if one were to affirm that they were uncreated, how could one know anything about them or investigate their properties? The right way, however, of thinking of the matter is as follows:—He, blessed be his name, has no quality which the mouth can utter or the mind conceive. Yet can some knowledge about him be obtained through that which proceeds from him. For we at any rate know that he has out of the hidden depths of his being produced the mystery of the true, brightly beaming light in the form of one "point" which, though being itself deeply hidden, produces another brightly shining light. It is the latter which is called "creation" *(Briah),* being indicated in the account of the creation *(Bereshith)* by the verb *Yehi,* that is to say: Let there be an extension of the originally existing substance. It must, however, by no means be imagined that the creation of something new is meant here. All that is implied in it is the extension of existence from out the first cause. We thus have literally a share in the God of Israel³, and know and recognize something of his great and exalted reality.

The creative thought (= the *Sefira Hokhmah*) is so deeply hidden that no one can form any idea of it. But the thought becomes extended and reaches the place whence the wind (or spirit, or breath) proceeds, and it stays there. This is the stage which man can to some extent comprehend, though his knowledge of it is but very slight; and it is on account of this understanding on the part of man that this *Sefira* is called *Binah.*

The stream then spread further still, "thought" being extended so as to reveal itself from out of *Binah* [understanding]. The result was the utterance of "sound," which consists of three elements, namely, fire, water, and breath . . . But the stream spread further still, and sound became speech, which consists of modifications of sounds. Now if thou contemplate "wisdom" (the second *Sefira, Hokhmah*) thou wilt find that the entire process, beginning with primal thought and ending with speech, is a complete unity, and that there is no break in it at all, all being one. Everything is clear to the understanding mind, and may the Lord be favorable to us and point out to us his straight ways [i.e. the right way of understanding his mysteries].

5.

The present chapter treats on the Names which may not be erased, these Names being the foundations of the worlds in all their varieties and mysteries. And verily we have already explained that all the successive spheres are the mystery of himself, blessed be he, their relation to one another resembling that between the flame and the coal from which it issues.

The first Name, *Ehyeh,* is the name of unity. As we have already explained, the mystery of the pure and impalpable ether has neither a name that is known, nor limiting boundaries, nor anything that man can take hold of. But the first existence which came forth out of this mystery is the all-embracing unity contained in the mystery of the "thought-point," which remains itself unknowable until its extension into that which comes after it. This is the reason why the mystery of this name of unity is *Ehyeh,* that is to say: "I am yet to be when the mystery of my existence becomes extended [or developed] . . ." This is, indeed, the mystery of the first name that was communicated to Moses at the bush at the commencement of his prophetic office . . . And it was because Moses was not satisfied until the full mystery of existence was revealed to him that later on the mystery of the name *Yahweh* was communicated to him . . . And verily the mystery of this name (namely, *Ehyeh*) is the first of the divine mysteries. For although there are ten special names of the Deity, none of which may be erased, and although, indeed, the total number of divine names is—as our teachers have said—seventy, to which correspond the seventy names of the congregation of Israel . . . yet is the mystery of this first name particularly unknowable and exalted above all else. And it remains thus hidden until there proceeds from it the mystery of "wisdom" whence all things are produced. This is the meaning of the phrase *Asher Ehyeh* which follows *Ehyeh,* that is to say, "which is yet destined to be revealed," as we have explained.

The mystery of the second name, namely *Yah,* involves a great

principle, "wisdom" being the beginning' of the name which pro-
ceeds out of the mystery of the pure ether. It is that which in
accordance with the mystery of *Asher Ehyeh* was destined to be
revealed. And verily the mystery of "wisdom" comprises the two
letters *yod* and *hay*. For although *Yah* is but half the name *(Yah-
weh)*, yet does it comprise all existence, the addition of the other
two letters of the name indicating the mystery of further extension
in accordance with the principles of existence.

Concerning the mystery of the third name, namely *Eloha*, it is
necessary to know that just as the name *Yah* is expressive of the
ether made palpable in the mystery of "wisdom" (the second
Sefira, Hokhmah), so also "understanding" (the third *Sefira,
Binah*), which is expressive of a further stage of the ether made
palpable, corresponds to a special divine name the composition of
which is as follows: The two remaining letters of the Tetragramma-
ton after *Yah* are *vav* and *hay*. To these are prefixed two other
letters forming the mystery of *El*. The whole name therefore is
Eloha. The name is also connected with the mystery of the soul,
as it is written; for although it is from Eden that the souls proceed,
yet it is their ultimate origin from above. And verily, the name
connected with "understanding" (the *Sefira, Binah*) is the living
Elohim, for he is the most exalted King, high above all else.

The fourth name is the mystery of the name of Unity expressed
by the Tetragrammaton, which denotes the complete extension of
existence . . . It is the peg, as it were, from which all things are
suspended; and it is the sum-total of all things, for it comprises all
that is above and below. In it is the mystery of his existence, blessed
be his name. It is also the name which more especially points to
his unity, blessed be he, in accordance with what we have said
regarding the mysteries of its letters.

* * *

The tenth name contains the mystery of *Shaddai*. In one sense
there are only nine names, for that of the pure and impalpable ether
(viz. the name *Ehyeh*) stands outside the number (being entirely
and absolutely unknowable). But however this be, it is to be re-
marked that some connect the name *Shaddai* with the word
Shoded [destroyer], expressing, as the name does, the quality of
justice. There is also the other explanation that *Shaddai* means
"He who said to the world, It is enough" *(Shaddai = Sheddi)*.

This would seem to fit in with phrases like: "And El-Shaddai shall give you grace," and "I am El-Shaddai, be thou fruitful and multiply," this promise not having been made to Abraham before he had undergone circumcision . . . As the renewal of the race cannot take place without either the "covenant" or the female, the two must be regarded as indissolubly united with each other. This is also connected with what has been said under the name *Sebā'ōth* (the eighth name), for it also points to the sign and the covenant in the midst of all his hosts. From it proceed all the exalted hosts both above and below. The sun is thus a sign among the hosts of other stars, none of the latter shining as brightly as the sun . . . *El Shaddai* thus points to the union of the moon with the sun[5] in order to produce offspring after their kind. This is the mystery of the saying, "I am El-Shaddai, be thou fruitful and multiply," and "And El-Shaddai shall give you grace." For thus [namely by this mystic union of *El-Shaddai*] are all good things bestowed on the world, grace and mercy being drawn down from on high, and all the worlds being blessed . . . Thus far concerning the mystery of the ten names, all pointing to the mystery of divine unity.

—Translated from the Hebrew
by George Margoliouth

from
MIQDASH MELEKH

(A Zohar Commentary)

R. SHALOM BUZAGLO (C. EIGHTEENTH CENTURY)

A Warning to those who wish to enter and walk in PaRDeS

Attend, oh man, to what the holy master ARI [Itzhak Luria] has to say at the beginning of his *Kanfey Yonah,* and I quote:

> Know that in order to help one understand, permission was granted to utilize the limbs of the body as a simile, as it is written "from my flesh do I see G-d." Yet you in your wisdom purify your thoughts to know that in the above there is nothing physical. Far be it. Anything that happens higher than the Azilut we have no permission to deal with, or to compare it with anything that has form and like-ness. It is all a means to explain things to the ear. In this way we utilize a simile. Yet he who is wise understands from his experience that no form exists there at all. However, from the ten sefiroth on downwards, we have permission to talk in simile and likeness.

In his commentary on the *Sifre Dezeniutha,* the ARI writes as follows:

> Do not let your thoughts seduce you into saying that in the space of the supernal Azilutic beings are visible colors and forms. Those who assume that there are will be called to the nether-world to be judged for having assigned thing-like dimensions to the Lord of Lords. There is no color or form in Azilut. He, who is exalted even over the highest, sees and is not visible. Yet, in truth, it is also that

form and color originate from there—but they do not appear except as they emanate downward. Having descended, fallen back from the high where they were rooted, they issue the colors white, red, black, etcetera . . .

. . . And when you see terms like "male," "female," "mating," and "kisses," you ought to know that by "male" is meant that attribute and mode which gives energy to the one who receives it, whom we call "female." Thus the mystery of the "mating," attributed to the sefiroth, is the connecting and the cleaving of the "male" who issues the energies with the "female" receiving them in union. In this sense are the hard rigors of the "female" sweetened by the grace of the "male" (as this is also written about in the book *Mavo Sh'arim,* Gate 3, Part 2, Chapter 2).

So, too, in the creation of the world when the mode of judgment was merged with the mode of compassion; this itself was in the mystery of the "mating" and "kissing," and in this sense does spirit cleave to spirit in the essence of the sefiroth. And what is meant by the mystery of "pregnancy"? The "female" receives from the "male" the root of what is to become and fixes its form in the form of the spirit. When it is yet in the "male," it exists in a subtle and undefined manner. In the "female" it develops to assume manifest existence in actuality. So the *Zohar* states, *Ki Tazria,* 73:

"They are all contained in Hokhmah. From there they issue only on specific paths to Binah where they become fixed. This then is what scripture means by: 'And by Understanding do they become established' and 'All of them were made by Hokhmah' [in Binah]."

The mystery of "birth" and "nature" refers to the coming of existing beings from their subtle beginning into concrete existence and fulfillment.

Know, therefore, that the wise ones of the Zohar and the ARI needed to utilize these terms and descriptions, borrowed from the body repertoire, in order to clarify such mysteries which can not be expressed except by means of these terms and physical analogues. For further understanding, permission was granted to utilize analogues of the physical body because the countenance of man is so amazingly made and ordered, fashioned so in the silhouette of the supernal beings.

The supernal ones are in the manner of the light of the "names." For example, "Abba"—father—[hokhmah] gives off light in the simile of the male's gestalt[1]. The Names are the ones who mate and mingle, mix and interact, connect and reflect, and influence with the light energies. In this sense are the sefiroth named by the lights of the "names" [of Divine light]. This is all total spirituality and has nothing to do with physical light, like that of a candle or that of the sun. Far be it.

The reason why we are permitted to use the word "light" in speaking of the Divine and the spiritual is because it is the most subtle of all senses, the most precious.

Look and see what the book *Pli'ah* [pg. 13] has to say about this:

> One born of woman can not attain these modes. If he could conceive of them, this conception would constitute a limitation of the Divine. Even the modes themselves [the sefiroth] can not confine the light of the mode which transcends it. How much more so with the Ain Sof that gives them all life. It cannot be limited by understanding. How much more so when it comes to mankind.

So when we conceive of these things, it is not they whom we know—but their effects on our scale of observation. So we do not know the sefiroth themselves—nor their power which the Ain Sof has invested in them to conduct the affairs of those here below . . .

*   *   *

Now you may ask: What is the point of attempting to climb the dangerous mountain of the Lord? Is it not better to be satisfied studying the manifest simple part of the Torah? Your answer is that each serious student of the wise has an obligation to know Him, be He blessed, in order to recognize his Creator. As it says in the Zohar, *Canticle,* pg. 18:

> Wisdom is this which a person needs to have in order to know. One way is to contemplate the mystery of His Master. Another is to know one's self. Who am I? How was I created? Where do I come from, where am I going? How is the body fixed to function? How must I give an account of myself before the Ruler of All? A third way is to know the secrets of souls. What is the soul within me? Where does it come from? Why did it come into this body made from a stinking drop? A fourth way is to know and contemplate the world one is in. What is its purpose? And then to seek to know the supernal mysteries of the higher worlds and to know one's Master. All of these paths of contemplation are within the mysteries of the Torah . . .

So it is through the wisdom of kabbalah that one can get to understand the mystery of One-ness and the arcana of Divine conduct, and one can get a hint of how the limbs and attributes and appellations written in the Torah refer to the Creator. How the sefiroth evolve from the infinite Ain Sof, be He Blessed. How they are unified and mated through the Torah and the commandments. And the rungs of the souls and the angels, what heaven and hell are all about. What the qlippot [shells] are and the sparks they contain which need to be freed to return to their holy sources. Hayyim Vital in his *Liqutey Torah* [*Parshat: Vayera*], states that our entire intent is on *t'shuvah* and our good works are to draw down the influence into the ordered universe of *Yosher*. So, too, are the 613 commandments the mirror of the 613 veins and limbs of man and, in this way, the silhouette of G-d. In this way can a person gain the end of his fulfillment in the mysteries of the Torah and find grace and good sense in the eyes of G-d and man.

—Translated by Zalman M. Schachter

Part Seven

It is impossible that anything that comes out of a man's mouth should be in vain and there is nothing that is completely ineffective . . . for every word that is uttered creates an angel . . . Consequently, when a man leads a righteous and pious life, studies the Law, and prays with devotion, then angels and holy spirits are created from the sounds which he utters . . . and these angels are the mystery of maggidim, and everything depends on the measure of one's good works.

—R. Hayyim Vital

INTRODUCTORY NOTE

Hayyim Vital was the foremost disciple of the remarkable Isaac Luria (1534–1572) who founded a new school of mysticism which exerted a profound influence on the Jewish world and formed the theoretical basis for much of the Hasidic thought. Luria, or ARI, "the Lion," was a talmudic scholar and a highly original mystic who lived an ascetic life and imparted his teachings to a very small circle of disciples. It was Vital's notes on the master's teachings which form the basis of the standard exposition of the Lurianic Kabbalah, *Etz Hayyim* ("Tree of Life"), a work sub-divided into several books, e.g. *Peri Etz Hayyim* ("Fruit of the Tree of Life"), the *Sefer ha-Kavvanot,* and the *Sefer ha-Gilgulim* ("Book of Metempsychoses").

According to Luria the special primordial act of creation consists in *tzimtzum,* a self-concentration of the divine life—a voluntary "contraction" or withdrawal of God from "Himself into Himself," thereby creating the possibility of existence outside the Divine, including that of evil. The basis of the world is the *Ain-Sof* (Limitless), which first enters actual existence in the form of light, as *Aur Ain-Sof* (Light of the Limitless). The "vessels" (Sefiroth) are not able to endure the inrush of divine substance and through the breaking of the "vessels" a state of chaos is produced, along with the element of evil.

Lurianic Kabbalah is directed above all things to the perfection of the individual soul and the improvement of all worlds. Both endeavors are united in the idea of *tikkun* (Restoration). There is a *tikkun* of souls, and even of dreams, and a *tikkun* of worlds; the world of future perfection is itself called *Olam ha-tikkun* (World of Tikkun) where all the fallen sparks and souls are restored to their proper place. The achievement of the cosmic *tikkun* is identified with the messianic consummation of history.

The doctrine of *tikkun* is associated with that of *gilgul,* or transmigration of souls, which is applied not only theoretically but also practically. The ARI recognizes the souls which he meets and can trace all the stages of their wanderings. "Looking at the forehead of a man he could tell at a glance from what particular source his soul was derived and the process of transmigration through which it had passed and what its present mission was on earth . . . He was able to tell men their past as well as predict their future, and to prescribe for them the rules of conduct calculated to make amends for their shortcomings in a previous existence." (Solomon Schechter, "Safed in the 16th Century" in *Studies in Judaism,* II, 238– 239.)

Besides regular reincarnation there are supposed to be exceptional cases of "soul pregnancy," *ibbur,* which takes place when either the soul of a deceased person which is already in a higher stage attaches itself to a soul still wandering on earth in order to support it, or when the former requires for its own perfection the cooperation of a human being still living on earth.

In Lurianic Kabbalah there is a great emphasis on the unique spiritual significance of every human act, since by his acts man fulfills a redemptive role. This intense awareness of participation in both a higher and direct reality (man as a dimensional process) is a further elaboration of Zoharitic teachings.

Means of attaining perfection were asceticism and chastisement, fasts, ablutions, special prayers and devotional exercises, recited with close attention for mystical combination of sounds. The purpose is to make contact with the name of God, *yihudim,* "unions." Out of such prayers and meditations a special liturgy was formed. The *Prayerbook of Isaac Luria* was subsequently adopted by the Hasidim.

HYMN TO SHEKINAH FOR THE FEAST OF THE SABBATH

ISAAC LURIA

I have sung
an old measure

would open
gates to

her field of apples
(each one a power)

set a new table
to feed her

& beautifully
candelabrum

drops its
light on us

Between right & left
the Bridge

draws near in
holy jewels

clothes of the sabbath
whose lover

embraces her
down to foundation

gives pleasure
squeezes his strength out

in surcease of
sorrow

& makes new faces
be hers

& new souls
new breath

gives her joy
double measure

of lights & of
streams for her blessing

O Friends of the Bride
go forth

give her many
sweet foods to taste

many kinds of
fish

for fertility
birth

of new souls
new spirits

will follow the 32 paths
& 3 branches

the Bride with
70 crowns

with her King who
hovers above her

crown above crown in
Holy of Holies

this lady all worlds are
formed in

all's sealed
within her

shines forth from
Ancient of Days

Toward the south
I have placed

candelabrum
(o mystical)

room in
the north

for table
for bread

for pitchers of wine
for sweet myrtle

gives power to
lovers

new potencies
garlands

of words for her
70 crowns

50 gates
the Shekinah

ringed by
6 loaves

of the sabbath
& bound

all sides to
Heavenly Refuge

the impure powers
have gone

demons you feared sleep
in chains

—Newly set by Jerome Rothenberg,
Rosh Hashonah, 5733

from
ETZ HAYYIM

(Tree of Life)

R. HAYYIM VITAL (1543–1620)

BRANCH 4

Know that when the Infinite desired to cause emanations and create and make his world composed of four worlds—emanating, creating, forming and making—and He saw there was no strength in the worlds to receive the Great Light of the Infinite and not enough in the nether worlds; but even in the actual Sephiroth, even of Emanation, they had not sufficient strength to receive the Upper Light, for the Sephira of WISDOM could not receive the Upper Light unless by means of the Sephira of CROWN and so on in each case. So all those Emendations were required, that are mentioned in Adra Minor and Adra Major and because of this, four Worlds had to be made— אבי״ע of Emanation, Creation, Formation and Making.

And the matter is, that in all the worlds there are both the essence of substance and its vessels and at the beginning the Infinite extended through the ten Sephiroth of Emanation by vessels. For the idea of spreading or expansion shows that the Light became denser and more compact than before and so we find that these ten Sephiroth are ten vessels which came into being by the expansion of the Infinite Himself, only the Light became more compact and became vessels by expansion. And after this expansion the ten vessels, then the substance or essence of the Infinite, were incarnated—and this is the inner meaning of substance and vessels.

When this aforementioned expansion reached the kingdom of Emanation, he who confers the High Emanation saw that there was no strength in the lower worlds to receive the light if it were further expanded; so then when the vessel of the Yod of Emanation was finished, a curtain or draping was made, separating the Emanation from other worlds lower than it.

Then the Infinite Light, blessed be He, that expanded to there, beat on that curtain and then by the strength of the blow of the descent that touched there, he returned to ascend by reflected light upwards to its place. Then the world of emanation was finished by or through vessels and the Infinite clothed Himself with substance as written above. Therefore where Infinite Light reaches in the above-mentioned way, is called the world of Emanation, for the light itself is only after it has become more dense, as written above.

As to the question of that light becoming more compact, one surely knows that anyone seeing a very strong light cannot bear it unless by moving a good distance away or by means of a curtain or by both together. Behold the CROWN which is in the Emanation lights therewith the Infinite without any curtain or moving away: therefore is the CROWN called Infinite. And WISDOM received through the CROWN; but UNDERSTANDING received the Infinite Light by being a distance away, for now the Infinite is far from it and can receive it. And in a lesser degree it does not get the light save by means of a window: a narrow aperture which is in the window passes the essence of the light without any curtain; but there is no broad way, only a very narrow one, but it is near, for from the UNDERSTANDING to the lesser degree is not far. Through the hole of the lesser degree, the light extends through the hole and window as the miniature, but is removed far.

So there are four aspects, by which the details of the Emanation can be divided spontaneously, but all of them are without a dividing curtain at all and the whole is therefore termed the world of Emanation for the Infinite Light extends throughout it all without a curtain.

And, indeed from there downwards the Infinite Light does not extend, only the illumination going out from it through the curtain. And thus the dividing curtain and draping between Emanation and Creation, as referred to, on account of that beating of the Upper

Light that reaches up to there and beats against that hanging, and from the strength of those ten Sephiroth of Emanation which came as far as there and struck their light there, lights sparked forth, passing through the curtain, and came below the ten Sephiroth of Creation from the sparkle of reflected light of the ten Sephiroth of Emanation upon them, through the curtain.

And by the strength of the ten Sephiroth of vessels are made ten Sephiroth of other vessels, and by the strength of the ten Sephiroth of substance (essence) ten Sephiroth of Creation were made with the aspect of other substances in creation. And similarly, at the end of Creation another curtain was made and on account of the striking on the curtain of ten Sephiroth of Creation, with aspects of both substance and vessels, were made the ten Sephiroth of Formation and so from Formation to Making by means of that curtain.

By this means one can understand how one is called Emanation, one Creation, another Formation and the fourth Making, because there is a curtain separating each one, and no one is in any way similar to another.

In truth, the difference between Emanation and three worlds is in the fact that with Emanation the Infinite Light pierces and passes through it to the end of the Emanation without any curtain at all; but below this point there is a curtain and the difference between Creation and Formation is that the former has one curtain, the latter two, and Making has three.

But indeed, in the details of the world itself, as there are four aspects in Emanation in their detail, as mentioned before, so there are four aspects in Creation itself and in Formation itself.

Indeed regarding the four aspects I have seen, there is one difference, according to Rabbi Gedaliah, and it is this—there are only three degrees, for the first three get the light from afar, and the last gets it from near, through a window, and KINGDOM from afar and through a window. So you can understand what is written in the Tikkuné Zohar, that the life and soul and body are one, for the Infinite does not pass there save by means of a curtain.

I have also found a third explanation of the mystic difference that is to be found in Emanation: it is that a larger format extends the Infinite Light near until it comes very wide and extensive. But singly the light also comes from near Infinite Light, but through a window (i.e., narrow) and not wide as it comes to the larger format. And as to the smaller format, the light comes to it from afar and also narrow through a window; but the width of the window in the smaller format was the same as that of each one separately.

But the aperture through which the light comes from far and the window from which the light is drawn is smaller and narrower than the window of the small format (miniature). All these aspects are not through a curtain at all, but between Creation and Emanation there is a dividing curtain.

BRANCH 5

You know that we have no power to do anything before the emanation of the ten Sephiroth, nor to imagine any likeness or shape at all, God forbid; but in order to make things intelligible we must speak by way of parable and comparison. So that even if we speak of the fact of description, as before, it is only to make matters intelligible.

Know, therefore, that the ten Sephiroth are two distinct matters: first, the extension of the spiritual, and second, the vessels and the limbs through which the substance extends. And lo, it is necessary that all this should have its root above these two aspects and so we must speak in the order of the steps from the top to the end.

Behold, we shall begin and say that the Infinite (En Soph), Blessed be He, has no form whatsoever, God forbid, as has been explained; but when He thought to create the worlds in ten steps, by a form of order, He emanated and continued from it the extension of many lights that they should be the roots of emanation to emanate further thereafter.

To assess and compare this matter, you know, already, that there are four bases for everything, those being sight, hearing, smell and speech; and they are the secret of the soul (Neshamah) and NRN (soul, spirit, breath).

We shall commence to explain from the mysticism of the soul onwards; afterwards beginning with what precedes it, we say that if we compare and illustrate the ears, that there is a thin wind in them. This one can prove, for when a man closes his ears, he hears inside them a sort of echo on account of the wind gathered inside. Then wind comes out from the nostrils and is felt more than from the ear. Then from the mouth, where air coming out is stronger and felt more than the others; and according to the importance of the matters and their aspects, so is their fineness. For the ear, being the mystic of Binah, understanding the vapor emitted is very thin, thinner than that from the nose, and that from the nose is finer than that from the mouth, which is below it in degree.

But, if we put it into language of parable—it is that from the mysticism of the ear is extended the breath and wind from within and without. This is the real Neshamah (soul): the breath from the nose is Ruach (spirit) and that from the mouth is the mystic of the Nephesh (the vital spirit of life).

Now, after we have spoken of how the existence of soul, spirit and life-vitality from ear, nose and mouth were emanated, we will next explain the existence of their vessels (Kelim), the physical body incorporating them.

We have already explained that from the aspect of actual sight is made the soul for the soul; but the sight is not the "sod" of the vapor which extends below as with the ear, nose and mouth. The reason for this is that the soul spirit and life-breath, which are the lights of the ear, nose and mouth, extend downwards; but the soul to soul is the look of the eye which does not extend but remains in its place as the surrounding light, as already mentioned, and has only a very fine close observation. This is the mystic of looking and observation. It is indeed not like the vapor of the ear, nose and mouth, whose essence and substance extend downwards. So from the hidden meaning of this sight are made thirty vessels which is the body, ten of them for the vapor of the ear known as Neshamah (soul), ten more for the vapor of the nose known as Ruach (spirit) and the remaining ten for the vapor of the mouth known as Nephesh (vitality of life).

But the vapor itself which is the light of the face (or inner light) cannot spread out downwards because the sight aspect extends from the eyes which are the highest of all: therefore with this sight alone, the vessels came forth, which is quite different from the ear, nose and mouth since it was impossible to emanate any substance from them if it were not from the vapor actually going forth from them.

But this observation is such that the sight extends through this life-vitality, spirit and soul, as mentioned before, and on account of this observation the roots of the vessels were made.

And this is the mystic of "And God saw the light and He divided for the one emanating, called God looked and contemplated, who is Aleph Koph, through the light of the soul, called Aleph-Tar. For the kingdom is Aleph Tar [i.e., embracing all—Translator] and this is the mystic of the "life vitality" which is made from the vapor of the mouth. But the Spirit and soul are called light Aleph Tar light, the life-vitality plus the soul and spirit and when the Emanator observed and saw the Nephesh—life-vitality called Aleph Tar, then the roots of the vessels went out and this is "And He divided" for the hidden mystic of body is the vessel which gives and does —dividing and border and limit to the lights.

And, indeed, in the matter of this sight there is direct light and reflected light; for in the beginning the sight extended to the end of the tenth aspect of the Nephesh—life-vitality, and afterwards, returning upwards, it divided and became "vessels" clothing the Nephesh in all its parts.

This, then, is the direct light, which had strength to make vessels with the "sod" of the head, which is Gimel-Resh, the three firsts. Yet it could not be recognized until this sight touched the actual Nephesh and where it touched the making of the body to the head was completed, which are the three firsts.

But, vessels to the body which are the seven lower ones did not yet have strength in this sight till the Nephesh touched and encountered the Nephesh (life-vitality) itself. And by means of the removal of the two from down upwards—the ring-streaked light and the light of the eyes, the light was reflected and clothed the seven lower ones.

BRANCH 6

Know, that the existence of the full picture of man in the world must contain the four aspects which include all the emanations and all the worlds and these are: ע״ב = 72 as follows Yod (20) He (15) Vav (22) He (15); ס״ג = 63 as follows Yod (20) He (15) Vav (spelled with Aleph) (13) He (15); מ״ה = 45 (All with Aleph) Yod (20) Ha (6) Vav (13) Ha (6); ב״ק = 52 Yod (20) Heh (10) Vav (12) Hoh (10).

These four forms of the Tetragrammaton divided into four full forms are the following four aspects: The Taamim (accents) are ע״ב (72), the points are ס״ג (63), the letter crownlets are מ״ה (45) and the letters are ב״ק (52).

And each one of these four forms is made up of all of them, and in each of them is the aspect Tenta (טנת"א) i.e., Accents, points, crownlets and letters.

And lo, the aspect of the skull of primordial man, which is "head," to that of the place of the ears, is called by name ע"ב (72) and that is the underlying meaning of the taamim (accents) as mentioned before, although in this aspect alone, the whole Tenta טנת"א is included, but we are not permitted to speak of this. For, although we call these parts by names such as man, head, ears and so on, it is only so that our ears can understand and make them intelligible to us. Therefore we give names in such a high place but the principal name substitutes are from the world of emanation and below, which is the larger aspect of emanation and below, for from there onwards is the aspect of Parzuph (face or visage); but from the larger aspect there is no face aspect whatsoever, our use of these terms being only for the sake of clarity.

Now, from the aspect of "ears" and below we shall begin to explain with the utmost brevity. Know, then, that from the ears downwards begins the name ס"ג (63); it has already been explained that this also comprises Tenta (Accents, points, crownlets and letters, as above) and it is known that the first two are always divided into three parts and there is a range of accents and punctuation above the letters and also below the letters as well as in the middle of the letter. Behold the inner light which was in primordial man went out through the above-mentioned holes, the vapor exuded from the head through the holes of the hair. We have already mentioned above that we are not allowed to speak or to be occupied with this matter so we will start with the vapor coming out of the ears downwards, which is the category ס"ג (63). It is said that through the orifices of the ear go out the light of the innermost part of the first Man.

It is clear that when the vapor goes out, it becomes somewhat thicker so we see that the light which remains in the innermost recesses of primordial Man is greater than that which goes out from him; but it is certain that this latter light is great in the aspect of vessels and body of the first Man—this is quite simple.

Now when the light went out through the ears—both right and left—these lights spread outside from the place of the ears to that of the pointed end of the chin and extended from where the hair of the beard sprouts on the cheeks on both sides of the face; and opposite it, there spreads out and extends this light until it reaches down to the pointed end of the chin and there the lights coming out of the two ears join up, not completely, but with a small space remaining between.

After that the middle accents came and they are in the aspect of the light proceeding from the nose of first Man and חוטם (Chotem), i.e., nose, has the numerical value of ס״ג (63). From here, too, there proceeds and extends a light from both nostrils, right and left, the right encompassing. The internal left as we have mentioned in connection with the ear: and they extend directly to the breast of this primordial man and this is the main part of the light, but, indeed its illumination extends to the back and so surrounds completely the primordial Man.

Behold, these lights, the internal ones, approach their outer surrounding lights more than the lights proceeding from the ears, as the holes of the nostrils are near, but nevertheless, divided into two—and are not joined, so that with these lights too there was not the aspect of vessels.

And the addition of these, more than the lights of the ears, was the shape of the letter Vav which is within the letter He, which, in the ear, was included in it, is now revealed and what was then the aspect of He became now the aspect of two letters, Daled and Vav, to teach that the going out of the letter Vav outside and its being revealed is the mystic miniature form which was here revealed.

But, in truth, not only was Vav made but it was also divided into six parts which are six Alephs. The reason for this is that five faces are included in the letter He, which are in major form, father and mother minor and, its female and they are known as Yachneran, Unit, Living Creature, Soul, Spirit, and Living Soul. So we find that the miniature is the aspect of Spirit, as is known and as the verse says, "Everything which had the spirit of the living breath in its nostrils" which is the nose. Thus by this nose was revealed the aspect of the miniature and was divided into six ends but the letter "daled" remains one joined letter and the letter Vav is divided into six Alephs.

And as the letter Vav is divided where the hole of the right nostril is, so is it also divided in the left nostril and among all of them there are twelve Alephs which together with the nose itself makes 13, equal to the letter Vav [(16)(1)(6)]. And similarly, these two Vavs with the nose, whose shape is like an Aleph, as is known, for the two holes of the nose are two Yods and the wall dividing them is shaped like a vav, so that its shape is א (Aleph) and with the two aforementioned vv it becomes Vav—to teach us that above the aspect of head where there is the brain is ע״ב —72 (the Tetragrammaton with Yods as explained above) and here the name ס״ג —63 and there is no difference between these two forms of His name except in writing the vav fully, as is known.

And these two vavs have the aspect of middle accents in the middle of the word and they are a Psik, a disjunctive accent and a Maqueph, a conjunctive one, as is known, for the Psik teaches us, the vav of the he which was cut off and became six Alephs, as above, so comes about the name Psik. And when you join the Psik with the Maqueph they are one daled teaching us the letter daled of the letter he.

And behold, this daled we have mentioned before is not cut off but there is another meaning to it—and this is it that when you take the he which is in the right ear whose number is the ten Sephiroth, as above and it is of the aspect of one "Yod" and it is joined and united with the "he" which is in the right nostril whose shape is daled, vav, as aforementioned, so that altogether it is the shape of Yod, vav, daled and that is the picture א , Yod on top, vav in the center, and daled at the bottom.

Also if you take yod which is in the hole of the left ear and join it with vav, daled which is in the aperture of the left nostril you get Aleph, beth whose shape is yod, vav, daled, so you have two Alephs with the picture יוד , Yod, vav, daled.

And if you draw one picture, joining yod of the left ear, with vav which is in the left nose and yod which is in the right ear, then the Aleph has the form of yod, vav, yod. Also if you join yod of the right ear, vav of the right nose, yod of the left ear, then you have four Alephs with the above.

And these teachings revealed something the daled of the he in the nose, which is partially revealed but not completely as vav of the he, but the main completion of the revealed daled is downwards, by the light of the mouth, as will be explained, by Divine help.

After that the lower accents and vowels which are beneath the letters came and they are the aspect of lights going out from the mouth of primordial man outwards and the lights are completely joined or fused as they come out from only one pipe-like exit. This is because the farther the lights go away and spread out downwards the more one is able to reach them and receive them so that there is no fear if the surrounding and the inner lights join together.

And lo, since the surrounding and the inner lights have already fused together, therefore begins to be formed from here the Kelim (vessels) aspect, but they are the acme of purity, as I have already explained. Therefore until now only one vessel was revealed although the lights are divided into yod (ten).

And these lights are called Akuddim (streaked). This is according to the verse, "And saw in a dream, and, behold, the he-goats which leaped upon the flock were streaked, speckled, and grizzled" [Gen. 31:10, 12] and further, "for I have seen all that Laban (i.e., white) doeth unto thee." In this verse all the aspects we are discussing are alluded to here, for Laban (white) is the underlying name for the upper whiteness which was the first of all the emanations and this made the aspects of "streaked speckled and grizzled" for the requirement of the emanation which would follow them which was known by the name of Jacob.

And he commences with "streaked" because they are the lights proceeding from the mouth of primordial man through which began the revelation of the formation of the vessels to be yod (ten) lights both inner and surrounding, bound and joined together within one vessel, which is therefore known as "streaked" from the verse "And he bound Isaac," that is, he tied him [making streaks or marks on the flesh—Translator] as is written by Divine help: but the upper lights of the ears and nose were not made clear nor elucidated in the verse since the formation of the vessel had not yet been revealed through them. Afterwards we shall explain speckled and grizzled.

Now, behold when the inner lights joined with those encompassing within the mouth, when they went out of the mouth together, bound together one beat against the other and stamped and kicked against the other and from these beatings there was born a formation of Kelim (vessel) aspect—so this place is known as פ"ה month for month has the numerical value ס"ג (63) and כ"ב (22), i.e., number of letters, to hint that what was made anew in this place was to do with the revelation of the bringing into being of the Kelim (vessels) which were revealed here by the twenty-two letters.

—Translated from the Hebrew by The Work of the Chariot

from
SHA'REY K'DUSHAH

(The Gates of Holiness)

R. HAYYIM VITAL

GATE 4

Here, greatly condensed, are the conditions for prophecy:

It has already been stated that there are dents which damage the vegetative soul and there are those that damage *Chaya*,[1] etc.

All this must be refined.

First of all, one must do *T'shuvah*[2] and return from all trespasses or vices, never to relapse into them again.

One must carefully keep all of the 248 Mitzvoth which apply to our times. This too has already been stated in Part 1.

One must take special care to set permanent times aside for the study of Torah, both day and night, so not even one day be wanting.

Then you must pray with perfect intention each of the three daily prayers, to perform the benedictions and the grace after the meal with their intentions, to honor the Sabbath in all its details, and to love one's neighbor as oneself with a perfect heart, and to read the Sh'ma, the prayers, and to observe the Mitzvoth of the Tzitzith and T'fillin. One must also be guarded to keep the 365 negative commands, especially those which bring with their transgression either the death-penalty by a court of man or heaven, or excommunication—and so with any of the "thou-shalt-nots" in the rabbinic minutiae. Special watchfulness is necessary against tale-bearing, slander, empty talk and mockery; the lewd casting about of one's eyes, of all kinds of accidental seminal emissions and all kinds of approach of menstruous women, and of oaths even to swear to the truth. The keeping of the Sabbath is the most important of them all.

You must also be guarded from all vices, for they defile the elemental soul. Remove yourself to the very extreme from the vice of pride and liken yourself to the very lowest threshold upon which all step. The virtue of humility must become second nature in you so that you will feel neither joy in being honored nor pain in being defamed, so that both will be equal to you.

Be guarded from anger, even if you be smitten on the cheek. There is no greater obstacle to *Ru'ach Ha'kodesh*[3] than anger and fussiness. You must refrain from such, even to the very extreme, even before members of your own household.

So also must you guard yourself from melancholy. Prophecy does not rest on even the most deserving one when he is melancholic. Be glad in your portion even at such times when you are beset by suffering. As it said, "Love the Lord thy G-d with thine whole heart."

Then study Torah for Her sake with all your strength. Intend to do this only to give pleasure to your Creator. Be extremely gladsome when busy with the Torah and the Mitzvoth, as it is said, "I rejoiced over Thy word as one who finds great treasure." By doing so, you will draw great power to flow down into all the worlds. The root of all is the "awe" before Him, be He blessed, which you must generate at every moment in yourself in order not to sin. This you can achieve by visualizing the Name before your eyes as it is written, "I have [be]held YHVH facing me." Intend to adhere your mind to Him and not to be separated even for a moment from Him. This is the mystery of "cleave unto Him."

GATE 5

Deal with how-ness [function] and its content.

It is well clarified that "Light" is in the form of Man radiating in all four worlds: *Atziluth, B'riah, Yetzirah,* and *Assiah*[4]—to the very end of the four elements in this lowly world which itself is conjoined with the "Light" which is called the ten spheres. They are invested into this "Light" of the most high "Man," which is called the "Light of the Quarry whence souls are hewn." Even the lowest souls are there included. When they descend into this world to become invested in bodies of flesh, they leave their roots cleaving to the main root from which they are hewn. Only the branches of the roots descend by spreading downwards to become invested in bodies. This can be compared to a tree whose branches are at one with the roots which nourish them. When man transgresses a Hareth transgression, he cuts the branch from the "tree" and the "roots" and remains cut off in this world like the spirit of an animal. This is the mystery of "surely shall that the soul be cut off," and this too is the mystery of "For every man is a tree of the field," and this too is the mystery of why the souls of the Tzaddikim are twice called: Abraham, Abraham, Jacob, Jacob, Moses, Moses. Once their name is used to denote the root which remains cleaving to the tree on high. This is what is called Man's Mazal (star-planet or, more correctly, flow-from fount), as the Sages told us how Moses, our Master, saw the Mazal of Rabbi Akiva sitting and expounding. From there the flow of the Mazal proceeds to the branch which descended and invested itself in the body.

The root is most high in the very head of the world and the emanation of the branch is very long, spreading through all the worlds with only part of it investing itself in the energy of the body. In each world through which the branch spreads, it leaves a root. Hence, each soul has countless roots in different worlds, one higher than the other. Through your actions you may merit to raise them all. Thus all the roots one has in the Universe of Assiah make up one's whole soul of Assiah, and the same holds true on their own levels with the roots in the other rungs.

Thus the concept of Prophecy can be understood when a man has purged himself of all sin, the defilement of the Yetzer Hor'a [evil inclination], preparing himself to adhere to a particular supernal root of his being and realize it in full.

However, even if you have become worthy of this, you need to divest your soul completely and totally from all things of matter and the senses. Only then will you be capable of adhering to and realizing the spiritual root. However, this divestment—which is written about in many books—is not a complete divestment from "doing," in which the soul leaves the body. That is sleep and what is realized in it is a dream. The presence of *Ru'ach Ha'kodesh* in man is in the waking state, when his soul is *in his body*, not when it has left him. What is meant by divestment is a complete removal of thought.

In thought there resides a power of M'dammeh [association, fantasy and illusion] which makes for conceptualization. This M'dammeh comes from the elemental animation soul. This M'dammeh must be arrested and cut off from association, from weaving thoughts and mental rehearsals of worldy cravings—as if one's soul has left the body. Only then can you turn the M'dammeh into the direction of one of the upper worlds, into the direction of one of the roots of your soul, proceeding from one to another until your describing will attain your Supernal Source.

There you will become impressed by the thought forms of the "Lights" which will form themselves according to your ability to receive them in the very same quality of apperception which you have for things of this world which are not before your eyes. Then think and intend to receive light from the ten spheres from that point tangential to your soul. There you intend to raise the ten spheres up to the Infinite so that from There an illumination will be drawn down to them—to the very lowest level. When this light is drawn down to them, they rejoice and become more luminous from that light drawn down unto them by the root of the soul which has its hold on them—in the measure that it deserved.

Then you intend to lead it downward, step by step, so that the light will reach the intellective Soul which is in the body. From there it will reach into the animating soul and its associative powers, wherein the content becomes construed in material thought-forms in your association. Then you will understand them in the same manner as if you had seen them with the eye of flesh.

At times, this light becomes construed in the form of an angel which addresses you. A displacement and projection occurs towards the outer periphery of the sensorium. Thus you see, hear, smell and speak with your physical senses as it is written, "The Spirit of G-d spoke [through] me and this word was on my tongue." For the "Light" has become materialized and has taken form through the physical senses.

At other times your prophecy will be only with the spiritual senses, through the power of M'dammeh alone. This only comes as a result of diverting the physical M'dammeh.

In this way prophecy can be compared to a dream in which the rational soul has left the body and ascended, rung by rung, and arriving it beholds and then returns, descends and draws within itself the "Light," draws it into the animating soul and its power of M'dammeh where things become construed and take on further shape. But after the soul has left the body this does not apply.

There are two different kinds of prophecy: (a) The prophecy whose feat of prophecy is like a trance. They achieve light which flows downward into the rational soul and is drawn into the animal soul where it becomes shaped into projections of the five inner senses and their associating power. But with such seers, their outer senses become overwhelmed. They fall to the ground and have no strength to contain all the light in themselves. This kind of prophecy is called "dream," although we do not mean actual dream, but rather a "trance"; (b) The second prophecy is a perfect prophecy in which the senses are not overwhelmed, wherein it all assumes its proper shape and this is the prophecy of the quality of Moses. The cause of this is that the prophet has fully clarified and refined the substance of his body which has been completely changed by the holiness of his actions. It attains to the level of his soul. All defilement passes away from it leaving it so pure and good that it proves his body was never confining for the powers of his soul.

It has already been explained that the soul has many roots in the worlds above, depending on the level of its origin, and depending on that is also the level where the prophet will draw forth his prophecy. Consequently, if the root of the soul originated in a higher place, the person will have need to amend all the other rootlets below it in able to draw forth prophecy from a level he has already mended. Thus you will understand why there are so many levels of prophecy. The numbers of these levels is infinite. You realize, therefore, that it is the desire to be raised to the higher levels which opens the channel for the influence of thoughts to be attained as well as the intelligence being attained—to become united with the soul and to be drawn downward.

You will realize that content is verily light and substance of the spiritual which comes down into the mind and through the rational soul. This influx and very real light is what is called "thought." When you realize it fully, you will see what this means in terms of prayer intentions and the good thoughts of men—and also the reality of evil thoughts which mean cleaving onto evil with one's mind. Thus you realize that prophecy is a gift which, by necessity, is given to each person who attains to holding onto the end of the branch of the tree. He who is capable of shaking a branch of the tree is capable of moving the entire tree. Yet the only way in which the upper branches will be moved is when a man has merited to draw on himself the supernal light. With his thought is he able to draw down even those supernal and sublime lights. He that has not merited and purified himself will not be capable of drawing down supernal light. The lights will not agree to come to him and become incorporated in his thought. Vanity is developed without purification and this is no help.

—Translated from the Hebrew
by Zalman M. Schachter

from
SEFER HA-GILGULIM

(Book of Transmigration)

R. HAYYIM VITAL

After having explained the nature of the original inclusion of all souls in the First Man *(Adam Ha-Rishon),*[1] and the manner in which these souls, through his sin, were clad in the Shells *(Kelipoth),*[2] we shall now explain the matter of the transmigration of the souls *(Gilgul Neshamoth).*

The original intermixture of Good and Evil necessitates two processes: first, the separation of the good from the evil by the fulfillment of the three hundred and sixty-five negative commandments; and second, the restoration of the good by the fulfillment of the positive commandments.

There is no member of the body of the Primordial Man that is not constituted of two hundred and forty-eight limbs and three hundred and sixty-five sinews; the total of which is six hundred and thirteen. One might assume that it would be sufficient if the sparks of a limb corporately fulfilled the six hundred and thirteen commandments, even though each of the sparks did not individually fulfill them. But this is not so. The limbs are also divided into six hundred and thirteen sparks or more (as mentioned above),[3] and each spark is composed of all. Therefore, each spark of a soul *(Nizoz Neshamah)* must individually fulfill all six hundred and thirteen commandments of the Torah which correspond to the six hundred and thirteen limbs or sinews of man. If a commandment is not fulfilled, one must then transmigrate, as was mentioned in *Tikkunim, Tikkun* 70.[4]

Certainly there is a distinction between someone who has already fulfilled all six hundred and thirteen commandments by means of sparks of that limb which is the source of his soul—even though he himself did not fulfill all of them—and someone who has not yet fulfilled the six hundred and thirteen commandments even by means of sparks of his source, and this is a simple thing.

Moreover, all six hundred and thirteen commandments must be fulfilled by deed, by speech, and by thought. Speech was alluded to in the verse, "this is the law of the whole-offering,"[5] etc., as our masters, blessed be their memory, said: "Everyone who deals with the law of whole-offering"[6] etc. If some spark of a soul has not fulfilled even one aspect of those three—deed, speech, and thought —it must transmigrate until it fulfills all of them.

Also, whoever did not deal with the Torah in its literal meaning *(Peshat),* allegoric meaning *(Remez),* sermonic *(Derash),* and esoteric interpretation *(Sod),* contracted *(notarikon)* into *Pardes,*[7] must transmigrate until he delves into all of them; each and every one according to what he can conceive, and according to the aspect of his root *(shoresho),* the portion given to him on Sinai, as is already known.[8]

Thus one can find an answer to some problems and doubts arising in what we have explained. There are righteous people, lesser in degree than others, who have rested in the next world, and there are righteous people who are very great, such as Moses our master, of whom it is said in *Tikkunim*[9] that his duration lasts until sixty myriad generations. The reason for this distinction is that Moses needs to complete his portion, which is very great, and his transmigrations are not completed so soon [as others'].

Through this, one can also understand that there are righteous people who die in their youth, such as Rabbi Bun, not because of a transgression for which one has to die *(kareth),*[9a] but rather because he had already completed what he needed to complete of all the six hundred and thirteen commandments and other things; therefore he died in his youth. This is what our masters, blessed be their memory, intended saying: "Rabbi Bun endeavored to complete in twenty-eight years what a veteran sage did not endeavor in seventy years,"[10] and understand this.

And you shall also understand from this [why] there are righteous people for whom death is hard, such as Moses, our master, peace be upon him; and there are [those for whom it is not]. The reason is that Moses, our master, peace be upon him, has not yet fulfilled all the six hundred and thirteen [commandments] dependent on the land, on the Temple, and was not [willing] to return in a transmigration (although he had to). Death was bitter to him. Thus one can see why Moses, our master, peace be upon him, had to transmigrate. But the righteous who have completed all they need are serene in death, and that is what is written in Daniel: "but you go [your way] to the end and rest,"[11] since he already had no need to transmigrate anymore.

Similarly, one will understand from this the long delay in Redemption, since many transmigrations are necessary until every spark fulfills its six hundred and thirteen commandments and all the above-mentioned aspects.

Thus you shall also understand what was said in the Gemara: "A certain Rabbi asked another Rabbi: 'In what was your father most careful?' He answered: 'In *zizith.*' "[12] There are righteous people who are more fastidious in one commandment than in another. This would seem to be a contradiction, because our sages, blessed be their memory, said: "And be heedful of a light precept as of a weighty one."[13] But they were sages and knew what they were lacking, therefore in those commandments they had fulfilled in earlier transmigrations they were not so strict, [as in other precepts]; or else there is no end to it. Since a person has already fulfilled some commandment in an earlier transmigration, he no longer has to fulfill it. This is said only in commandments involving no personal obligations, such as commandments dependent on the land, and the beginning of the shearing, and the like; however, it is surely incumbent upon him to fulfill in all transmigrations those commandments involving personal obligations, such as *sukkah, shofar, lulav, tefilah,* and the reading of the *shema',*[14] and the like, and understand this. The rest of the people who do not know why they came into the world and what they lack should fulfill all of them. Therefore they have admonished: "Be heedful of a light precept as of a weighty one."[14a]

One can also understand from this that there are [people] whose whole desire and endeavor are in the literal interpretation of the Torah; there are those who deal [with the Torah] in a homiletic way; some in allegory; some in numerology; and some in the way of truth; everything according to what [unfulfilled aspect] for which a person was transmigrated this time, since those things once fulfilled in other transmigrations require no further fulfilling.

Likewise one can understand all other problems and doubts related to the matter of people and their transmigrations.

After we have explained the [matter of the] roots of the souls, and how each spark needs to complete all the six hundred and thirteen in the above-mentioned way, there is also a need to understand that man should know the root of his soul—wherefrom it flows—as said in Zohar on Canticles in the verse: "Tell me love of my soul"[15] etc. Also one needs to know why he came to the world, since you already know that "all Israel are guarantors to each other,"[16] the reason being as mentioned above in Chapter One, that all the souls of Israel were in First Man *(Adam haRishon);* but they are guarantors only for the revealed things, as the Scripture said: "What is revealed belongs to us and to our children."[17] Also they are guarantors only if they were able to protest but did not, as is well known.[18] However, there is a special consideration according to the innermost [meaning] and it is that all of one root are guarantors to each other in all particulars. Also not only will they suffer punishment for him as we will explain;[19] this is not so in other roots; even though they are revealed and [a person] has the ability to object—he is punished in this world only, not being required to return in a transmigration or in an impregnation *('ibbur)*[20] for this, as we shall explain.[21]

Therefore it is found that all the six hundred and thirteen sparks of souls included in one root of those seventy small roots which exist in each and every limb of the First Man, as mentioned above in Chapter Three,[22] all are full guarantors to each other, because all these six hundred and thirteen sparks are considered one soul. Understand this well because it is a great law of transmigration. Hence if any spark of those six hundred and thirteen sinned or caused any blemish, all the six hundred and thirteen sparks of that root need to remove the blemish, and are not called perfect and restored—even if they restored at the time all that is needed—until the blemish of that spark is healed; therefore, all those sparks need to participate with it in the secret of impregnation, as we will explain with the help of God,[23] in order to help it [that spark] complete all the six hundred and thirteen sparks absolutely. And

when the six hundred and thirteen are perfected, they have no
other obligation to whoever is from another root, even though the
soul were from the seventy small roots in the limb of First Man.

One should also know that of those six hundred and thirteen
sparks some are closer to each other than others. Hence, it is the
closest spark which will impregnate one or transmigrate into one
and help it, as we will explain, with the help of God, in Chapter
Five.[24] All six hundred and thirteen sparks were [originally] called
one soul, but because of the sin of the First Man, or of man himself,
they were to split as a rock shattered by a hammer into six hundred
and thirteen sparks or more, as mentioned above.[25] And by this one
can understand what was found in the books of the kabbalists "so
and so transmigrated into so and so." It indeed seems strange to
say that such a great person would need to return and transmi-
grate, especially so if he returns into a person much baser than he
was in the beginning. But since all six hundred and thirteen sparks
are guarantors to each other, sometimes it will happen that a very
great spark will transmigrate into a very small one in order to help
him and perfect him, since he is his guarantor from his root. Thus
each one of those six hundred and thirteen sparks or more which
exist in the same inheritor is called after all the sparks in the same
root even though they are not [perfect]; since necessarily, in every
root there are great sages and little ones, and people who perform
the commandments and boors and evil ones, like a tree which has
a trunk and branches, leaves and fruit and husks, and all of them
are one soul. Know that in each and every root there must be six
hundred and thirteen sparks which are in the body of the soul and
[its] essence, in the secret of its two hundred and forty-eight limbs
and three hundred and sixty-five sinews, and all of them are sages;
it is impossible that the number of the sages will be less than six
hundred and thirteen. Although the rest of the flesh in those limbs,
such as the branches, leaves, and the trunk of the tree, are the
ordinary people who exist in each root, the fruit of the tree are the
sages, and they in particular are the six hundred and thirteen. And
all this is in the soul *(nefesh),* and another six hundred and thirteen
are in the spirit *(ruah),* and thus also in the breath-of-life *(ne-
shamah),* etc. It is this way in all portions of the universes of
emanation, creation, formation, and activation *(ABY'A).* And see
Chapter Two,[26] and understand this very well, because this knowl-
edge is greatly needed, so that your mind will not be confused. The

reason is this: in each and every particular root there is a particular face of the six hundred and thirteen limbs and sinews; and as there is a very great difference between the roots, some being from the head and some being from the feet, such is also the case with the sparks of the roots themselves; there is a big difference among them.

Do not be astonished by this since we have found that all evil people and all participators in foreign worship were born from First Man, Noah, Abraham, and Isaac, and their kind. How can this be possible in the world? The fact is that the soul is constituted of two hundred and forty-eight limbs, and each and every limb has flesh, brains, blood, skin, hair, and nails. Whoever is the aspect of the inner brain will be very great, thus extenuating to the hair and nails, which are the shells of that limb. Therefore, do not be astonished if we say that in the root of Abraham's soul and the like there are sparks of evil people, men of low value. And understand this well so that I will not need to remind you about it every time, and see Chapter Thirty-Two.[27]

There are many commandments which not every spark has the capability to fulfill. The reason is that all the souls, even those which are from one root, do not come in one family or one tribe; rather, one comes in the transmigration of a priest or a Levite, and one in the transmigration of a judge, and one in the transmigration of a literalist and the like. Because there are special commandments for the priest, for the Levites, for the kings, or judges, not every spark has the ability to fulfill all six hundred and thirteen commandments. Likewise, there are also other commandments such as redemption of the first-born son, or the commandment of levirate marriage or *ḥalizah*,[28] which a man cannot fulfill if he has no first-born son. And there are other commandments that each person can fulfill and is obliged to, such as the reading of the *shema'*,[29] *tefilah*,[30] and *zizith*[31] and the like. But there are other commandments which a man is not obliged to pursue, such as gleaning, forgotten sheaf, the corner of the field, the beginning of the shearing. If a man has a field and ewes, he is obliged [to fulfill the commandments which are relevant], but if he does not have them, he is then exempted. And there are commandments which are dependent upon the building of the Temple, such as the sacrifices, etc.

Now we shall explain them. A man must be zealous in the

fulfillment of all the commandments he is capable of fulfilling in his transmigration, such as phylacteries and the like; and he should buy a field and fulfill the tithes, etc. If he does not fulfill them he must transmigrate and fulfill them in all ways. There is a distinction concerning those commandments which are obligatory even without the Temple but which a man is not capable of fulfilling, such as redemption of the first-born, levirate marriage and *ḥalizah*. If a man had an opportunity to fulfill them but did not, they are like the rest of all other commandments whose fulfillment is in man's hands. Therefore he should have to have a full transmigration in order to fulfill them. But if he did not have an opportunity to fulfill them, he would not have to transmigrate because of them. Rather it would be sufficient for him to enter in the secret of impregnation in some person who is from his root and thus related to him in transmigration, as mentioned above.[32] Thus a man will have the chance to fulfill the commandment vicariously, and afterwards leave [the man he inhabits], and this will be sufficient.

The commandments dependent upon the building of the Temple require that all the sparks which came before the Temple was built or in the time of the Temple, transmigrate into priests or Levites or Israelites until they are all restored. However, the sparks that did not enter the world until after the Destruction need to transmigrate in the time of the coming of the Messiah prior to the next world, which is the seventh thousand; since the main reward and punishment is at that time. But since the soul in itself cannot fulfill the commandments, then first will come the messianic days, in order to fulfill all the commandments depending on the existence of the Temple. Thus one can understand what Rabbi Ishmael ben Elisha meant, when he slanted the candle on Saturday evening and said: "When the Temple will be built I will bring a fat sin-offering," etc.[33] And this is sufficient and understand it very well.

—Translated from the Hebrew
by Yehuda Shamir

from
PARDES RIMMONIM

(The Garden of Pomegranates)

R. MOSES CORDOVERO (1522–1570)

We saw [fit] to put forth a good explanation acceptable to the mind of the enlightened [mystic] in the present Chapter concerning these three concealed [Zaḥzaḥoth].

The point is that His thoughts are not our thoughts and His ways are not our ways.[1] When man imagines in his mind to cause some existence to come into being, his thought will not activate [it]. Even though he will imagine and draw in his mind the form of the existence he wants to actualize—nevertheless it will not be actual until he acts and it will be achieved *(in actu)*. Now, the actuality is found to be more complete than the potentiality *(in potentia)*, because the potential is lacking existence and has no existence and perfection at all, and the actual is the essence and the existence and there is nothing apart from it.[2] Not so are the acts and actualizations of the King of the Kings of Kings, the Holy One, blessed be He. [This is so] because when it came up in His Will to give existence and emanate the pure and holy emanation—then it was emanated and drawn, all of it, in its essence, without any change in Him, God forbid; but an existence united with Him until there was no difference at all between the Emanator and that existence. But He and they are one thing and one substance, and one root.

Even if we relate that emanation *(ha-aziluth ha-hu)* to the aspect of the three, as we will explain that they are Primordial Light, Bright Light, and Shining Light *(Or kadmon vezah wumezuhzah),* the aspect of their distinction is not in the value of their essence but in the asset of their branches which spread and emanate.

The thing is, as we have already explained in the section Order of Emanation *(Sha'ar Seder HaAziluth),* that the emanation is included in Crown, Wisdom, and Intelligence *(Kether, Hokhmah, Binah),* because they are the Root of Mercy, the Root of Judgment, and the Root of Compassion *(Shoresh haHesed, haDin, haRah-amim).* Thus, also in the order of their emanation, Mercy and Lasting Endurance were in Wisdom *(Hesed, Nezah, Hokhmah),* included in each other and all is one. Thus Majesty in Power and Power in Intelligence *(Hod, Gevurah, Binah)* are included in each other. So the Kingdom is in the Foundation and the Foundation is in the Beauty and all is in the Crown *(Malkhuth, Yesod, Tifereth, Kether).*

Therefore, when the Will came up to emanate the emanation in the substance of the Root, three points were drawn, and they are *Kether, Hokhmah,* and *Binah.* In them the whole emanation was included.

The reason they are distinguished into three, while being united in a complete union—and [even] the existence of this distinction is impossible unless it is figuratively (metaphorically, *'al derekh hashalah)*—is because as the Root is one so the three points are one, and the points and the Root all is one. Indeed we relate to the three because they are Root and the source to three branches which are *Kether, Hokhmah,* and *Binah,* and not *Kether, Hokhmah,* and *Binah* really, but *Kether, Hokhmah* and *Binah* drawn in *Kether,* from the aspect of the existence of the beginning of their spread from the substance of the Root to the Crown.

Now it is found that Crown, Wisdom and Intelligence, draw bounty from their special, concealed source in the substance of the Root, which is the Primordial, Bright and Shining Light, which are united by perfect union . . .

. . . And if we relate the number three to it, it is because they are roots to three sources of their three branches, as we have explained, but in their substance, in their spread, they are united completely. This reality and union and source was revealed in the Simple Existence from the aspect of His Will toward the emana-tion, and our saying "was revealed" means the reality of the existence which was not emanating because of the concealment of the emanation in His substance. Now from the aspect of His spread in the emanation He emanates in those sources and this is their revelation. And not that they are revealed to the emanated, let alone to the created, let alone to the formed, let alone to the activated, because their reality is not revealed to another . . .

—Translated from the Hebrew
by Yehuda Shamir

from
KINATH SETARIM

(Lamentation of Mysteries)

ABRAHAM BEN MORDECAI GALANTE

"The paths of Zion mourn without *(darkhe Zion aveloth mibli)*"
etc.[1]

Know that thirty-two paths of Wisdom *(Hokhmah)*[2] are flowing
down from stage to stage, from thirty-two to thirty-two, down to
the Kingdom *(Malkhuth)*.[3] Those which are in it (in *Malkhuth*)
are called "thirty-two lower paths *(lamed-beth netivoth tatain)*,"[4]
as mentioned in a book which my teacher, blessed be his memory,
composed.

[God] holds all these as a covenant of the chosen *(berith yehidae)*
called Peace *(Shalom)*[5] and He causes them to be entered into the
Great Ocean *(yamma rabba)*, so that He comes into His strength,
as explained in *Parashath Mikez*, p. 196.[6]

Now the mourner bitterly bewailed and said: "the paths of Zion"
meaning those ways and paths that flow unto Zion, i.e. the Founda-
tion *(Yesod)*—they [the Paths] are mourning, because they do not
serve in this Attribute *(Middah)* to calm her (the *Middah*) from
the tumult of the waves of Judgment *(dinin)* rolling in it; they are
like a mourner who is forbidden in intercourse.

And this is the meaning of "without those who come for a
festival *(mo'ed)*," i.e. they do not come and flow unto this Attribute
called Festival.

202

This is perhaps what [our sages], blessed be their memory, alluded to in the Midrash: "R. Abdimi of Haifa said 'even ways are seeking their role—this is the meaning of the Scripture *the paths of Zion mourn.*'" This is the end of the quotation. He deduced from "they mourn" that now they are mourning, but at any other time they are not. Rather, they are seeking their role.

Another interpretation: The reason that "the paths of Zion mourn"[8] is "without those who come for a festival,"[9] i.e. without pilgrims for the three festivals, when every male was seen before the Lord God.[10] Through this they were awakening the Upper Male *(hazakhar ha'elyon),* and He would unite with His *Middah* (Attribute).

Then, this *Middah* would be called Elohim, since by means of it the Upper Mother *(Imma 'Ilaah)* beautifies her Daughter *(Bartha),* i.e. through being called Elohim. This is so because this name alludes to the union, as [Elohim] in reverse is *milah* (circumcision) and an extra Aleph (A), and indicates the unity by means of the presence of the males before the Lord God, as explained at the beginning of *Parashath Bereshith* (Prologue),[11] in the verse "these I remember."[12]

Now "the paths of Zion mourn"—those thirty-two paths of that Zion (the Upper Zion)—they are mourning. Why? "Without those who come for a festival"—because no one ascends for the three pilgrimages to awaken that Union.

Another interpretation: You already know that in the Foundation, i.e. that Zion, there are two paths! One toward the flow of good oil, and the other to the rest, to give abundance to the outer powers. Now [Jeremiah] is teaching us that the two paths were mourning in the time of the Destruction. Even the pure path (going toward the flow of good oil) was clad in sorrow and mourning, which is the Shell *(Kelippah).* They [both paths] do not enter into the Tabernacle *(Ohel Mo'ed)* as I have already explained. Since nothing enters nothing comes out. Therefore, "all her gates are desolate."[13] Her Gates which are fifty Gates of *Malkhuth* from the realm of the Jubilee, through which she brings out the souls and the existences, they are all desolate, because she has nothing to bring out, since whoever is granting peace in the house is inactive.

Another interpretation: *Shomemim* (desolate) comes from "*semamith* (a spider) which can be caught in the hand."[14] The interpretation is thus: It is as if the Shell called *Semamith,* which makes the world desolate *(meshomem)*, entered into those fifty Gates, in such a way that she made all those Gates full of Spiders and Cobwebs, like an entrance which is closed for some time and the spiders weave in it their webs since there is no one going out or coming in. It is possible that our masters, blessed be their memory, hinted [that] by saying " 'all her gates are desolate,'[15] that there were no incomers nor outgoers."[16] That is the end of the quotation. Their words seem to indicate that *shomemim* comes from *semamith* as I have explained.[17] This is in my opinion the secret of what our masters, blessed be their memory, said that Manasseh offered a spider *('akavish)* on the altar.[18] This is meant in the same way as the Zohar interpreted *Parashath Pinehas,* the verse "He scolded the beast *Kanah* (He created)." The interpretation of the saying of our masters, blessed be their memory, is "Gabriel came down and stuck a reed *(kanah)* in the sea" etc.[19] The meaning is: The Reed *(kanah),* which is the male in the Shell, ascended and took hold in the Upper Sea *(Yam ha'Elyon),* because he (the Reed) receives bounty from there. This is also the meaning of the statement that [Manasseh] offered a spider *('akavish),* i.e. Lilith the wicked, Semamith who desolates the world on the Upper Altar *(haMizbeah ha'Elyon),* to suck from it.

Do not let your heart fall when you hear these things, because they are not literal, God forbid, since it is written: "I am the Lord, My Name and Glory I shall not give to another;"[20] and how is it possible that the Shell will enter the Holy Place? Surely God does not do evil. They can not enter the Palaces, much less the Throne, much less the Emanation, except for the Tabernacle of the Boy,[21] in the secret of the departments where one entrance is opened, called the Hole of the Major Abyss *(Nukva diTehoma Rabba).* From there they come out and ascend through outer spheres vis-a-vis the Palace of Merit *(Hekhal Zekhuth),* the Palace of the Fear of Isaac, from the Side of the Shell of Esau, from which it came out, up to the Palace of Love *(Hekhal Ahavah),* and the Palace of Charity to Abraham, from the realm of the Shell of Ishmael; of which it came out. There worshippers of stars and constellations scream and demand until the force of their prosecution climbs up into the holiness. Then the King of Justice judges the people of the land, because He loves Justice, and the decree comes out in agreement between all of the ten Sefiroth. The destroyer has permission to lay waste. In the aspect of the entrance of this prosecution it is called the entrance of the Kelippah in the Holy Place. And keep this rule in your hand and bind it in your wings so it will not fall.

Another interpretation: "All her gates" are five gates which are five Sefiroth, five Salvations (yeshu'oth), which surround her from all her sides, as it is explained in the beginning of Parashath Bereshith (Prologue).[22] They are those who save her from any enemy attack and from ambush on the way. Now "all her gates" which guard it "are desolate," as if they are wondering and marvelling, since they do not believe "that enemy or invader would enter the gates of Jerusalem."[23]

"Her priests are sighing,"[24] i.e. Michael the High Priest and others under him who surround the Upper Altar of the Lord from its four sides, as stated in Parashath Zav, p. 36:[25] "There are six hundred thousand myriads of soldiers in each corner, one is in charge of them, all are clad in an efod (priestly garment), and are there to carry out the service of the Altar in correspondence with the lower priests."[26] Here the quotation ends.

All those priests sigh because the lower worship, which causes the Upper Worship, was annulled. Also they sigh because some have offered a Spider on the Altar; they are about to arrange its order, and they have seen the Abomination of Desolation (shikuz meshomem). And all these priests are in the World of Formation ('olam hayezirah).

Another interpretation: "Her priests (kohaneha)"[27] are her servants, according to the Scripture "and they serve (vekihanu) Me."[28] And they are the Seraphim in the World of Creation ('olam haberiah).

Another interpretation: Her servants of the World of Activation ('olam ha'asiyah). Each of them is in charge of some affair, and there are many of them.

"Her virgins,"[29] i.e. the seven virgins who are the Queen's companions, the feminine aspects of the Palaces of Formation (hekhaloth hayezirah), are sad. When there is intercourse between the Holy One, blessed be He, and His Shekhinah they (the above feminine aspects) are purified and rise and unite in one point, in its inside, in the secret of "see how the kings all gather"[30] etc. "they see,"[31] etc. "they are seized with trembling,"[32] etc.. However, now, with the lack of that union, they have remained sad and melancholy, and in sadness they lie down.

Another interpretation: "Nugoth" (sad),[33] that is 'agunoth (deserted) without intercourse. When the Temple existed those virgins were entered in the secret of the Upper Intercourse, as interpreted in *Tikkunim,* that when the Holy One, blessed be He, unites with His Shekhina, the angels of the Shekhina and the angels of the Holy One, blessed be He, unite in one.[34] This is the secret of "one called the other,"[35] "and they receive from each other"[36] etc. This is the Scripture "sad"[37]—deserted without union.

"How bitter is her fate,"[38] for as long as she has the bitterness of the *Dinin* (the powers of judgment), they (her powers) taste more bitter than death, and the Beauty *(Tifereth)* does not unite with her, in the secret of "and unto a woman"[39] etc. And therefore he said the reason "her virgins are sad"[40] and deserted without union is because she, the Shekhina, is bitter and wrapped in the dress of *Dinin.* And if she has no union—how will they have? "If Rabbi did not know—how would R. Hiya?"[41]

Another interpretation: "How bitter is her fate,"[42] you already know that there are two kinds of bounties *(shefa'im):* One to give abundance to the lower elements; it flows to a Category *(Middah)* according to the deeds of the lower elements, if they are better or worse, do plenty or less in that abundance. The second is an abundance from Him, blessed be He, to the sustenance of the substance of the ten Sefiroth. It is not dependent on the deeds of the lower elements, but always flows and comes out from before him—it never stops. Anyhow *Tifereth* in the time of the Exile does not want to receive that influx, so that He will be sad in the trouble of Israel. This is the meaning of "in all their trouble *zar lo*" the *vav* is grieved.[43] This is the meaning of "the Holy One blessed be He has taken an oath that He will not enter Lower Jerusalem,"[44] *Malkhuth,* (Kingdom). And likewise the emanation of the *Malkhuth,* from the influx to the aspect of its essence. She did not want to receive it in order to sadden herself. And this is "how bitter is her fate,"[45] she in her substance embitters herself from her own free will, seeing the measure of the trouble of Israel.

—Translated from the Hebrew
by Yehuda Shamir

from
RESHITH HOKHMAH

R. ELIJAH DE VIDAS

... there were great saints so absorbed in the Object of their longing that they did not feel any distraction besetting them. He who longs and yearns destroys all thought in himself which excludes the object of his desire; he is alive only to the fire burning within him. So full of longing that he eats, drinks and sleeps totally absorbed in his beloved. In the same way man ought to deport himself with G-d. This we can learn from the following tale told by Rabbi Yitzchak of Acco, of blessed memory, in his *Ma'assitoh Hap'rushim:*

"A princess went to bathe in the river and was observed by a low-born man, one of the slum dwellers. The thought which first flashed into his mind—'When will I be able to deal with her as I please?'—became an obsession. His desire for her grew mightily within him and finally he managed to have a word with her.

"Confessing his love—more in frustrated gestures and deep sighing than in well-put words—he proposed to her. The immensity of his love filled her with compassion and she answered that only in the cemetery could she meet him and be his own. She meant by this that the only place where rich and poor, aristocrat and beggar, are equals is in the cemetery. Their love would have to wait for death before it could be consummated.

"But he understood this only as being an appointment for a tryst. He sold all his possessions. What would he need of his own when

207

he became the princess's squire? And he went to the cemetery, making it his home.

"He meditated on the form of his beloved and day by day his fervor increased. The image of her became more lovely and bold. Whenever impatience took hold of him, he would tell himself: 'How difficult it must be for the princess to leave her palace—she gave me her word. If not today, tomorrow. She will come.' Thus he waited, beholding her constantly with his inner eye.

"From time to time he saw how they brought corpses to the cemetery and soon he became aware of the transitoriness of existence. It can not be the fleshly form of the princess which I love, he decided. There is something else about her, something very special and unique, something enduring and divine. And thus he began to contemplate the divine spark in forms which gives them such beauty and grace.

"In time he turned from the divine, which clothes itself in forms, to the loveliness of the eternally divine, which is without form or name. Daily he beheld the preciousness of the King, yearning to be absorbed into His very Being, rather than in any of His manifestations.

"No other thought entered his mind, so absorbed did he keep it on the object of his love. One can not be preoccupied with such single-minded yearning without being transformed into the very substance and being of the beloved object. And so, the former slum dweller, the low-born man, realized G-d. A G-d realized person, a Tzaddik, is soon felt by those who seek one. He attracts those who need him in the same manner as a flower attracts bees. Soon the cemetery became a place of pilgrimage for those who sought his blessings and direction. He was spoken of as the 'Tzaddik of the House of Life.'

"It so happened that the princess, who had already married, was barren. Like many others, she came to seek the blessing of the Tzaddik. When she stood before him, he greeted her and thanked her from the bottom of his heart. For all that he had realized he owed to his initial love for her. The Tzaddik freely bestowed his blessing upon her.

"Soon thereafter, he became so absorbed in His Being that he forgot to return to his flesh.

"At first, the people who came to seek him did not wish to

disturb him. They thought him to be in devekuth [absorption]. Only later did they understand he had 'left life for the living.' "

* * *

Rabbi Yitzchak of Acco continues: "He who has never loved a woman is likened to an ass or worse. For all service to G-d must begin with the discrimination and further sublimation of lofty feelings . . ."

And the *Reshith Hokhmah* continues, saying: "Thus the words 'desire' and 'learning' must be understood. He who fastens his desire exclusively to one thing in the Torah—so that day and night he thinks of nothing else—will surely attain to the highest and most amazing levels of the soul. Such a one needs no fasts and austerities. All depends on the steadfastness and intensity of his longing for Torah, which must be like one who longs for his beloved . . ."

—Translated from the Hebrew
by Zalman M. Schachter

THE CREATION OF MAN

R. ISAIAH HOROWITZ (C. 1565–1630)

The body of man is called Flesh whilst man par excellence refers to that which is inside, i.e. Soul. Man's soul is an expansion of God's name and the shape of his body is also marked by God's name. The body of man was created from the dust of the Lower Temple and the soul from the dust of the Upper Temple. The lower man *Ha-Adam Ha-Tahton* is called microcosm and he is formed in the shape of the great man *Ha-Adam Ha-Gadol,* the name of the mystery of emanation.

The soul of man consists of three degrees. (1) *Nephesh* from the Sephirah of Kingdom. (2) *Ruah* from the Sephirah of Glory and (3) *Neshamah* from the Sephirah of Intelligence. The *Neshamah* emanates from the bright splendour of His glory from the Upper Lights. The soul is brought about by a union of the Sephiroth— Glory and Kingdom—which indicates that the soul of a male and female are, originally, united and are twins in the embryo. One cannot be thought of without the other, the male part drawing its strength from the male Sephirah and the female from the female Sephirah.

The soul of Adam and Eve emanated from the two Sephiroth— Beauty and Kingdom in their roots—in accordance with the mystery of the Two Faces. The soul of Adam is the root of all souls from which descend 600,000 souls in every generation. And when death was decreed upon Adam's soul, death was also decreed upon the souls which came from it, because they all were in his potentiality. Man because of his soul is linked with God. Let us make man in our image (Gen. 1:26) and this is indicated in the word TsLM, *image,* its numerical value being 160. The Kabbalists call the evolution of emanations ETs, *tree.* God is called the tree of true life, the soul of all living. The numerical value of ETs, *tree,* is 160. The numerical value of Tetragrammaton according to the following calculation is also 160:

$$YOD \cdot HAY = 10 \times 5 + 5 \times 10 = 100$$
$$VAV \cdot HAY = 6 \times 5 + 5 \times 6 = \underline{60}$$
$$160$$

The Torah is also called tree, as it is written: *It is a tree of life to them that grasp it* (Prov. 3:18), and beloved is man who is created in God's image. Thus man and the Torah are linked with God's name.

God's name is imprinted in the shape of man from above to below and from below to above. The head resembles the letter *Yod,* the body is like *Vav,* and the five fingers of each hand correspond to the letter *Hay,* and similarly the toes on each two feet correspond to the two letters *Hay,* the genital organs to the letter *Vav,* and its crown to the letter *Yod.* The shape of the two eyes are like the letter *Yod,* and the nose like the letter *Vav.* The ten fingers represent the ten Sephiroth.

The three parts of the soul—(1) *Nephesh* (2) *Ruah,* and (3) *Neshamah* enter three different parts of the body, the liver, heart and brain. The *Nephesh* enters the liver which is the seat of life, the natural force which imparts sustenance to all parts of the body in accordance with their needs, the power which apportions food in accordance with its requirements, the power of growth and the power of begetting and the five senses—hearing, seeing, tasting, smelling and touching. The part of the *Ruah* is in the heart which is the seat of the will which guides its forces in accordance with its will as a king rules his people as he desires. The *Neshamah* which is in the brain is pure intelligence and rules over everything, the procedure being as follows. Before the heart wills anything it communicates with the brain where after due deliberation a particular action is decided upon and is passed on to the appropriate organs for the purpose of carrying it out.

God created man with a free will. Free will is given in the hand of man and all depends on his will. The choice lies in the power of a man to make an impression above and to open the fountain of the will according to his desire. The soul of man is able to perform many activities though they are contradictory in themselves such as love and hate, laughter and anger, etc. The soul possesses this ability, because it is accepted by all Kabbalists that the Sephiroth are also able to perform contradictory activities, at times they clothe themselves with justice and at times with mercy. The will of man is derived from the *Neshamah* whose soul comes from the emanation (of the Sephiroth).

The garment of the soul of man before he sinned was a holy body, pure and clean and inclining towards spirituality as it will be in the future when the body of man will be full of intellect and knowledge as before he sinned. Man by choosing evil changes his face and is likened to an ass and becomes like an ape. If man had not sinned he would not be material but intellectual and he would have remained in the Garden of Eden to work it and guard it. God created the world for the benefit of man. He made man upright, wholly good and to be a light, and had he not aroused evil, everyone would have agreed that it was better for man to have been created. But only after man had sinned, thus nullifying the object of creation, the problem arose whether man ought to have been created or not. When man, however, will improve spiritually he will be better than he was before. The garment of skin which is now dark will be changed into light and will be even more light than before.

—Translated from the Hebrew
by Rabbi Dr. Eugene Newman

Part Eight

Our highborn King will rule in Jerusa-
lem
over all of Israel's kin.
He is called Shabbati Zevi
from the tribe of Judah.
Because God himself chose to make him
King,
mark well and mark him high
Amen Amen Amen.

—Jacob Tausk of Prague

INTRODUCTORY NOTE

Three factors contributed to the spread of the Messianic belief in Israel: the loss of national independence and the attendant deprivations, the will to live dominantly and triumphantly as a rehabilitated people in its national home, and the unfaltering faith in divine justice by whose eternal canons the national restoration was infallibly prescribed. Helplessness in the face of overwhelming odds, a masterful love of life, and an unyielding hold upon the basic morality underlying all national experiences constituted the physical, psychic and ethical elements out of which the Messianic faith was fashioned. The Messianic ideal was a group conception into which political aspirations, religious imperialism and moral vindications merged.

In the beginning the Messianic ideal was temporal and political, colored by that intense mystico-religious imperialism of the nation which was the legacy of prophetism. The ideal evolved into supernaturalism as the task of national redemption and universal conversion appeared progressively more difficult of accomplishment through human effort alone. While the human character of the Messiah and his religio-political mission were never entirely lost sight of, certain miraculous potencies were added to his personality in proportion to the nation's realization of its own impotence. Only the intervention of a divinely endowed being, at the moment of the nation's deepest degradation, could destroy the wicked powers which oppressed it, restore the people, cleansed by suffering, to its ancient glory and rebuild the broken harmonies of the world. The nation could not save itself—except through repentance. Moral purification could prepare the way for the advent of the redeemer. But only as a penitent sinner could Israel play a part in the drama of its national salvation.

Messianism thrives on suffering. It is its soil and sap. And in Israel suffering was continuous throughout the centuries, if only the suffering which derives from the consciousness of the loss of national independence and a national home. The Jew never forgot, even when others did not cause him to remember, his exile.

Also he never forgot the divine promise of Redemption! In his darkest hour he never doubted it. He knew his exile to be a penance and atonement —a long and dreadful penance and an unprecedented atonement. But he also knew that in a world of providential justice no penance can be everlasting. "Behold, we who are in this long and bitter exile," writes Moses Albelda (16th century), "are warranted in hoping for our Redemption for three reasons: first, because of God's compassion, 'for the mercies of the Lord are unending'; second, because of the vindication of God's name which has been profaned among the nations; and, third, because of God's promise, for He is certain to keep His word."

. . . At times Messianic calculations seemed so real, so plausible and so clearly implied in prophecy as to set the whole nation agog with vivid expectation and stampede it into disastrous Messianic movements. At times these calculations were so authoritatively delivered as to cause the migrations of whole communities to the Holy Land on anticipatory Messianic pilgrimages. Some of the pseudo-Messiahs in Israel were as much the creation of these "literary" Messianic speculations of the people as the up-thrusts of the untoward political conditions of their times.

. . . The Shabbetian Movement swept through all the ranks of world Jewry, excited the highest hopes—and led to spiritual debacle and national humiliation. It had shaken the Jewish community to its very depths. The sober leaders of the people, once they had rediscovered their voice and their courage, determined not to permit such a thing to happen again. They frowned upon all further speculation inasmuch as such speculation always contributed to the rise of Messianic pretenders. Nevertheless speculation persisted, for the Messianic hope itself persisted among the people. It glowed like a flaming star in the darkness of their lives. The tragic conditions of the times, especially as they affected Polish Jewry, lent desperate urgency to that hope. The study of the Zohar, and of Lurianic Kabbalah generally, continued unabated. Such study always provided fertile soil for the Messianic complex. This was especially true among those circles which refused to abandon their belief in the Messianic role of Shabbeti Zevi even after his conversion to Islam in 1666 and his death in 1676.

Unlike all other Messianic movements since the time of Jesus, that of Shabbeti Zevi persisted even after his death; his followers spread Shabbetian doctrines, or those ascribed to him—some of them not without Trinitarian and Incarnational overtones—far and wide . . .

—Abba Hillel Silver in *A History of Messianic Speculation in Israel (From the First through the Seventeenth Centuries)*

DREAMS AND MESSIANIC REVERIES OF ABRAHAM HA-YAKHINI

ABRAHAM HA-YAKHINI (SEVENTEENTH CENTURY)

1.

In the month of Heshvan in the year 5413 (1652) I dreamed of an enormous camel pursuing me. Fleeing it, I entered a room and closed the door with a double bolt. The animal broke through the door, so I hid myself successively in many other rooms. In the last room there was a fragile light as transparent as a wave in which I wrapped myself. Having descended into the sea, I no longer feared the camel. There a young woman of great beauty came out to meet me, embracing me intimately and beseeching me not to forget that I was to be married to a queen who was, at present, hidden both by the sun and the moon. Much moved by this, I swore by her and believe I had relations with her. Immediately after, another young woman appeared, followed by the sun and the moon and I saw the resplendent queen who apparently was my destiny. Full of terror, I awoke, stirred by that vision in which nothing in me was hidden. I went to Tora!

2.

I had another dream in Heshvan 5413 (1652). I saw a terrible old man enter the room I was sleeping in. He was of average size. Seeing him I was seized by a great fear. Taking hold of me, it seemed he wanted to judge me; but I prostrated myself before him and begged him to tell me what it was all about without taking me away.

He sat down and I told him: Sir, for twenty years I have been smitten with Tora and withdrawn from wordly occupations. If I have sinned in relation to the norm, it's that I am only formed of clay and the evil instinct assails me at every turn.

Immediately the horrifying old man arose.

I asked him his name and he said: I am the Mishnah which punishes man; and I am the Tora which loves and cherishes you; so say no more.

But I continued confessing, all the while shaking with fear. Soon he transformed himself into a beautiful young woman who I held in my arms and embraced . . . with powerful hugs and many kisses. I woke up seized with great fear, my hair bristling and I was bathed in tears because of this great vision only God could understand or explicate. May it protect me from those who study Tora with disinterest. Amen.

3.

Yesterday evening, I saw myself in a dream coiffed in the turban of sultan Mahomet and carrying the handkerchief of that prince in my sash. Then I saw the tapestried beds, the royal ornaments, the gold and silver closets. I also perceived the breasts of a woman and pressed one of the nipples and milk ran out. I awoke. It was only a dream.

4.

The 15th of Sivan, 5413 (1652): I was out walking and near a window when I started to fall. I wanted to cry out. But I quickly regained my footing and thank God did not fall. I gave thanks to God and recited the acts of grace proper to such an incident in a high voice. My wife watched me cleaning the dirt in the house including the spiderwebs and other mustiness. I swept it into the fire.

Later, I saw myself in a dream dressed in a white *kiamiza* (nightshirt). It was the eve of Kippur, a little after the feast preparatory to fasting. The following night, I perceived a living water fountain impetuously overflowing. I also twice saw works bearing the name of R. Hanania inscribed in fire.

5.

Monday night of the week of Balak in the year 5423 (1663). I saw
a dream written in a book. The words YNN and ChNN and many
other names with the double *Nuns* which would indicate, as it is
known, that God was going to work miracles in my favor in order
that I be better able to serve and fulfill His desire. Amen!

A basket filled with large pears and chestnuts was given to me.
I also saw myself give ten piastres so that someone would open the
gate of the city for me—through which I passed to the harbor along
with many others. We were leaving Constantinople. I awoke then;
it was only a dream.

6.

*A*nd I will sing and celebrate the God exalted in His unique and
terrifying power by those around Him O Light of the Jews!

*B*ehold the gathering of aromatics and myrtle; the Holy One of
Israel had shaped a figure; he has squashed the enemy in his
press like raisins; a king who rules gloriously!

*R*apid as the hart he makes Tora letters leap; admirable in counsel
he pacifies all wrath; soon the elevation, soon the exaltation
—his truth a sword and shield!

*A*nd being rule and crown, glorified to the limits of his empire,
uplifted into the prodigious arcanas of Tora, he will find the
inmost sanctuary!

*H*ow detached he is from the magnificent primal holiness of the
divine soul; he is heir to the light of the awesome God himself,
to whom he is joined!

*A*crospire of God teeming with nobility; the empire has been
placed on his shoulders!

*M*ountains of nobility; a king in resplendency, a king in resplend-
ency, O scattered sheep!

—Translated from the French
by Jack Hirschman

THE COMMANDMENTS OF SHABBATI ZEVI

TEXT ATTRIBUTED TO ZEVI (C. 1665)

In the name of Shabbati Zevi.

Here are the Eighteen Benedictions of our Lord, King and Messiah Shabbati Zevi, may his Glory be uplifted!

1. The first is that one must carefully protect the faith of the Creator, who is singular and unique, and outside of which faith there is neither God nor Providence; neither superior nor judge, save him.

2. The second is that one believe in his Messiah who is the true Redeemer; there is no power of salvation outside him, Our Lord and King Shabbati Zevi, who comes from the house of David, may its Glory be exalted!

3. The third is that one never swear any false oaths in God's or his Messiah's name; for the Name of his Lord is within him and must not be profaned.

4. The fourth is that one must honor the Name of God and venerate it just as one does his Messiah whenever it is uttered; and that one equally have respect for his neighbor through the science of the Name.

5. The fifth is that one fly from congregation to congregation to proclaim the secret of the Messiah.

6. The sixth is that one never kill any man of any nation, no matter how detestable.

7. The seventh is that the 16th of Kislev be set aside for an assembly of all Shabbatian parts in a single house, where each man will relate to his neighbor what he has heard and understood of the Mystery of the Faith in the Messiah.

8. The eighth is that fornication not rule them; though this is a precept of B'riah (Creation), it should be set aside from this chapter because of thieves.

9. The ninth is that one never bear false witness, nor falsify against his neighbor, nor slander anyone, especially one of the Believers.

10. The tenth is that one is not permitted to initiate anyone into the Order of the Turban, who would enter it by force, for he who belongs to the group of fighting masters is one who enters spontaneously with a full heart and sincere will, without a desire to constrain in any way.

11. The eleventh is that one does not envy his masters nor covet what belongs to them.

12. The twelfth is that one be present at the festivities of the 16th of Kislev.

13. The thirteenth is that each man be charitable to the other and that each strive to make his neighbor's wishes as his own.

14. The fourteenth is that one read the Psalms every day in secret.

15. The fifteenth is that one must each month observe the birth of the moon, and pray so that the moon turn its face to the sun so that such stars be parzuf-to-parzuf [face-to-face; persona-to-persona; person-to-person].

16. The sixteenth is that one pay attention to the practices of the Turks, for then one will be able to sabotage them. Especially scrupulous should be the observations made during the Fast of Ramazan. It is not important to concentrate on the ceremonies which the Turks make to their devils, but everything noted should be acted upon.

17. The seventeenth is that one never make an alliance with the Musulmans, neither during his lifetime nor at his death, because they are an abomination and their women are reptiles, and this is referential to the saying: *Woe to him who sleeps with an animal.*

18. The eighteenth is that one make certain to circumcise his son and thus diminish the shame of the holy people.

Conclusion: These eighteen Ordinances that I have prescribed belong for the most part to the Law of *B'riah* (Creation) because the Throne is not yet strong at that point where Israel might take vengeance upon Samael and his legion. At such a time in the epoch, everything will become equal: the grade of restraint and the grade of permission, the grade of impurity and the grade of purity—all will recognize me, from the small to the large. In precaution of which the brothers who are believers but have not yet entered into the Mystery of the Turban—which is the struggle—should be careful to observe the grades of *B'riah* and *Atzilut* (emanation) and never diminish such observance, right to the time of the revelation. Then they will fathom the Tree of Life and all of them will become angels. May the Divine will permit such a revelation soon. Amen.

—Translated from the French
by Jack Hirschman

from

EIN SCHÖN NEU LIED FUN MOSCHIACH

(A Comely New Poem Concerning the Messiah)

JACOB TAUSK OF PRAGUE (1666)

In highly flavored melody
designed to free each pious Jew
living in the world
yet never hearing such a lordly song.
And the scholar too should take his due
through whom the world is liberated—
because God whose name should always be praised
has chosen us as the people of duration
and now has given us a Jewish King.
His many Prophets have stood up to announce it
and what they write puts strength in our limbs.
You will borrow sounds from this new age
and add them to the great poem of our King,
Shabbati Zevi,
a pious and valiant hero.
Our tribe is now filled with his Prophets
foreseeing us to the Holy Land in joy
where all the tribes are gathering at last
having endured exile's terrors.
You can read about it all my friend
if you care to buy the honored poem within

I call to that part of the land where our Brothers are of no conse-
   quence:
the Messiah is coming any day now.
Already one hears the hot gossip of the news.

Consider, loving brothers of all directions,
traveling the Israel road with me:
The Lord who has promised us
no longer keeps us in misery.
The horn of Messiah is raised to sound
the glory of his coming.
Amen amen.

I've heard and seen such peace in Amsterdam
to those who've seen the great Letters
telling of the new way;
how the Portuguese have had enough of prayerbooks
and now dance and leap for joy.
Amen.

God's built an Ark to stand forever,
the godless are powerless before it.
No mockery can destroy it
and these days one hears great music within it
in honor of our loving Lord and King
Amen amen amen.

* * *

They are sending messengers to every corner of the earth
with written proclamations.
No more hesitation.
Brothers will help brother who lack the money.
They will all together set off on the journey.
Amen amen.

Everyday new leaflets tell us of the wonders that are happening.
Our trades are dropped, the stores are closed,
we're on our way to liberty,
Amen amen.

Brothers, don't delay,
no penny can save you.
When you come to see me in the Holy Land,

it's not a purse that'll be born
but the dear Lord that has been promised us
Amen amen.

Jews, beloved Brothers, all are happy.
The dear Lord has given us a King
to lead the hope within us.
Oh we've hoped for so long.
Amen amen.

My brothers from all over the world,
hearing the music of peace,
come riding day and night to Jerusalem.
Their trade is dropped,
they come to me penniless.

Dear Lord God
let our wandering be done.
Misery has been our endurance,
now let's be on the move
to the true home.
An end to the misery we've been led through.

* * *

Our King came to the capitol of Turkey where our Brothers
waited to be freed;
he told the Sultan directly,
he would wear the crown,
but the Sultan didn't yet know the Jewish God
so he would hear none of it,
he was like Pharaoh with hardened heart,
yet our King performed wonders before the Sultan
who grew frightened of such a man
amen amen.

Ours is a Just God, spoke our King,
while you are like Pharaoh
who would neither let go
nor weep with his servant.
The Jewish faith is just.

Then Turk and heathen together cried aloud:
Jews, take what you want and go in peace.

For they dreaded our God, dear Brothers,
the One who fashioned the world
Amen amen.

* * *

From the first small leaves
his writings foretold
the 4th day of Sivan in 426
how deliverance was at hand,
it must be striven for.
Now bend with every penance
for the Messiah comes this year
Amen amen.

You Jews, Brothers, root of all that begins me:
we're headed for the Holy Land to dance and weep and leap and
         be free.
We'll forget all griefs.

* * *

Listen to what the highborn King Shabbati Zevi has done:
the Turks threw him into prison
but as soon as he entered
the light glowed,
the four walls began to burn all around, red as fire.
Men in prison with him beheld the glow.
The Turks then wanted to set him free immediately
but our King would not leave the jail.

* * *

Don't be occult, Brothers, Israel is alive.
I've seen it written in the great and good mail
and now there's no more sorrow.

* * *

True God, I praise you deeply for what you've given.
We've hoped so long to live in such joy;
we've suffered so many lashes.
Now assemble us at the great spread of creation.

God will eye the Jewish blind,
limb the lame and heal the sick.

God will turn all grief to glowing light.
Driven hearts will be gay.
O He is the mighty alone
Amen amen.
His loving care is known, I hear and see it.
And I will also reveal the Scribe:
his name is Jacob Tausk of Prague
called to the task,
who made this beautiful first with the Alephbeth,
then with the tongue of His Seal
Amen amen.

Listen now, my Brothers,
be well prepared for that ripe time of the new Jerusalem
and may it be sung forever
Amen amen.

This poem has a happy end:
Beloved God has sent us to the Holy Land
Guided by His Good Hand.

—Translated by Jack Hirschman

TRANSLATORS' NOTES

SHIUR QOMA

1. Both texts before me have 236 ten thousand thousands (rebaboth alaphim), I think, however, that alaphim is not correct, superfluous, because the total would be much greater than the component parts: twice 118 ten thousands.

2. The eye measures are missing in the Lemberg edition (1865).

3. In Lemberg the measure of the Skull is given as 30 rebaboth, i.e., 30 ten thousand parasangs.

4. In the text the reading is: the ten thousands of thousands of Israel. That is much more than the number of the Israelites at the time of the Exodus, to which expressions like this in Midrashic literature refer. I therefore translated "tribes"; the tribes in Israel were divided into groups of thousands (see Judges 6:15, I Samuel 10:19, Micah 5:1). The author here used a phrase from Bemidbar 10:36.

5. "Who know this mystery": perhaps, "he who possesses this secret."

6. Various names are inserted at this point, perhaps the name of the person using the prayer.

7. The name of what? Usually names are given for both sides.

8. The Height of YHVH of 2.36×10^6 parasangs is 1.4×10^{11} OLAM. If we take the current astrophysical dimensions of the OLAM as 10^{23} miles or 1.6×10^{28} cm (2×10^{19} light years) this leads to the dimensions of 1.4×10^{34} miles or 2.2×10^{39} centimeters for YHVH's height.

9. The number of 10^{15} parasangs for the total measure is considerably greater than the 2.36×10^6 parasangs given previously for the height of YHVH in Section 1.

10. "The holy palms." The text has KALFE HAQESETH. My translation is based on the correction made by S. Wortheim in Bote Midrashoth I, p. 43, note 179. He suggests the reading KPE HAQODES.

11. This is the only reference in the SHIUR QOMA to the way beyond YHVH, to His AIN PANEKA (Nothing Presence), NOT (AL) form, behind the Throne.

Another reading: "If Your presence go not with me, carry us not up hence."

HOKMATH HA'EGOZ

1. In Eleazer's view the throne of glory (and the angels) arose from the reflection of the Divine light of the Shekhinah in the cosmic waters. That light produced a radiance which became a fire and thus caused the throne (and the angels) to come into being.

2. This term denotes in Eleazer's terminology the "great fire" of the *Shekhinah* as distinct from the lesser fire produced by the radiance of the *Shekhinah* in the cosmic waters. The throne and the angels arose from the lesser fire.

3. The green color of the external shell is but the appearance of the "brightness" *(nogah)* or of "torches" *(lappidim)* as seen from the distance.

4. I.e., dry, and the two inner shells stick together.

5. Which corresponds to the image of the inner shell, and symbolizes surrounding darkness.

6. In the *Hekhaloth* literature the *cherubim* occupy a higher place than the *hayyoth*. Cf. H. Odeberg, *3 Enoch*, Cambridge, 1928, pp. 148–9. Eleazer's view seems to be different.

7. The existence of one *hayyah* above the four *hayyoth* may be suggested by the use of the singular instead of the usual plural in Ezek. 1:22, 10:15, 20. This would represent an analogy to Eleazer's doctrine of the "special cherub" *(ha-keruv ha-meyuhad)* which Scholem traced to the use of the singular in Ezek. 10:4 (cf. *Major Trends*, p. 113). On the other hand, the angelology of the *Hekhaloth* literature already knows Hayli'el, prince of the four *hayyoth* and Keruvi'el, prince of the *cherubim* (see Odeberg, *ibid.*).

8. I.e. the "visible glory" *(kavod nir'eh)* as distinct from the "inner glory" *(kavod penimi)* which has no shape, only voice. Cf. Scholem, *Major Trends*, pp. 112 ff.

9. On the dangerous properties of the nut in Jewish folklore cf. Gaster-Heller, *Beitrage zur vergleichenden Sagenkunde*, MGWJ, 80, N.F. 44, 1936, quoting *Sefer Hasidim*, ed. Bologna, fol. 119b, 1160 (not contained in the Parma recension, ed. Wistinetzki) and *Yalqut Hadash*, fol. 89a, no. 52: The nine leaves are the abode of evil spirits. Eleazer of Worms possibly alludes to this belief. For the phallic significance of the nut see Manhardt, *Wald-und Feldkulte* I, 184 (quoted by Gaster-Heller).

10. I.e., as distinct from the one clothing the kernel.

11. I.e., of the nut, between the surrounding darkness of the cosmic waters. The throne actually arose from the fire produced in the cosmic waters.

12. See note 7. The haggadic motif of God wearing *tefillin* (*B. Ber.* 6a), which plays an important part in Jewish mysticism, is here applied to the "visible glory."

DOCTRINE OF ETHER

1. It should here be explained that Moses de Leon identifies the ether with the first *Sefira, Kether,* the "point" (or first connection of substance) being according to this system the second *Sefira, Hokhmah;* and the third *Sefira, Binah,* is styled "the mystery of the inner sanctuary" by means of which the second *Sefira* can be comprehended. The first *Sefira* itself remains absolutely hidden from the understanding.

2. The idea of the jubilee year is here brought in as signifying a period or stage in the process of development of the cosmos out of the *Ain-Sof.*

3. This is the only one of the distinctly pantheistic features of the work. Moses de Leon's system, like that of most other Kabbalists, may, in fact, be summed up as "All is One and One is All."

4. I.e., part of the full name, which is *Yahweh,* as is explained soon after.

5. There is here a curious reminiscence of some parts of Babylonian and general Semitic mythology.

MIQDASH MELEKH

1. The term used by the author is Parzuf. This term comes from Persephone—in Greek referring to masks of actors. A model not without merit in this area of kabbalah which refers to the role that light assumes. In many ways the best way to translate the word "parzuf" is the meaning it has assumed in the literature of kabbalah and Habad, i.e., configuration and figure-ground totality.

SHA'REY K'DUSHAH

1. Man's soul constitutes five degrees: Nefesh, Ruach, Neshama, Chaya and Yechida. Each of them includes all the others.

2. Repentance: literally, "return," indicating that the concept of teshuvah means a return to God and to the right path.

3. The Holy Spirit.

4. The world of emanation; the world of creation; the world of formation, the world of angels formed from the emanations of the Briah; the world of action.

SEFER HA-GILGULIM

1. *Cf. Sefer HaGilgulim,* Chapters I & III.

2. *Op. cit.* in note above (1), Chapters I & II.

3. In the beginning of the paragraph.

4. *Ibid.,* 131a.

5. Lev. 6:2.

6. *Cf.* Talmud Babli, *Menahoth,* 110a. *Ibid.:* "Everyone who deals with Torah."

7. From Persian: orchard. In Talmud: Paradise. In the Zohar: the four methods of interpretation, following Christian interpretation.

8. *Cf. Sefer HaGilgulim,* Chap. I.

9. *Ibid., Tikkuna* 69, pp. 111b–112a.

9a. Divine punishment by premature death.

10. *Cf. Eccl. Rab.* V (on Eccl. 5:11). R. Bun son of Hiya is said to have studied Torah in twenty-eight years as a veteran sage cannot do in a hundred.

11. Dan. 12:13.

12. *Zizith* is a fringed garment (*cf.* Num. 15:38).

13. Mishnah, *Aboth,* 2:1. Cf. E.E. Urbach, *HaZal etc,* Magnes Press, Jerusalem, 1969, pp. 301–320.

14. Sukkah = a booth to dwell in during the Feast of Tabernacles. Shofar = a ram's horn. Lulav = a palm branch, one of the four species used in the Feast of Tabernacles. Tefilah = prayer, the eighteen benedictions serving as the core of daily prayers. "Shema" = "Hear," the Biblical passages recited as a proclamation of Unity (Deut. 6:4–9; 11:13–21; Num. 15:37–41).

14a. *Aboth,* 2:1.

15. Song 1:7. *Zohar Hadash.*

16. Cf. Talmud Babli, *Shevu'oth,* 39a.

17. Deut. 29:28.

18. *Vide Shevu'oth,* 39b.

19. *Sefer HaGilgulim,* Chapter V.

20. *Cf.* Chap. V.

21. *Ibid.*

22. *Cf. ibid.*

23. *Sefer HaGilgulim,* Chap. V.

24. See there; also another possibility.

25. Chapter I and the present Chapter earlier.

26. Should be Chapter III (and Chapter I). Chapter II deals with the dominion of evil over good.

27. On Adam's transmigration in the Patriarchs, and Cain's in the Egyptian, Korah and Jethro.

28. Removal of the sandal of a brother-in-law to free a widow from levirate marriage.

29. See note 14 above.

30. *Ibid.*

31. Note 12 above.

32. See passage with notes 24 & 25 above (in the text).

33. Talmud Babli, *Shabbath,* 12b.

PARDES RIMMONIM

1. Cf. Isa. 55:8.
2. Cf. Kaddari, M.Z., *MiYerushath Leshon Yeme HaBenayim*, Dvir, Tel-Aviv, (1970), pp. 14–17, for the Aristotelian source *(De Anima)* and the Arabic expression *Haraja* which influenced Hebrew *(Yaza min hakoah el hapo'al)*.

KINATH SETARIM

1. Lamentations 1:4 reads: "The paths of Zion mourn without those who come for a festival, all her gates are desolate. Her priests are sighing, her virgins are sad. How bitter is her fate!"
2. *Cf. Sefer Yezirah.*
3. There are nine *sefiroth* from *Hokhmah* to *Malkhuth* and thirty-two paths in each *sefirah.*
4. R. Moses Kordovero, *Pardes Rimmonim,* XII, ch. 1; the reason is that *Malkhuth* is the lower *Hokhmah.* Quoted by Horodezki, S.A., *Torah HaKabbalah shel Rabbi Moshe Kordovero,* Eschkol, Berlin (1924), Introduction, pp. 66–67.
5. Isa. 66:12. Zohar I, 193b. The symbols peace, river, and Joseph are related to the *Sefirah Yesod.*
6. Zohar I, 196b, where "by thy strength" is interpreted as through the higher soul *(neshamah)* or through the wife, a concept one can relate to Carl Jung's concept of the *anima* (see *Man and His Symbols*).
7. *Lamentations Rabbati* (I.31) on Lam. 1:4.
8. Lam. 1:4.
9. *Ibid.*
10. *Cf.* Exod. 34:23. Passover, Pentecost, and Tabernacles.
11. Zohar I, 2a.
12. Ps. 42:5.
13. Lam. 1:4.
14. Prov. 30:28. Translated as "lizard." The context is: "Four things there are that are smallest on earth yet wise beyond the wisest: . . . the lizard, which can be grasped in the hand, yet is found in the palaces of kings." Cf. Korān, The Spider.
15. Lam. 1:4.
16. *Lam. Rab., ibid. (cf.* note 7 above).
17. Lines 63ff. above. *Cf.* also p. 104 in the book, where Galante comments on *'al har Zion sheshamam. Har,* Mountain, is considered a surrounding aspect to Zion (in *Malkhuth*) Har is attacked by *semamiyoth,* powers of evil. Galante's interpretation there relates the spider, symbol of evil, to the spider, the animal. Spider is a general term for a whole category of creatures; they have no bones, as stated by Galante, who indicates evil has no substance, but unlike his statement, some of them live more than

twelve months. I am grateful to Prof. Osmond Phillip Breland of the Zoology Dept. in the Univ. of Texas at Austin for this information.

18. *Cf.* Talmud Babli, *Sanhedrin,* 103b. The Talmud refers to King Amon (642–640) not Manasseh (698–642).

19. Zohar III *(Ra'ya Mehemna)* 251b–252a. *Cf.* also *ibid.* 235a–236a. In that place they have built Rome!

20. Isa. 42:8.

21. Metatron, the Angel of the Countenance.

22. Zohar I, 1a.

23. Lam. 4:12.

24. Lam. 1:4.

25. Zohar III. 30a–b; 34b.

26. *Ibid.* 30a.

27. Lam. 1:4.

28. Exod. 28:41. *Ibid.* 40:15.

29. Lam. 1:4.

30. Ps. 48:3(4).

31. *Ibid.* 48:6(5).

32. *Ibid.* 48:7(6)

33. Lam. 1:4.

34. I did not find the quotation but *cf. Tikkuna* 18 (also 6 and Introduction).

35. Isa. 6:3.

36. Pseudo-Jonathan (Aramaic *Targum) ad loc.*

37. Lam. 1:4.

38. *Ibid.*

39. Lev. 18:19. The prohibition on intercourse during the period of menstruation.

40. Lam. 1:4.

41. *Cf.* Talmud Babli, *'Erubin* 92a, *Yebamoth* 43a. R. Hiya was a disciple of Rabbi Yehuda haNasi, usually called Rabbi.

42. Lam. 1:4.

43. Isa. 63:9(!). The last letter of *lo* is taken to stand for its numerical value (6) rather than a pronominal marker ("to six" rather than "to Him").

44. *Cf.* Talmud Babli, *Ta'anith* 5a, Rabbinovicz, R., *Dikduke Soferim,* III, München, 1870, 10(19).

45. Lam. 1:4.

Poet and novelist, editor and publisher, musician and teacher, David Meltzer has long been involved in the Kabbalah as a uniquely committed social, hermeneutic, and personal practice. He lives in the San Francisco Bay area and, since the 1950s, has played an essential role in the poetry world there.

From 1968 to 1978 he edited *Tree,* a bi-annual journal which combined classical Kabbalistic and modernist/postmodernist confrontations and dialogue with specific Kabbalistic themes such as the Shekinah, Yetzirah, Raa/evil, the Messiah.

He also has been the publisher of Tree Books whose list offers, among other works, the first U.S. publication of a section *of The Book of Questions* by Edmond Jabès, translated by Rosmarie Waldrop; Marcia Falk's translations of the great Yiddish poet, Malka Heifetz Tussman; works by Jack Hirschman, Nathaniel Tarn, Jerome Rothenberg, Rose Drachler, Max Jacob, and the traditional Kabbalistic authors, Abraham ben Samuel Abulafia and Eleazer of Worms, selections of whose work appear in this anthology.

David Meltzer's work in poetry has been published in many separate volumes, including *The Art, The Veil* (Milwaukee: Membrane Press, 1981)*; The Name: Selected Poetry, 1973-1983* (Santa Barbara: Black Sparrow Press, 1984); *Arrows: Selected Poetry, 1957-1992* (Santa Rosa: Black Sparrow Press, 1994); and the forthcoming *No Eyes: Poetry, 1995-1998* (Santa Rosa: Black Sparrow Press).

His prose includes two recently republished works, originally written in the 1960s: *Orf* (NY: Rhinoceros Books, 1995); and *The Agency Trilogy* (New York: Richard Kasak Books, 1996); and a new novel, *Under* (NY: Rhinoceros Books, 1997).

As editor he has also published several previous anthologies: *Birth: An Anthology of Ancient Texts, Songs, Prayers, and Stories* (Berkeley: North Point Press, 1981)*; Death: An Anthology of Texts, Songs, Charms, Prayers, and Stories* (Berkeley: North Point Press, 1984); *Reading Jazz* (San Francisco: Mercury House, 1995) and a companion volume, *Writing Jazz* (San Francisco: Mercury House, 1997).

In the 1960s he was the leader of a psychedelic band that included the late Tina Meltzer and the poet Clark Coolidge, whose *Serpent Power* was recently reissued on CD by Vanguard Records.

He is currently working on *The Rabbi's Dream Book*, a documentary fiction, and has taught in the Graduate Poetics Program at New College of California since its inception.